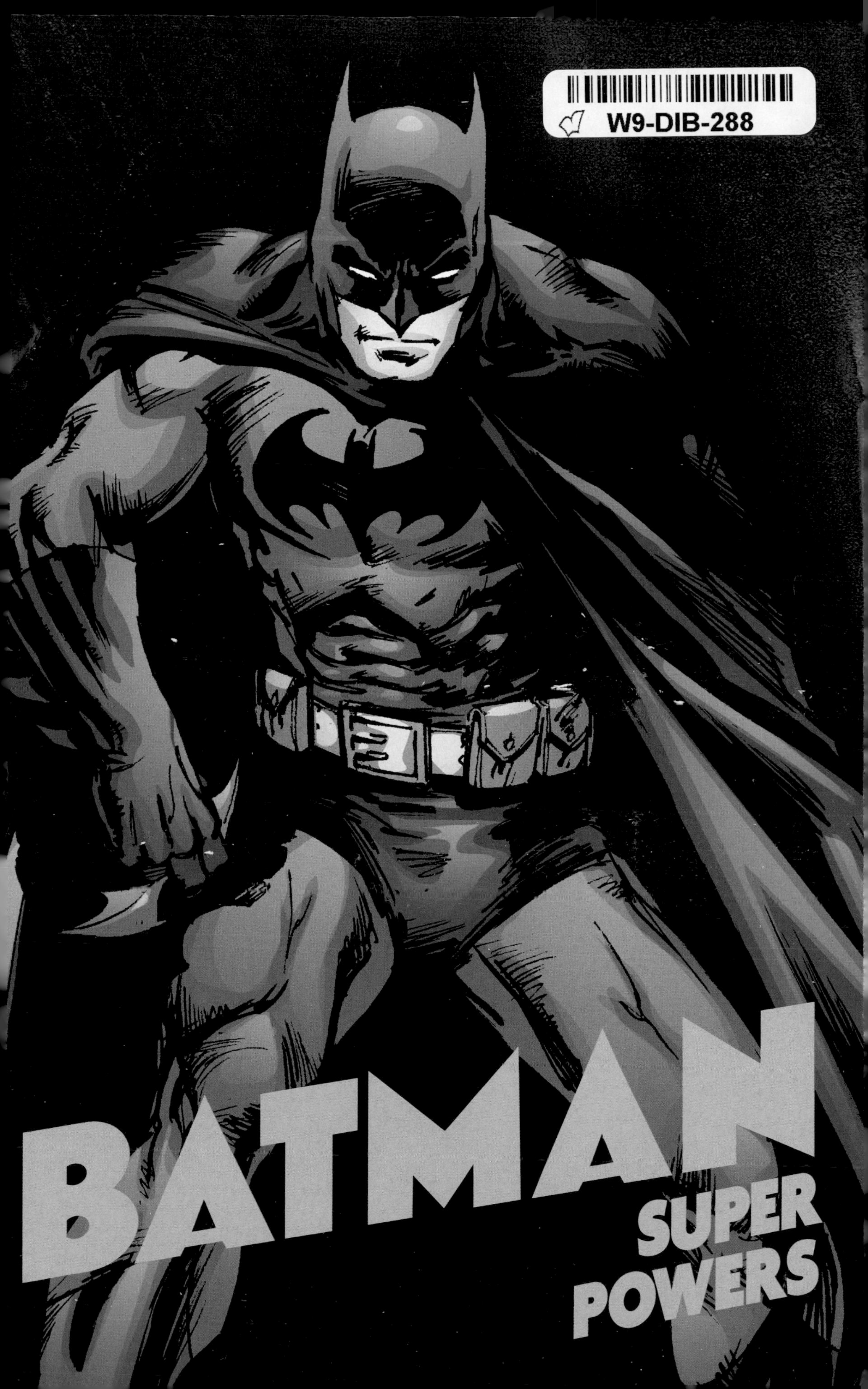
BATMAN
SUPER
POWERS

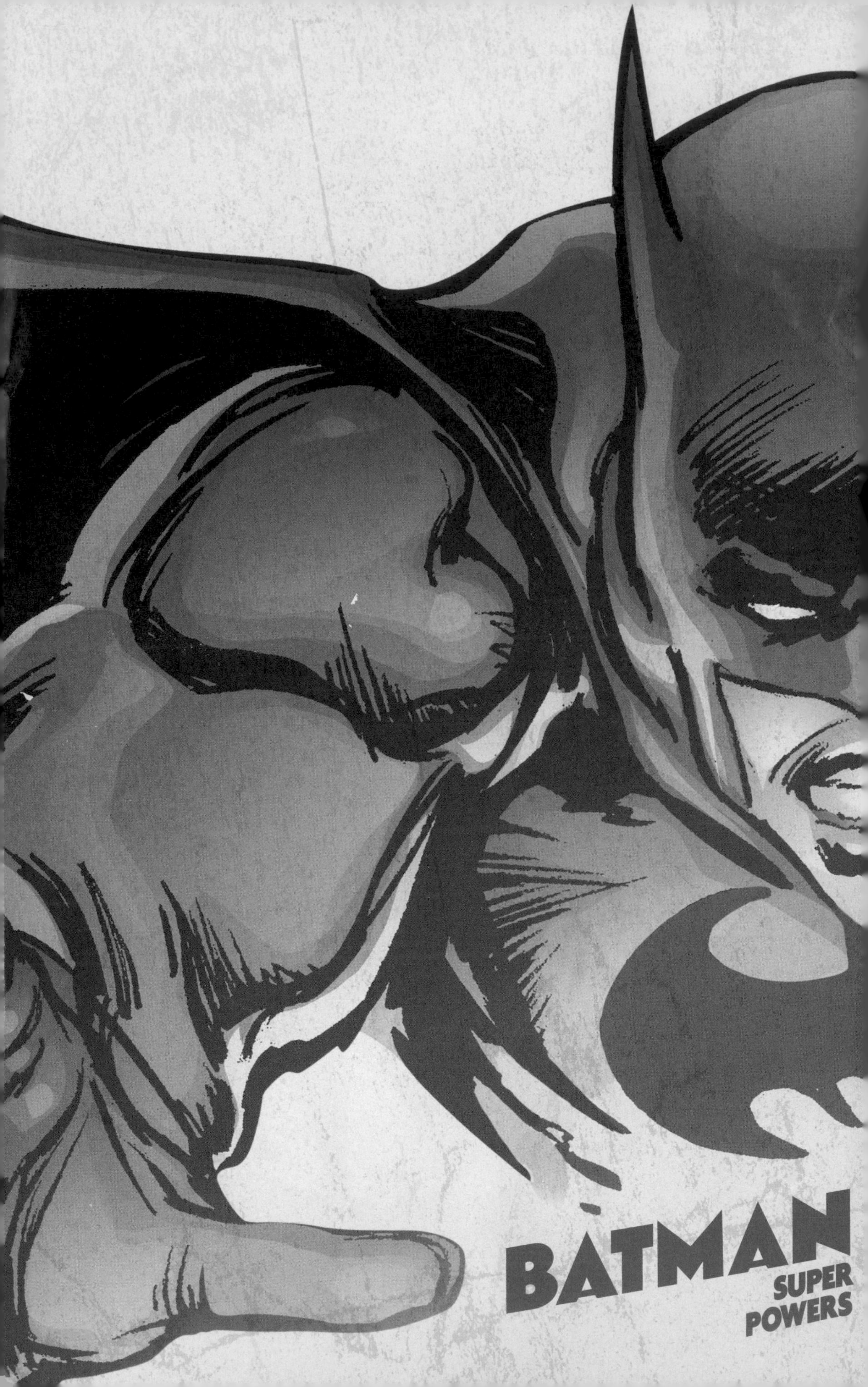
BATMAN
SUPER
POWERS

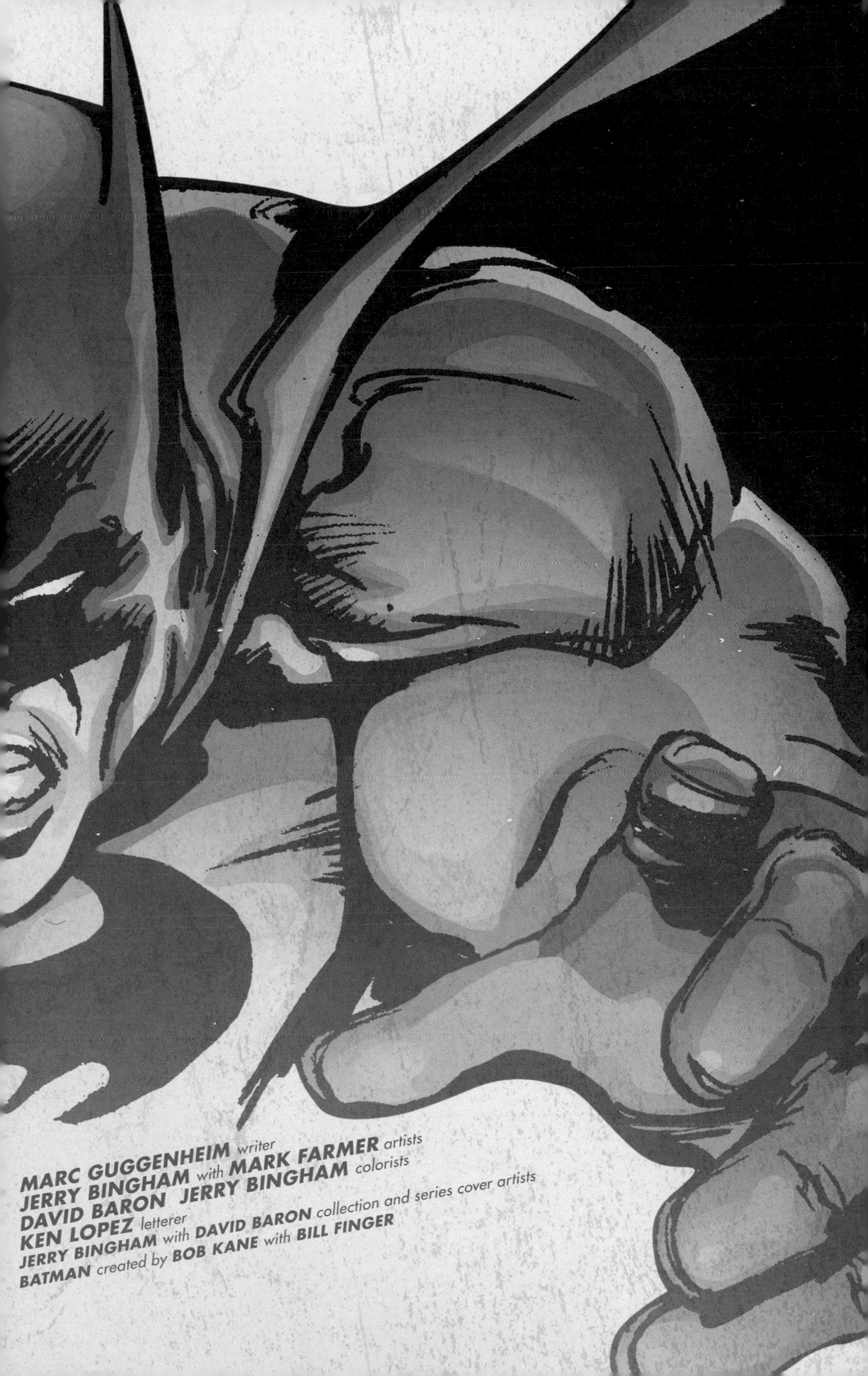

MARC GUGGENHEIM writer
JERRY BINGHAM with **MARK FARMER** artists
DAVID BARON JERRY BINGHAM colorists
KEN LOPEZ letterer
JERRY BINGHAM with **DAVID BARON** collection and series cover artists
BATMAN created by **BOB KANE** with **BILL FINGER**

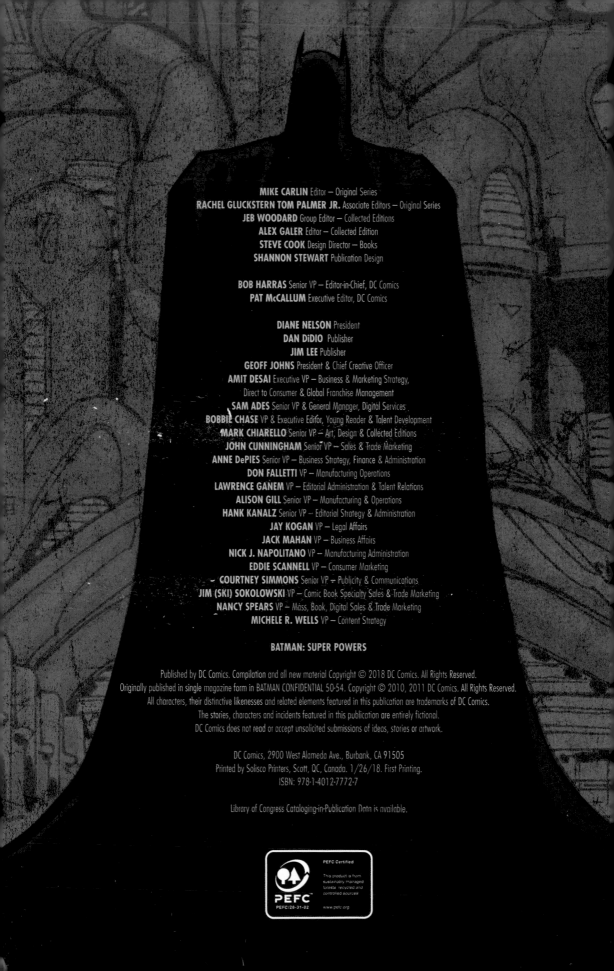

MIKE CARLIN Editor – Original Series
RACHEL GLUCKSTERN TOM PALMER JR. Associate Editors – Original Series
JEB WOODARD Group Editor – Collected Editions
ALEX GALER Editor – Collected Edition
STEVE COOK Design Director – Books
SHANNON STEWART Publication Design

BOB HARRAS Senior VP – Editor-in-Chief, DC Comics
PAT McCALLUM Executive Editor, DC Comics

DIANE NELSON President
DAN DiDIO Publisher
JIM LEE Publisher
GEOFF JOHNS President & Chief Creative Officer
AMIT DESAI Executive VP – Business & Marketing Strategy,
Direct to Consumer & Global Franchise Management
SAM ADES Senior VP & General Manager, Digital Services
BOBBIE CHASE VP & Executive Editor, Young Reader & Talent Development
MARK CHIARELLO Senior VP – Art, Design & Collected Editions
JOHN CUNNINGHAM Senior VP – Sales & Trade Marketing
ANNE DePIES Senior VP – Business Strategy, Finance & Administration
DON FALLETTI VP – Manufacturing Operations
LAWRENCE GANEM VP – Editorial Administration & Talent Relations
ALISON GILL Senior VP – Manufacturing & Operations
HANK KANALZ Senior VP – Editorial Strategy & Administration
JAY KOGAN VP – Legal Affairs
JACK MAHAN VP – Business Affairs
NICK J. NAPOLITANO VP – Manufacturing Administration
EDDIE SCANNELL VP – Consumer Marketing
COURTNEY SIMMONS Senior VP – Publicity & Communications
JIM (SKI) SOKOLOWSKI VP – Comic Book Specialty Sales & Trade Marketing
NANCY SPEARS VP – Mass, Book, Digital Sales & Trade Marketing
MICHELE R. WELLS VP – Content Strategy

BATMAN: SUPER POWERS

DC Comics, 2900 West Alameda Ave., Burbank, CA 91505
Printed by Solisco Printers, Scott, QC, Canada. 1/26/18. First Printing.
ISBN: 978-1-4012-7772-7

Library of Congress Cataloging-in-Publication Data is available.

PEFC Certified
This product is from sustainably managed forests, recycled and controlled sources
PEFC
PEFC/26-31-02
www.pefc.org

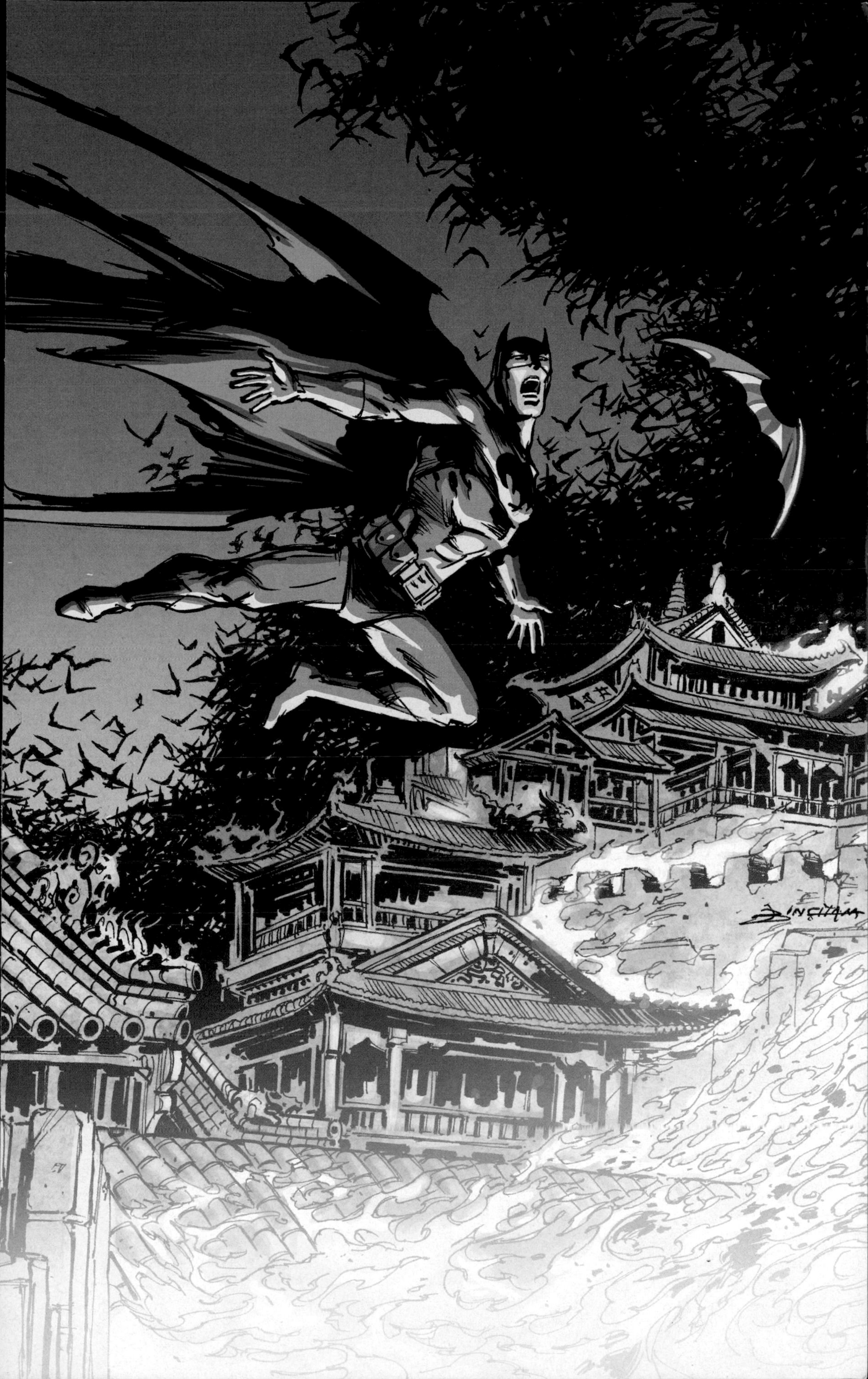

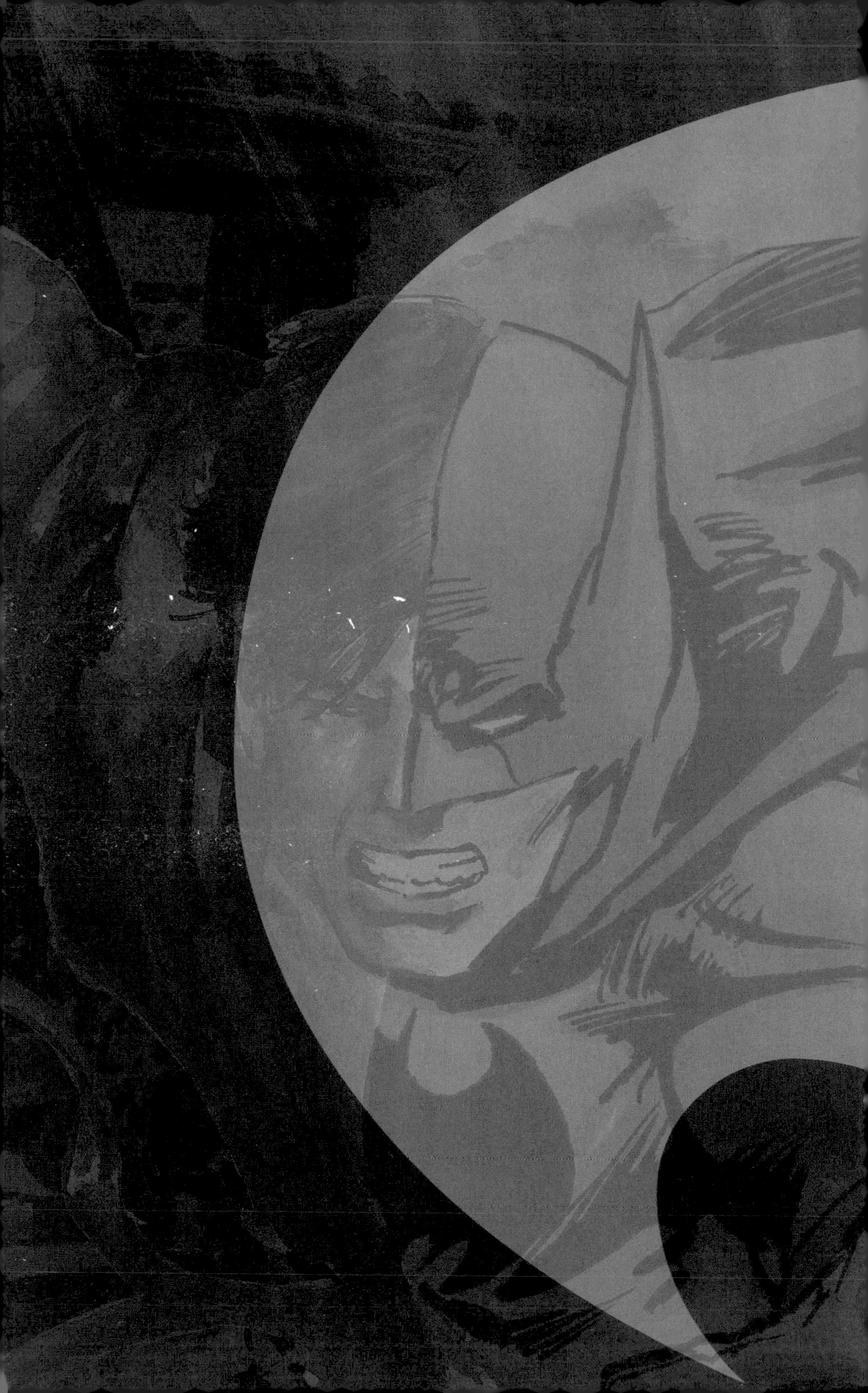

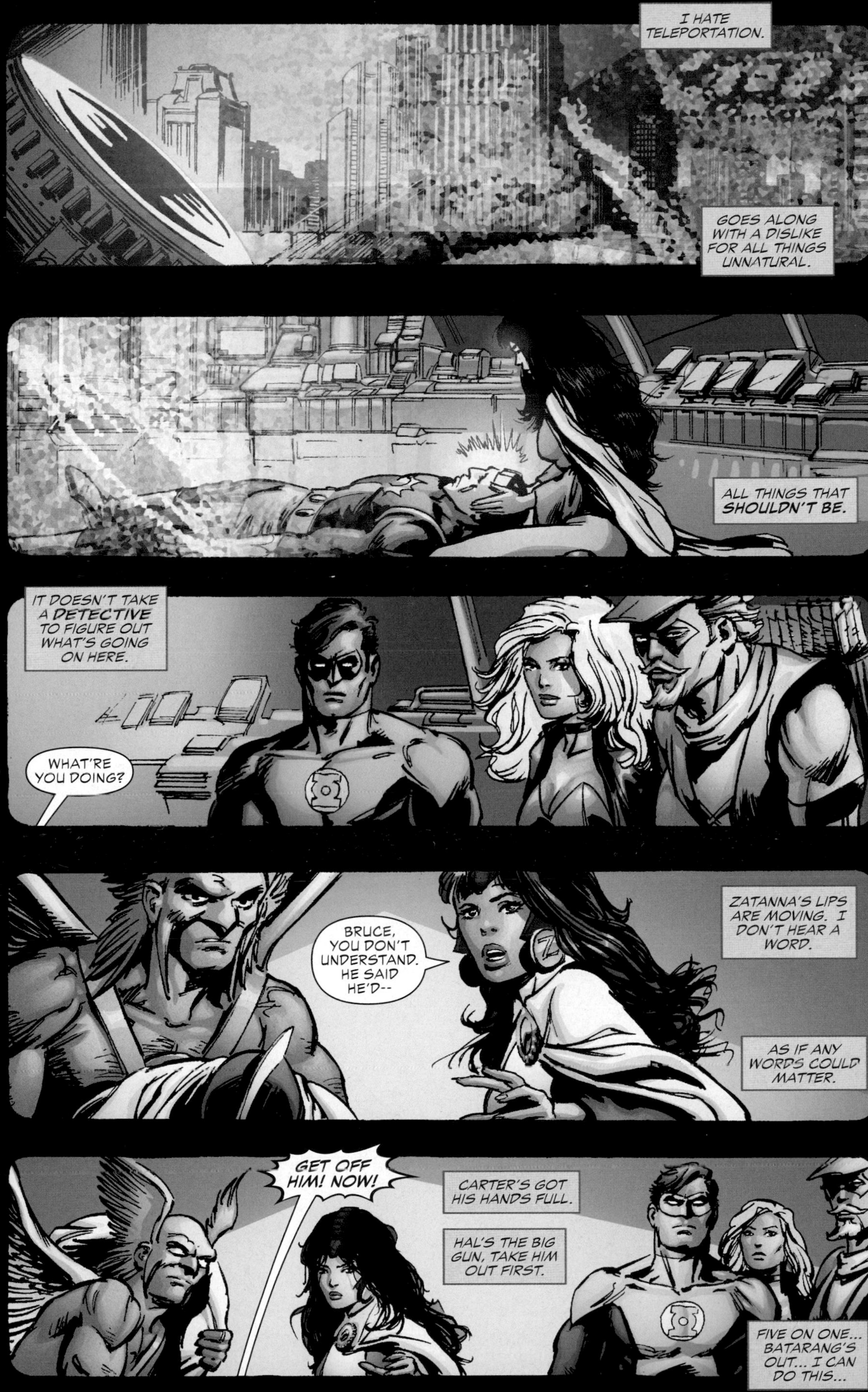
I HATE TELEPORTATION.
GOES ALONG WITH A DISLIKE FOR ALL THINGS UNNATURAL.
ALL THINGS THAT SHOULDN'T BE.
IT DOESN'T TAKE A DETECTIVE TO FIGURE OUT WHAT'S GOING ON HERE.
WHAT'RE YOU DOING?
BRUCE, YOU DON'T UNDERSTAND. HE SAID HE'D--
ZATANNA'S LIPS ARE MOVING. I DON'T HEAR A WORD.
AS IF ANY WORDS COULD MATTER.
GET OFF HIM! NOW!
CARTER'S GOT HIS HANDS FULL.
HAL'S THE BIG GUN, TAKE HIM OUT FIRST.
FIVE ON ONE... BATARANG'S OUT... I CAN DO THIS...

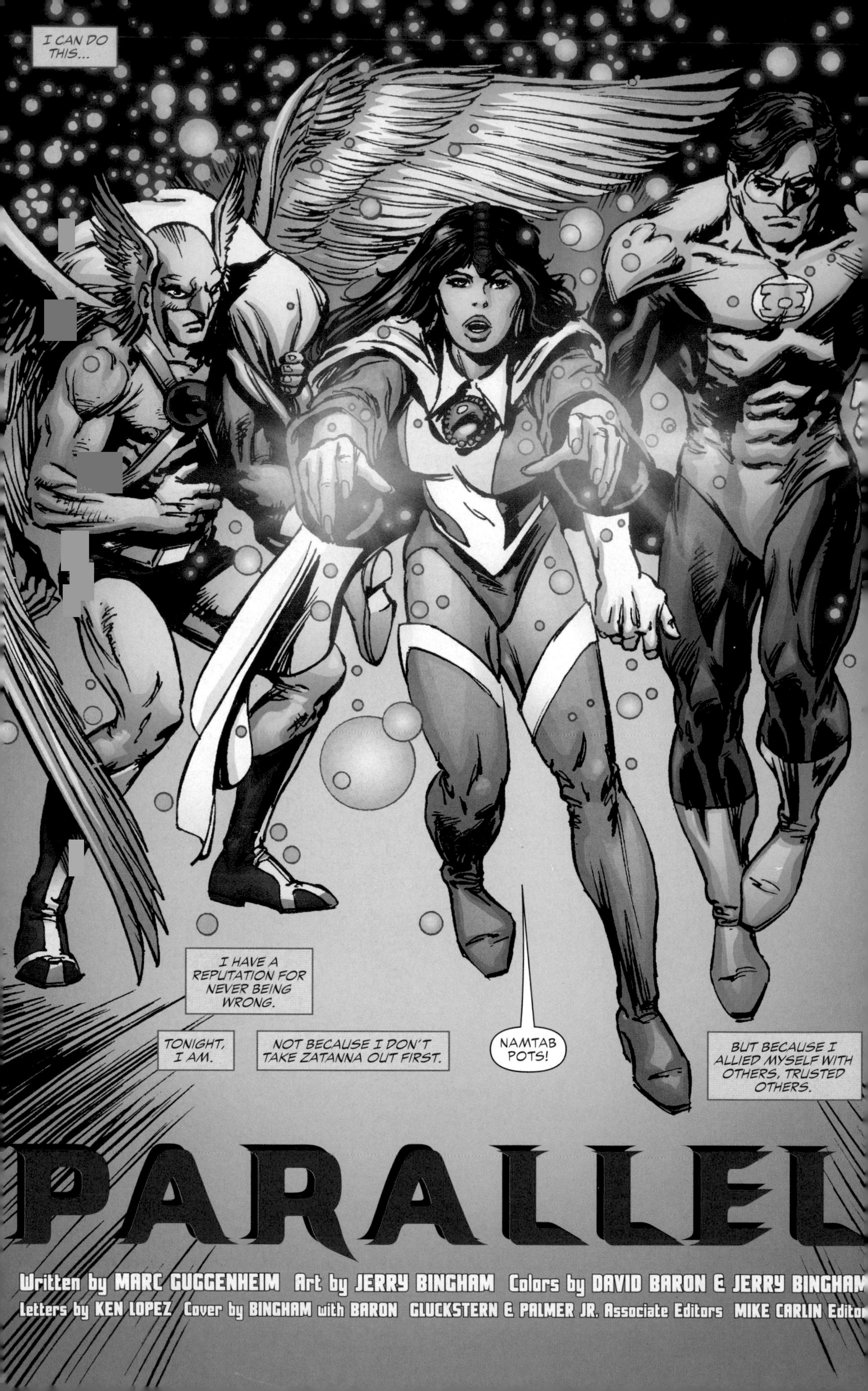
I CAN DO THIS...
I HAVE A REPUTATION FOR NEVER BEING WRONG.
TONIGHT, I AM.
NOT BECAUSE I DON'T TAKE ZATANNA OUT FIRST.
NAMTAB POTS!
BUT BECAUSE I ALLIED MYSELF WITH OTHERS, TRUSTED OTHERS.
PARALLEL
Written by MARC GUGGENHEIM Art by JERRY BINGHAM Colors by DAVID BARON & JERRY BINGHAM
Letters by KEN LOPEZ Cover by BINGHAM with BARON GLUCKSTERN & PALMER JR. Associate Editors MIKE CARLIN Editor

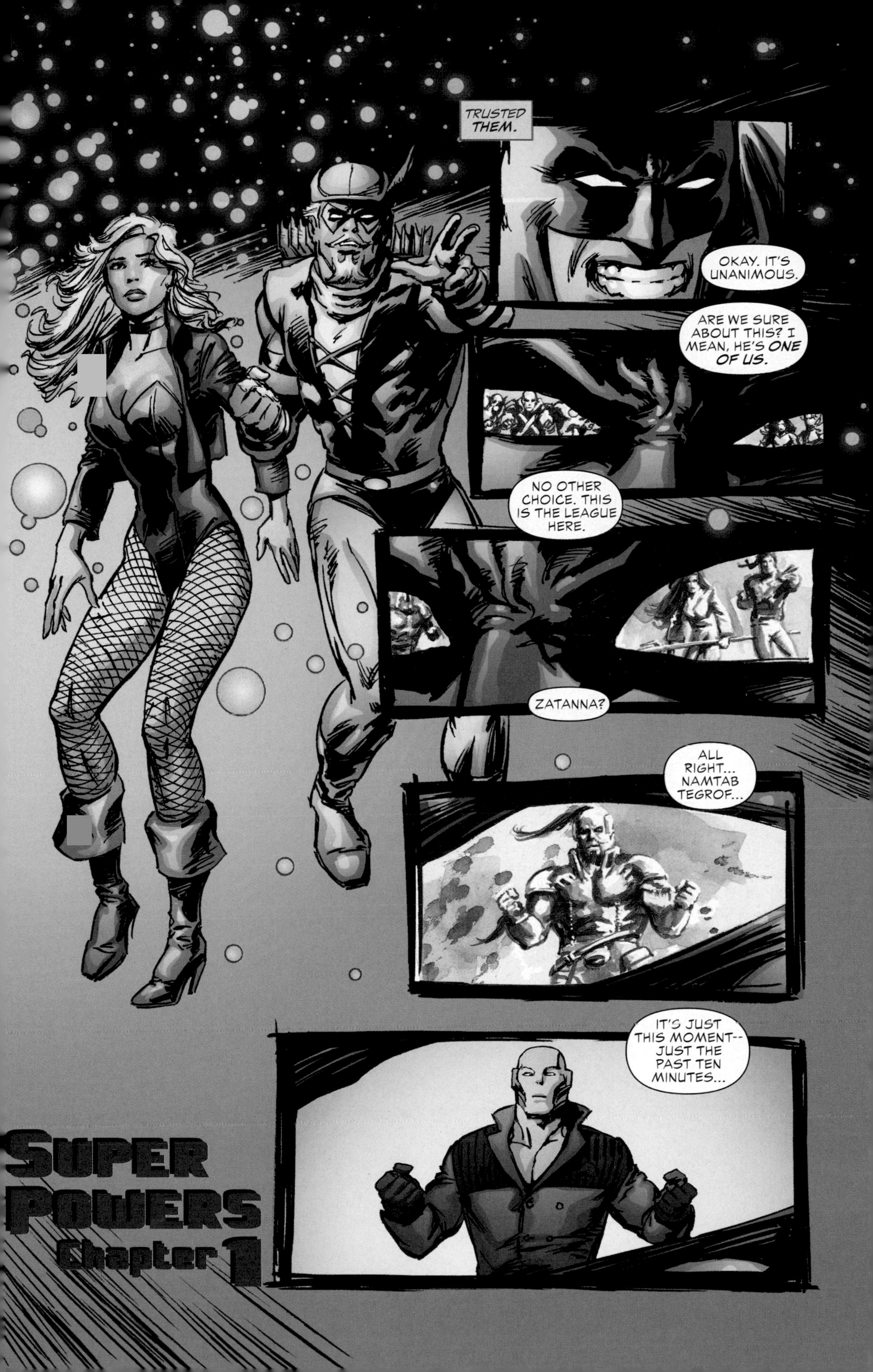
TRUSTED THEM.
OKAY. IT'S UNANIMOUS.
ARE WE SURE ABOUT THIS? I MEAN, HE'S ONE OF US.
NO OTHER CHOICE. THIS IS THE LEAGUE HERE.
ZATANNA?
ALL RIGHT... NAMTAB TEGROF...
IT'S JUST THIS MOMENT-- JUST THE PAST TEN MINUTES...
SUPER POWERS Chapter 1

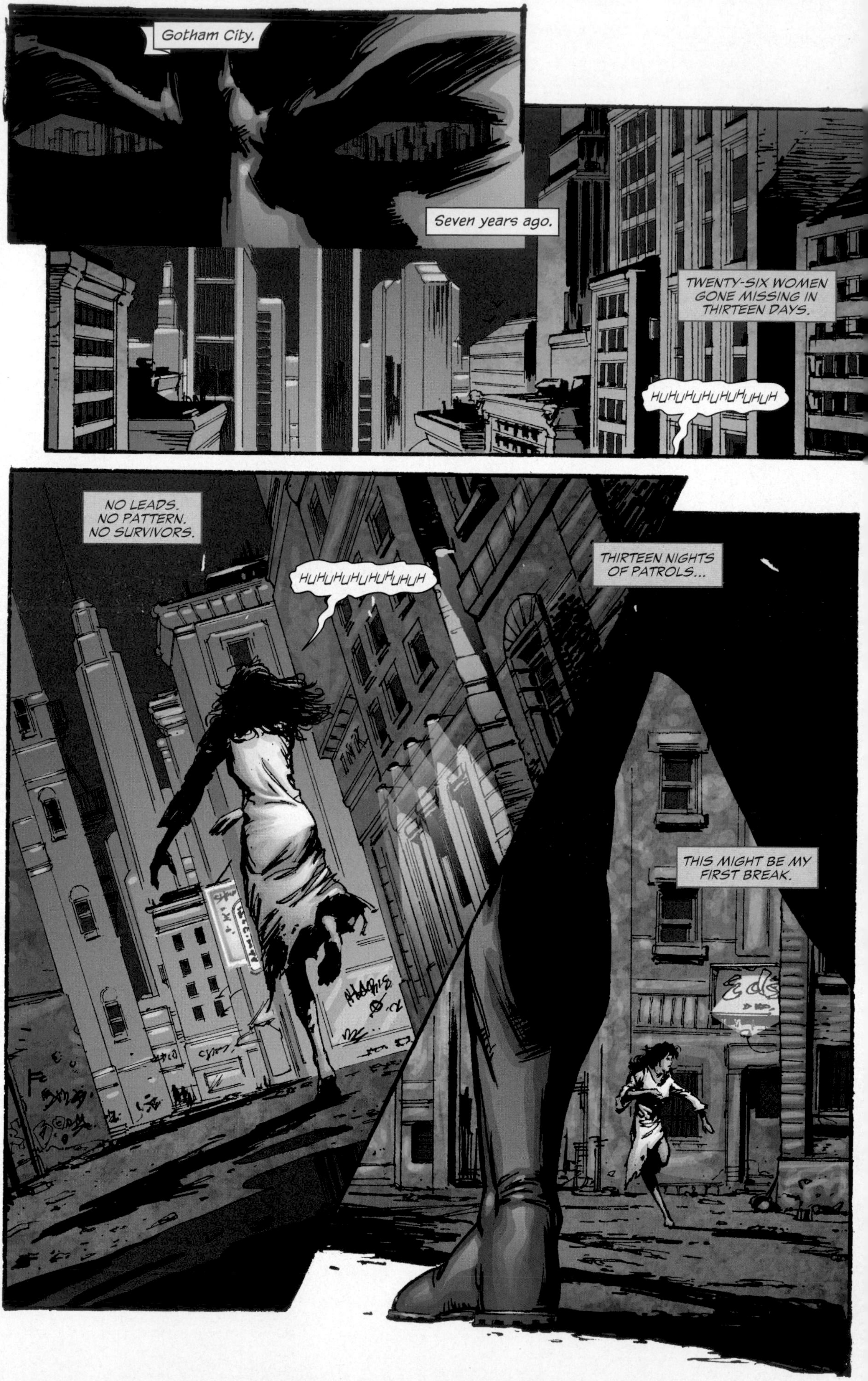

Gotham City.
Seven years ago.
TWENTY-SIX WOMEN GONE MISSING IN THIRTEEN DAYS.
HuHuHuHuHuHuHuHuH
NO LEADS. NO PATTERN. NO SURVIVORS.
HuHuHuHuHuHuHuHuH
THIRTEEN NIGHTS OF PATROLS...
THIS MIGHT BE MY FIRST BREAK.

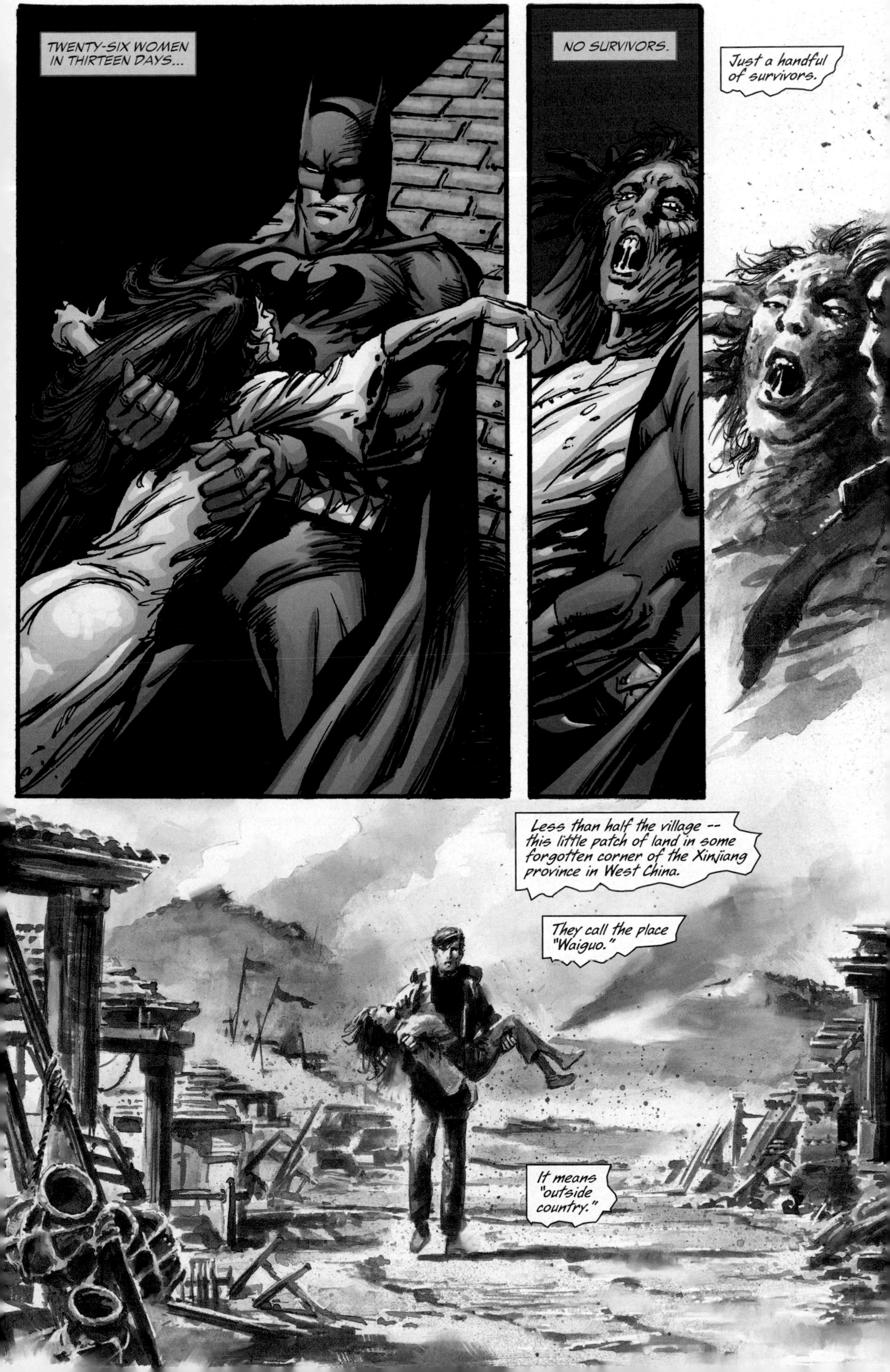
TWENTY-SIX WOMEN IN THIRTEEN DAYS...
NO SURVIVORS.
Just a handful of survivors.
Less than half the village -- this little patch of land in some forgotten corner of the Xinjiang province in West China.
They call the place "Waiguo."
It means "outside country."

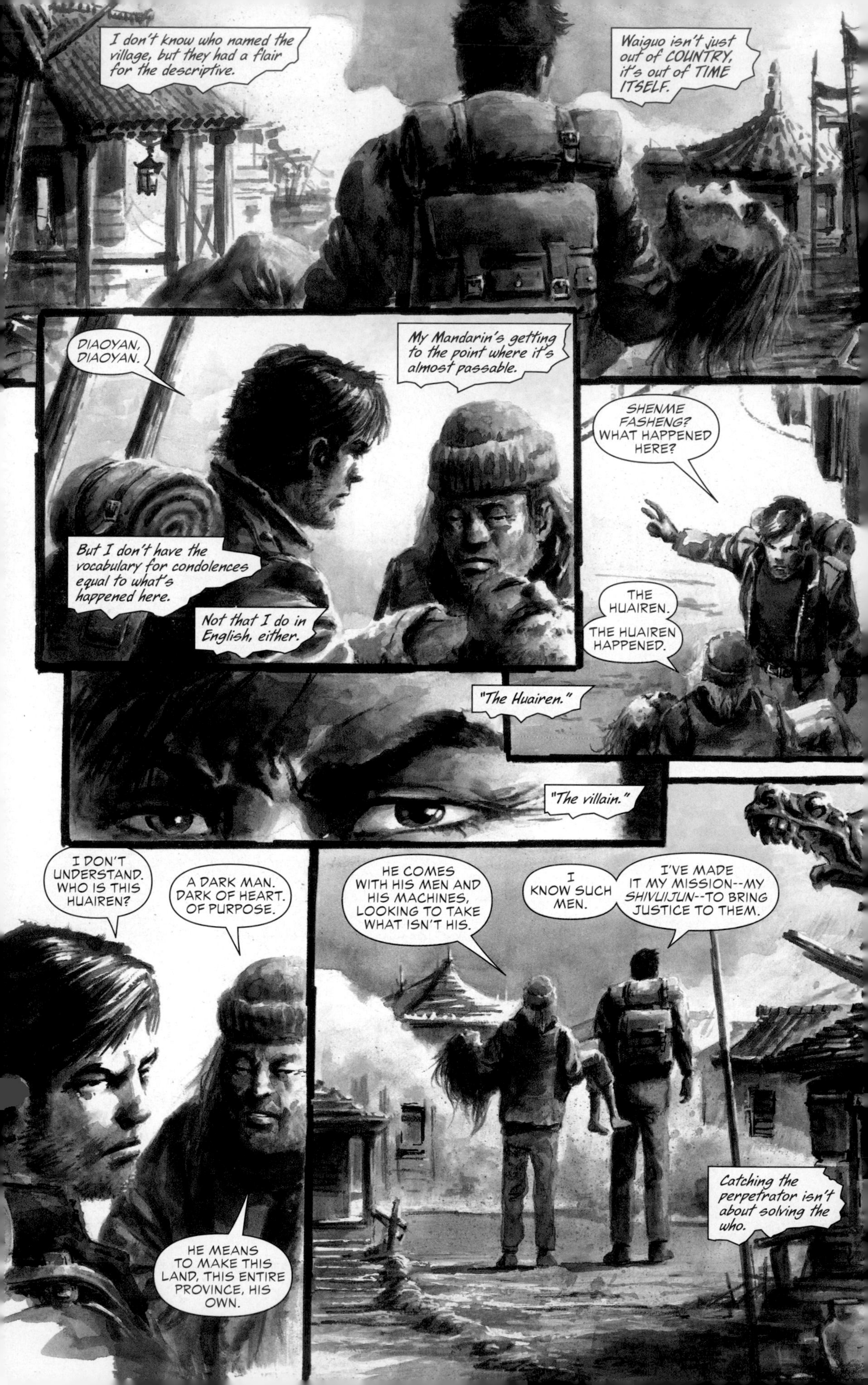
I don't know who named the village, but they had a flair for the descriptive.
Waiguo isn't just out of COUNTRY, it's out of TIME ITSELF.
DIAOYAN, DIAOYAN.
My Mandarin's getting to the point where it's almost passable.
But I don't have the vocabulary for condolences equal to what's happened here.
Not that I do in English, either.
SHENME FASHENG? WHAT HAPPENED HERE?
THE HUAIREN.
THE HUAIREN HAPPENED.
"The Huairen."
"The villain."
I DON'T UNDERSTAND. WHO IS THIS HUAIREN?
A DARK MAN. DARK OF HEART. OF PURPOSE.
HE MEANS TO MAKE THIS LAND, THIS ENTIRE PROVINCE, HIS OWN.
HE COMES WITH HIS MEN AND HIS MACHINES, LOOKING TO TAKE WHAT ISN'T HIS.
I KNOW SUCH MEN.
I'VE MADE IT MY MISSION--MY SHIVUIJUN--TO BRING JUSTICE TO THEM.
Catching the perpetrator isn't about solving the who.

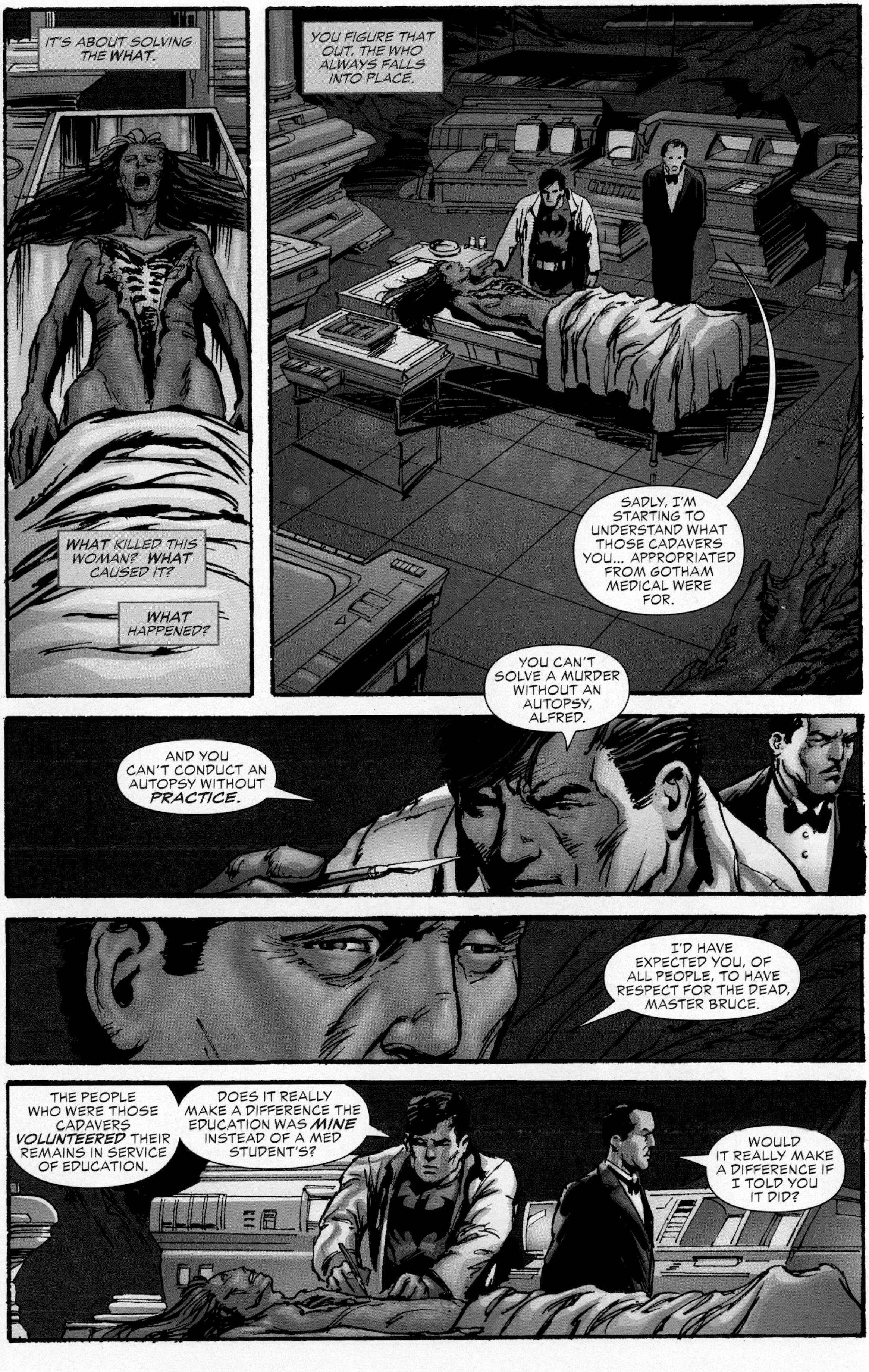
IT'S ABOUT SOLVING THE WHAT.
WHAT KILLED THIS WOMAN? WHAT CAUSED IT?
WHAT HAPPENED?
YOU FIGURE THAT OUT, THE WHO ALWAYS FALLS INTO PLACE.
SADLY, I'M STARTING TO UNDERSTAND WHAT THOSE CADAVERS YOU... APPROPRIATED FROM GOTHAM MEDICAL WERE FOR.
YOU CAN'T SOLVE A MURDER WITHOUT AN AUTOPSY, ALFRED.
AND YOU CAN'T CONDUCT AN AUTOPSY WITHOUT PRACTICE.
I'D HAVE EXPECTED YOU, OF ALL PEOPLE, TO HAVE RESPECT FOR THE DEAD, MASTER BRUCE.
THE PEOPLE WHO WERE THOSE CADAVERS VOLUNTEERED THEIR REMAINS IN SERVICE OF EDUCATION.
DOES IT REALLY MAKE A DIFFERENCE THE EDUCATION WAS MINE INSTEAD OF A MED STUDENT'S?
WOULD IT REALLY MAKE A DIFFERENCE IF I TOLD YOU IT DID?

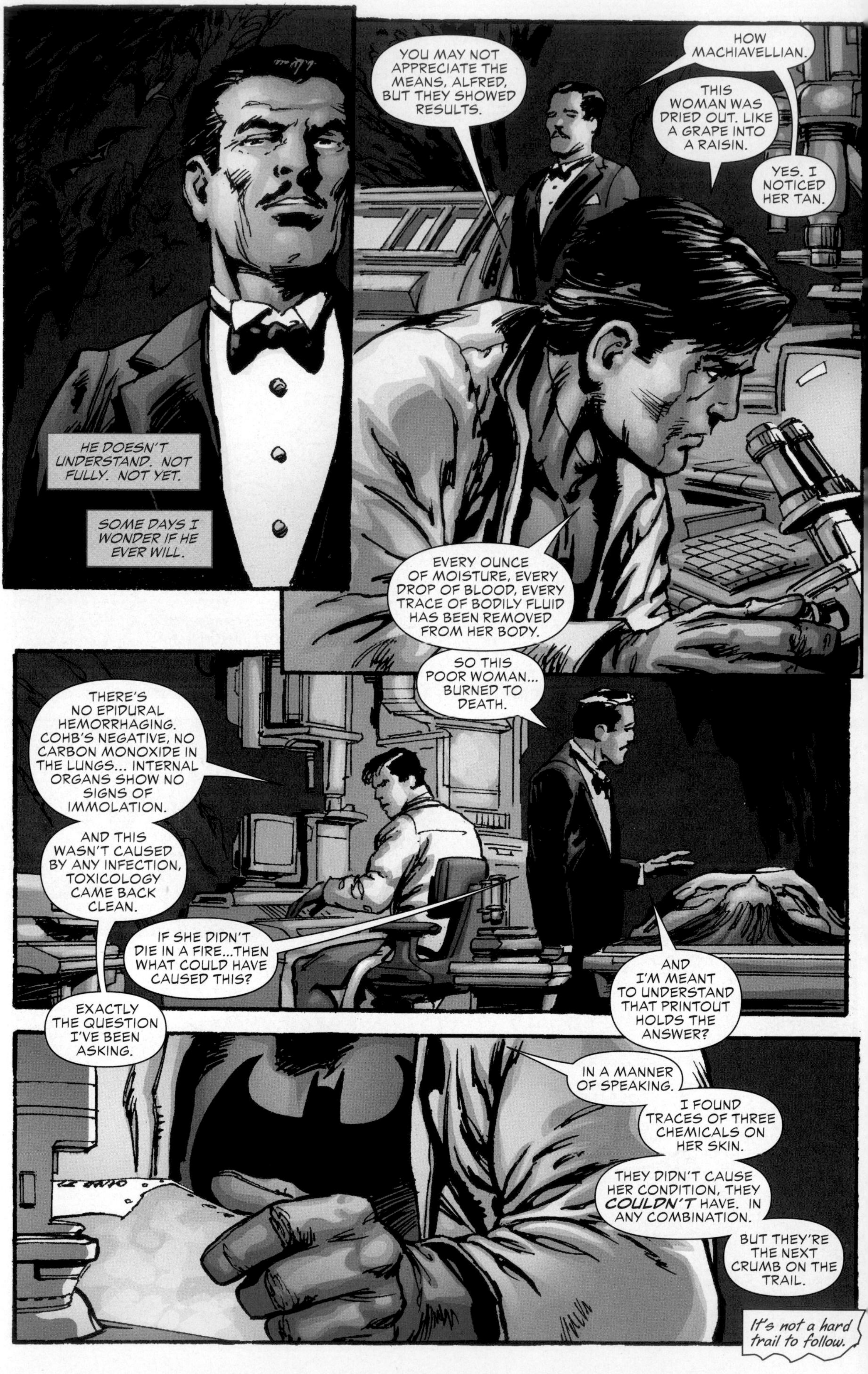
HE DOESN'T UNDERSTAND. NOT FULLY. NOT YET.
SOME DAYS I WONDER IF HE EVER WILL.
YOU MAY NOT APPRECIATE THE MEANS, ALFRED, BUT THEY SHOWED RESULTS.
HOW MACHIAVELLIAN.
THIS WOMAN WAS DRIED OUT. LIKE A GRAPE INTO A RAISIN.
YES. I NOTICED HER TAN.
EVERY OUNCE OF MOISTURE, EVERY DROP OF BLOOD, EVERY TRACE OF BODILY FLUID HAS BEEN REMOVED FROM HER BODY.
SO THIS POOR WOMAN... BURNED TO DEATH.
THERE'S NO EPIDURAL HEMORRHAGING. COHB'S NEGATIVE, NO CARBON MONOXIDE IN THE LUNGS... INTERNAL ORGANS SHOW NO SIGNS OF IMMOLATION.
AND THIS WASN'T CAUSED BY ANY INFECTION, TOXICOLOGY CAME BACK CLEAN.
IF SHE DIDN'T DIE IN A FIRE...THEN WHAT COULD HAVE CAUSED THIS?
EXACTLY THE QUESTION I'VE BEEN ASKING.
AND I'M MEANT TO UNDERSTAND THAT PRINTOUT HOLDS THE ANSWER?
IN A MANNER OF SPEAKING.
I FOUND TRACES OF THREE CHEMICALS ON HER SKIN.
THEY DIDN'T CAUSE HER CONDITION, THEY COULDN'T HAVE. IN ANY COMBINATION.
BUT THEY'RE THE NEXT CRUMB ON THE TRAIL.
It's not a hard trail to follow.

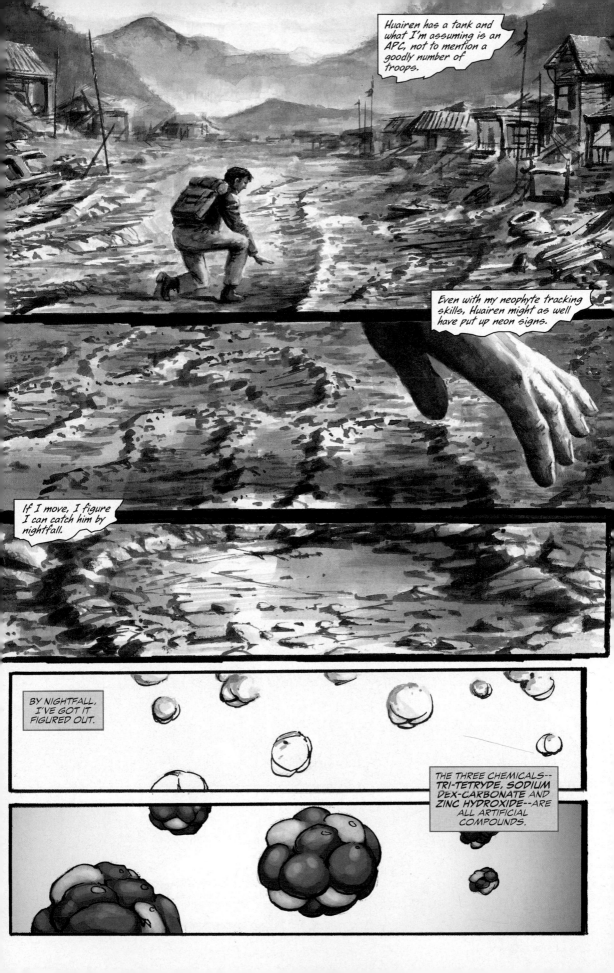

Huairen has a tank and what I'm assuming is an APC, not to mention a goodly number of troops.

Even with my neophyte tracking skills, Huairen might as well have put up neon signs.

If I move, I figure I can catch him by nightfall.

BY NIGHTFALL, I'VE GOT IT FIGURED OUT.

THE THREE CHEMICALS-- TRI-TETRYDE, SODIUM DEX-CARBONATE and ZINC HYDROXIDE--ARE ALL ARTIFICIAL COMPOUNDS.

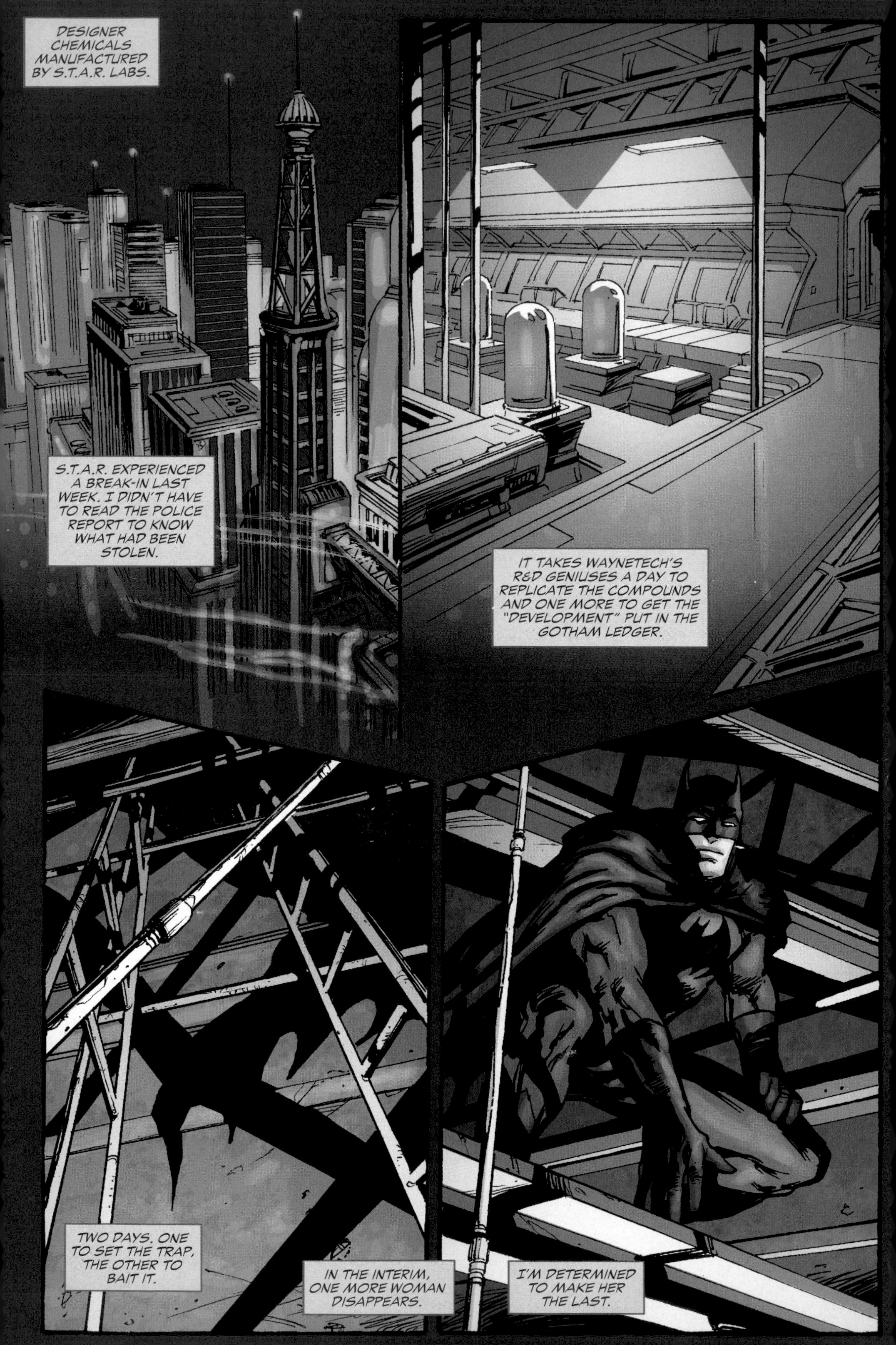
DESIGNER CHEMICALS MANUFACTURED BY S.T.A.R. LABS.
S.T.A.R. EXPERIENCED A BREAK-IN LAST WEEK. I DIDN'T HAVE TO READ THE POLICE REPORT TO KNOW WHAT HAD BEEN STOLEN.
IT TAKES WAYNETECH'S R&D GENIUSES A DAY TO REPLICATE THE COMPOUNDS AND ONE MORE TO GET THE "DEVELOPMENT" PUT IN THE GOTHAM LEDGER.
TWO DAYS. ONE TO SET THE TRAP, THE OTHER TO BAIT IT.
IN THE INTERIM, ONE MORE WOMAN DISAPPEARS.
I'M DETERMINED TO MAKE HER THE LAST.

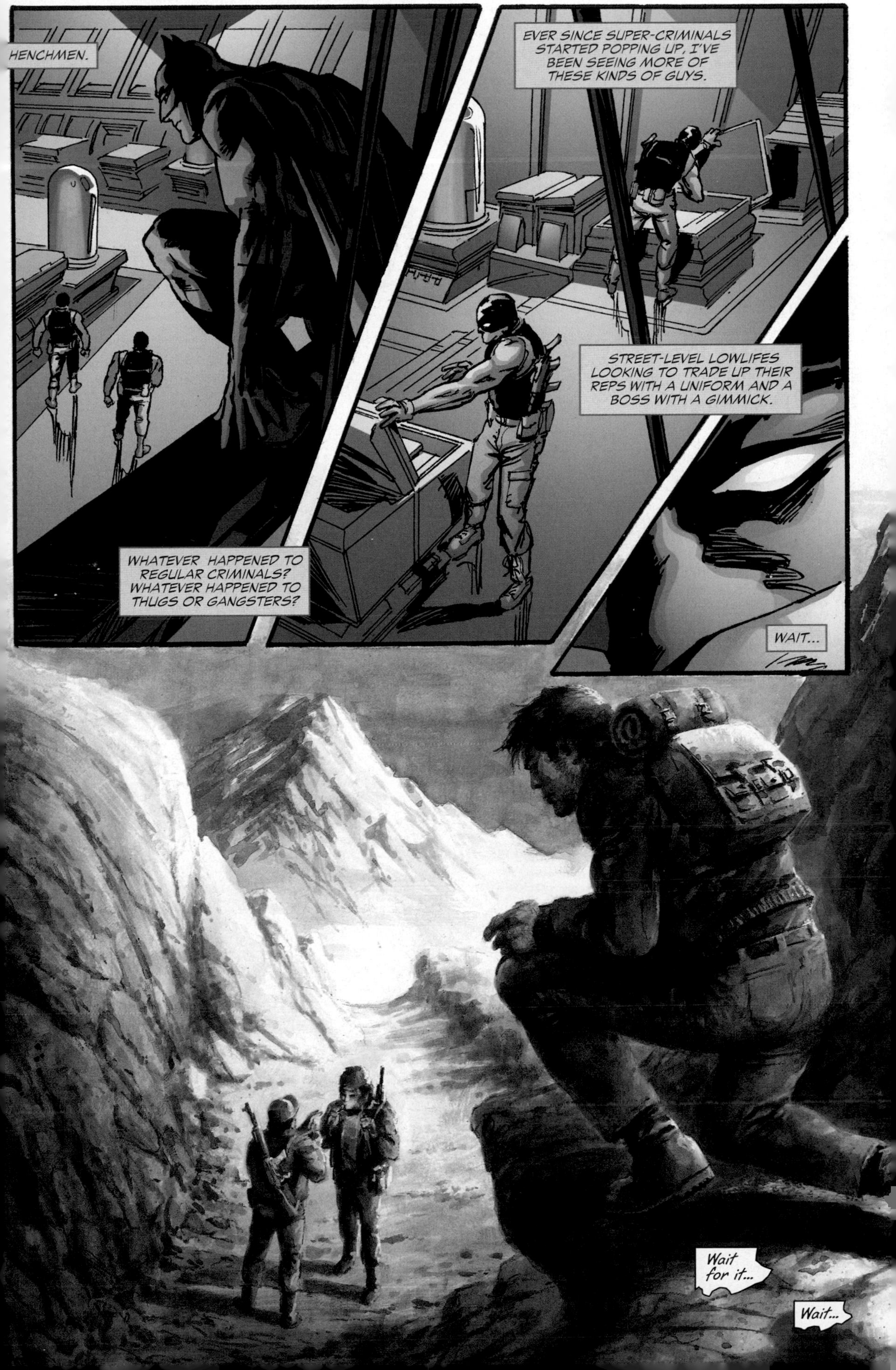
HENCHMEN.
EVER SINCE SUPER-CRIMINALS STARTED POPPING UP, I'VE BEEN SEEING MORE OF THESE KINDS OF GUYS.
STREET-LEVEL LOWLIFES LOOKING TO TRADE UP THEIR REPS WITH A UNIFORM AND A BOSS WITH A GIMMICK.
WHATEVER HAPPENED TO REGULAR CRIMINALS? WHATEVER HAPPENED TO THUGS OR GANGSTERS?
WAIT...
Wait for it...
Wait...

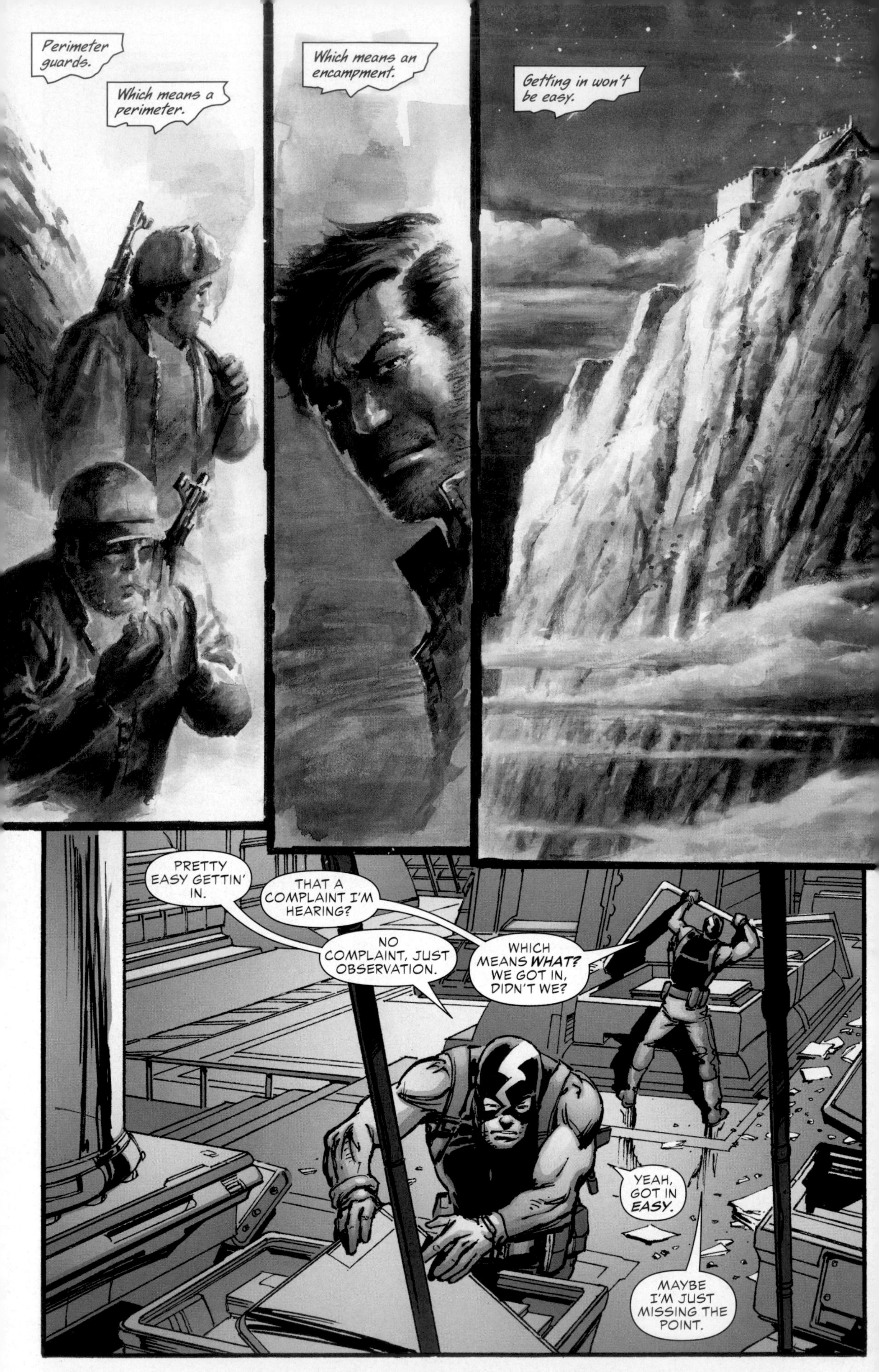
Perimeter guards.
Which means a perimeter.
Which means an encampment.
Getting in won't be easy.
PRETTY EASY GETTIN' IN.
THAT A COMPLAINT I'M HEARING?
NO COMPLAINT, JUST OBSERVATION.
WHICH MEANS WHAT? WE GOT IN, DIDN'T WE?
YEAH, GOT IN EASY.
MAYBE I'M JUST MISSING THE POINT.

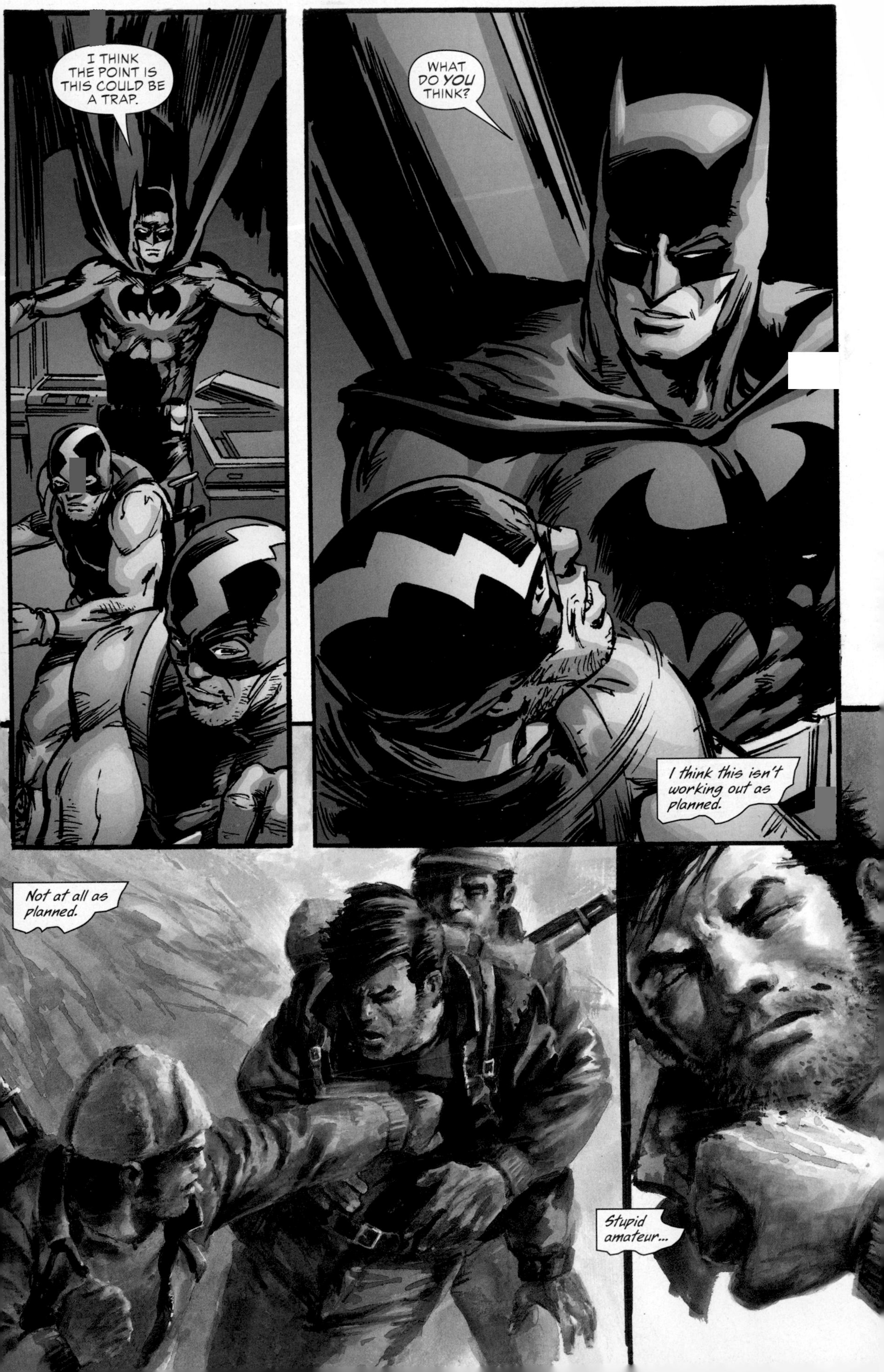
I THINK THE POINT IS THIS COULD BE A TRAP.
WHAT DO YOU THINK?
I think this isn't working out as planned.
Not at all as planned.
Stupid amateur...

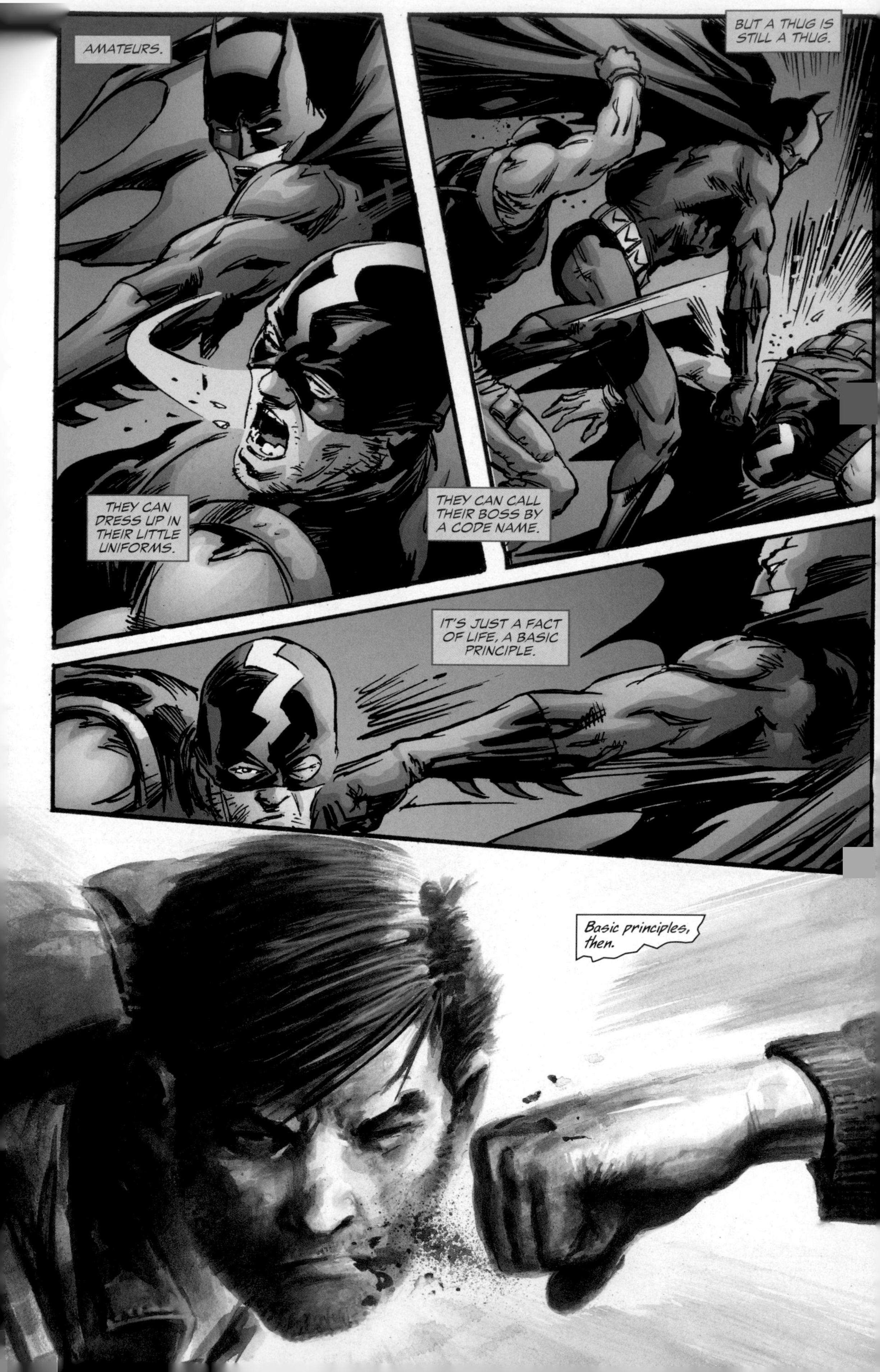
AMATEURS.
BUT A THUG IS STILL A THUG.
THEY CAN DRESS UP IN THEIR LITTLE UNIFORMS.
THEY CAN CALL THEIR BOSS BY A CODE NAME.
IT'S JUST A FACT OF LIFE, A BASIC PRINCIPLE.
Basic principles, then.

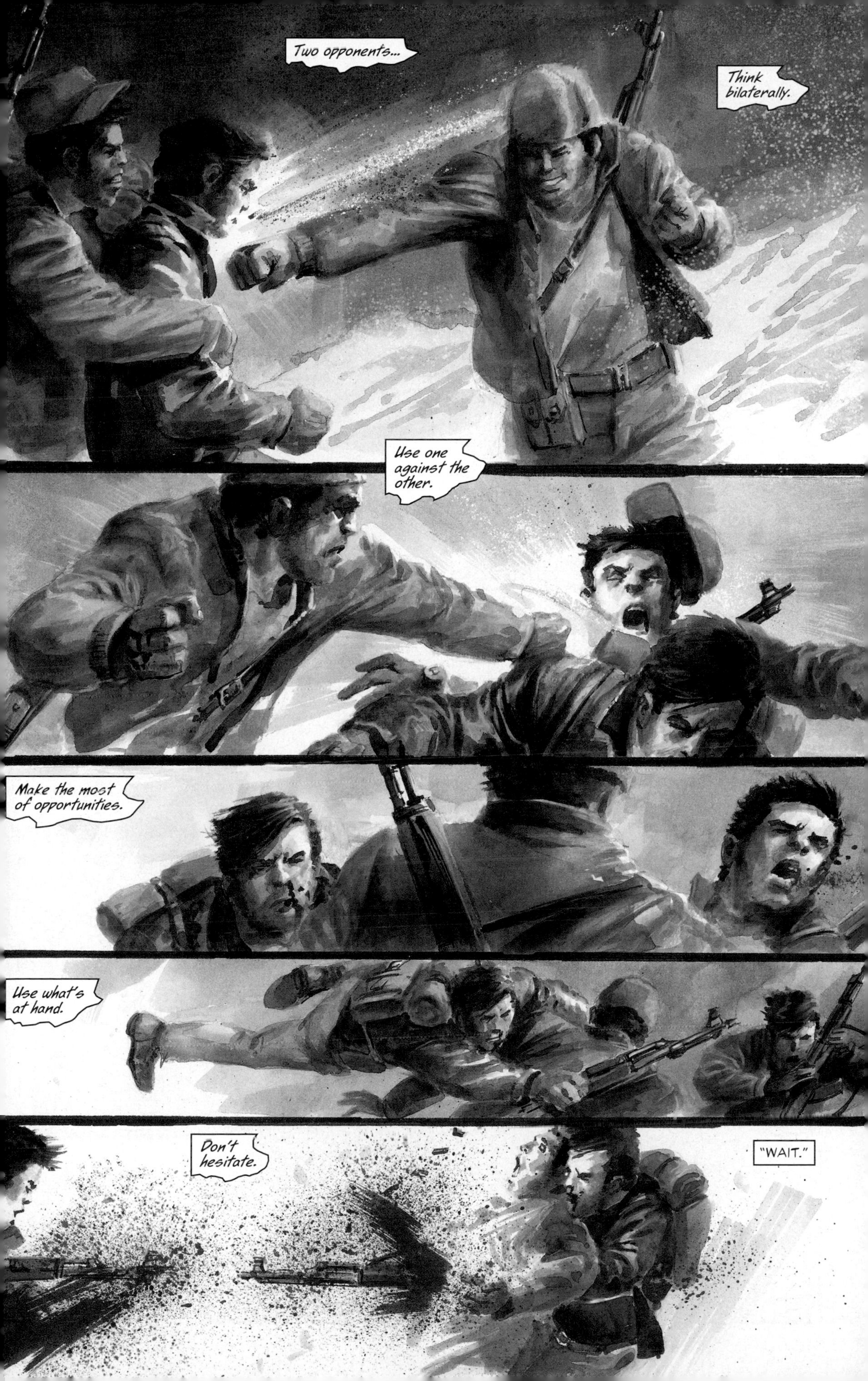
Two opponents...
Think bilaterally.
Use one against the other.
Make the most of opportunities.
Use what's at hand.
Don't hesitate.
"WAIT."

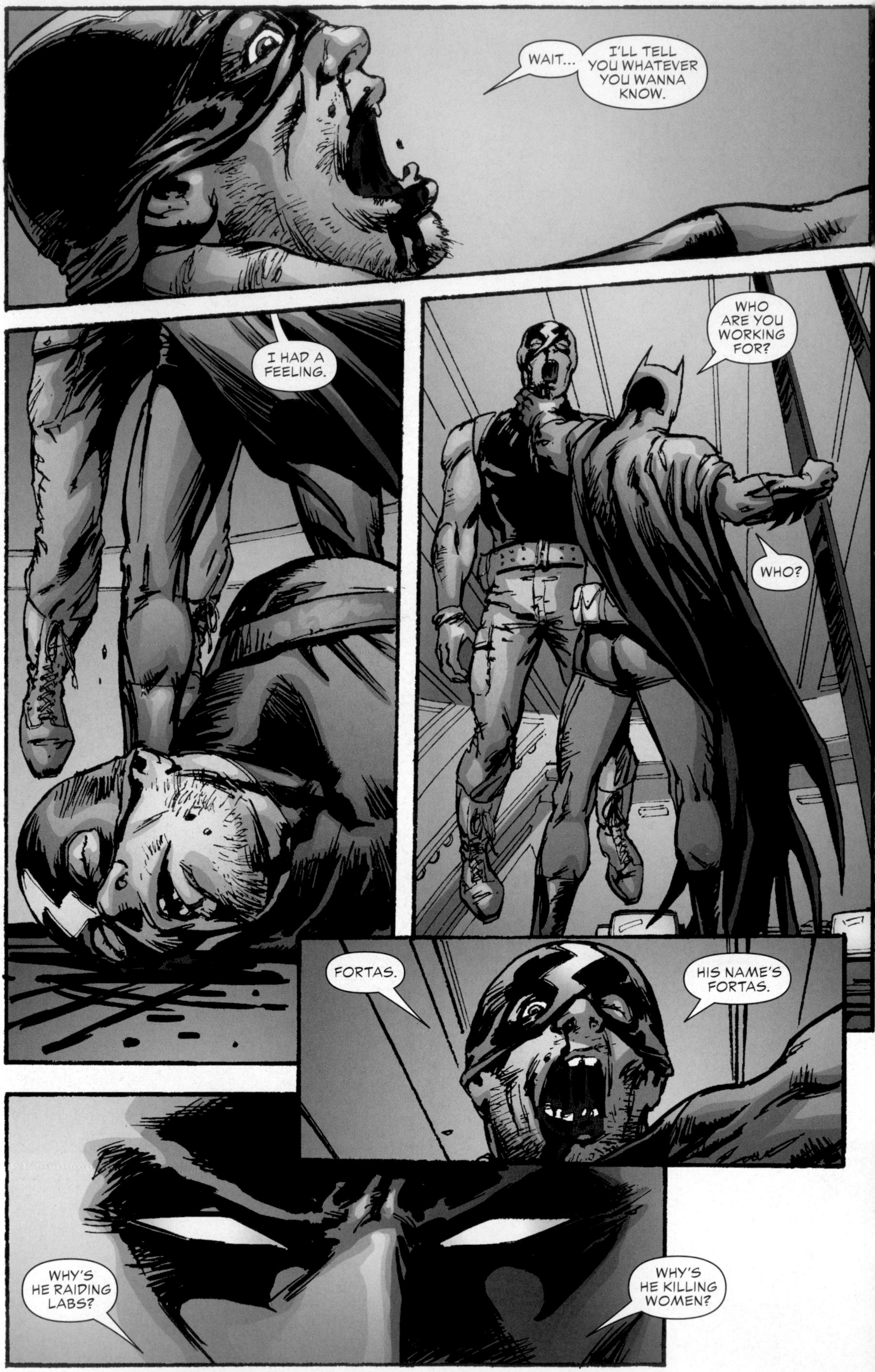
WAIT...
I'LL TELL YOU WHATEVER YOU WANNA KNOW.
I HAD A FEELING.
WHO ARE YOU WORKING FOR?
WHO?
FORTAS.
HIS NAME'S FORTAS.
WHY'S HE RAIDING LABS?
WHY'S HE KILLING WOMEN?

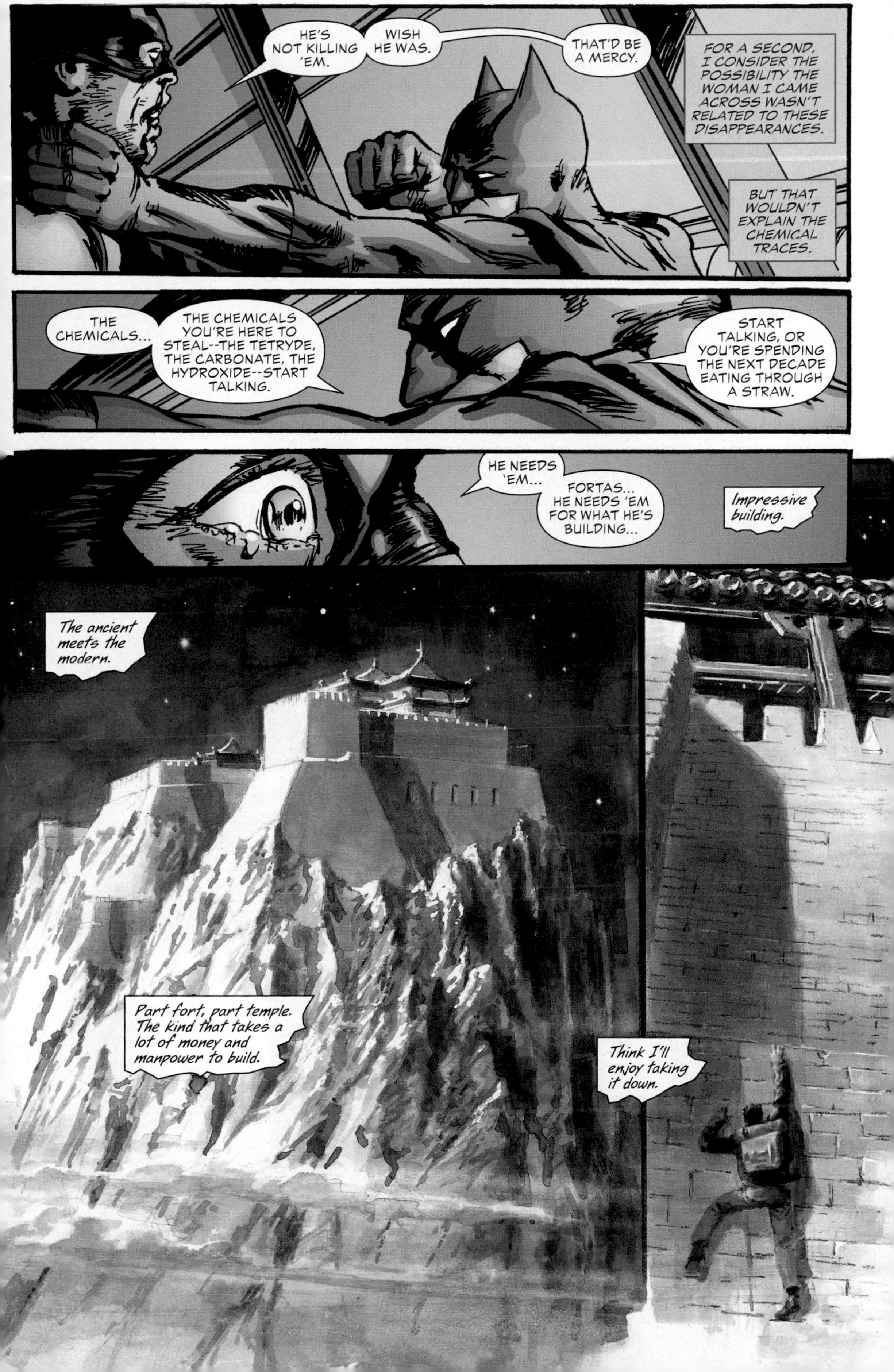

HE'S NOT KILLING 'EM.
WISH HE WAS.
THAT'D BE A MERCY.
FOR A SECOND, I CONSIDER THE POSSIBILITY THE WOMAN I CAME ACROSS WASN'T RELATED TO THESE DISAPPEARANCES.
BUT THAT WOULDN'T EXPLAIN THE CHEMICAL TRACES.
THE CHEMICALS...
THE CHEMICALS YOU'RE HERE TO STEAL--THE TETRYDE, THE CARBONATE, THE HYDROXIDE--START TALKING.
START TALKING, OR YOU'RE SPENDING THE NEXT DECADE EATING THROUGH A STRAW.
HE NEEDS 'EM...
FORTAS... HE NEEDS 'EM FOR WHAT HE'S BUILDING...
Impressive building.
The ancient meets the modern.
Part fort, part temple. The kind that takes a lot of money and manpower to build.
Think I'll enjoy taking it down.

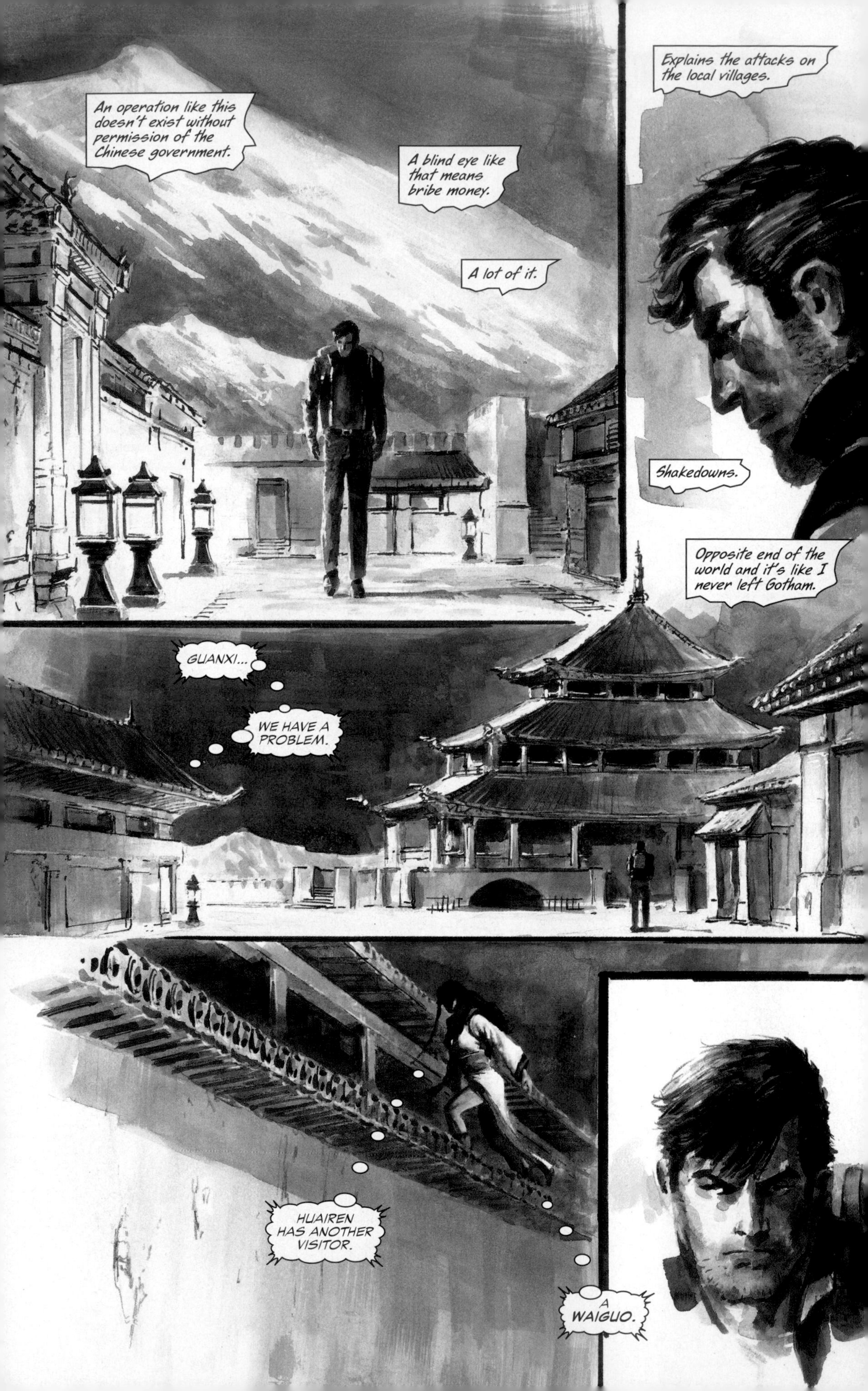
An operation like this doesn't exist without permission of the Chinese government.
A blind eye like that means bribe money.
A lot of it.
Explains the attacks on the local villages.
Shakedowns.
Opposite end of the world and it's like I never left Gotham.
GUANXI...
WE HAVE A PROBLEM.
HUAIREN HAS ANOTHER VISITOR.
A WAIGUO.

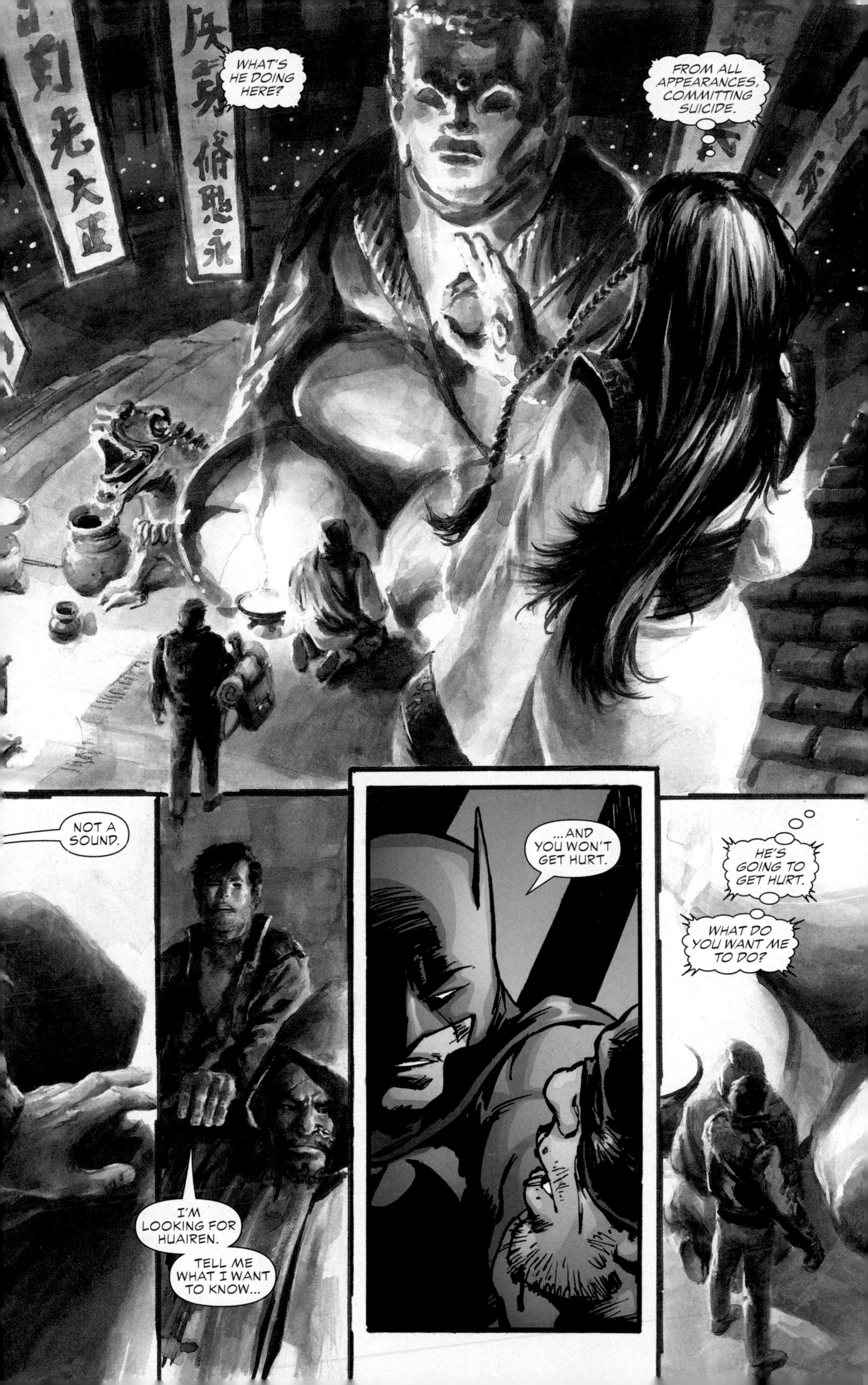
WHAT'S HE DOING HERE?
FROM ALL APPEARANCES, COMMITTING SUICIDE.
NOT A SOUND.
I'M LOOKING FOR HUAIREN.
TELL ME WHAT I WANT TO KNOW...
...AND YOU WON'T GET HURT.
HE'S GOING TO GET HURT.
WHAT DO YOU WANT ME TO DO?

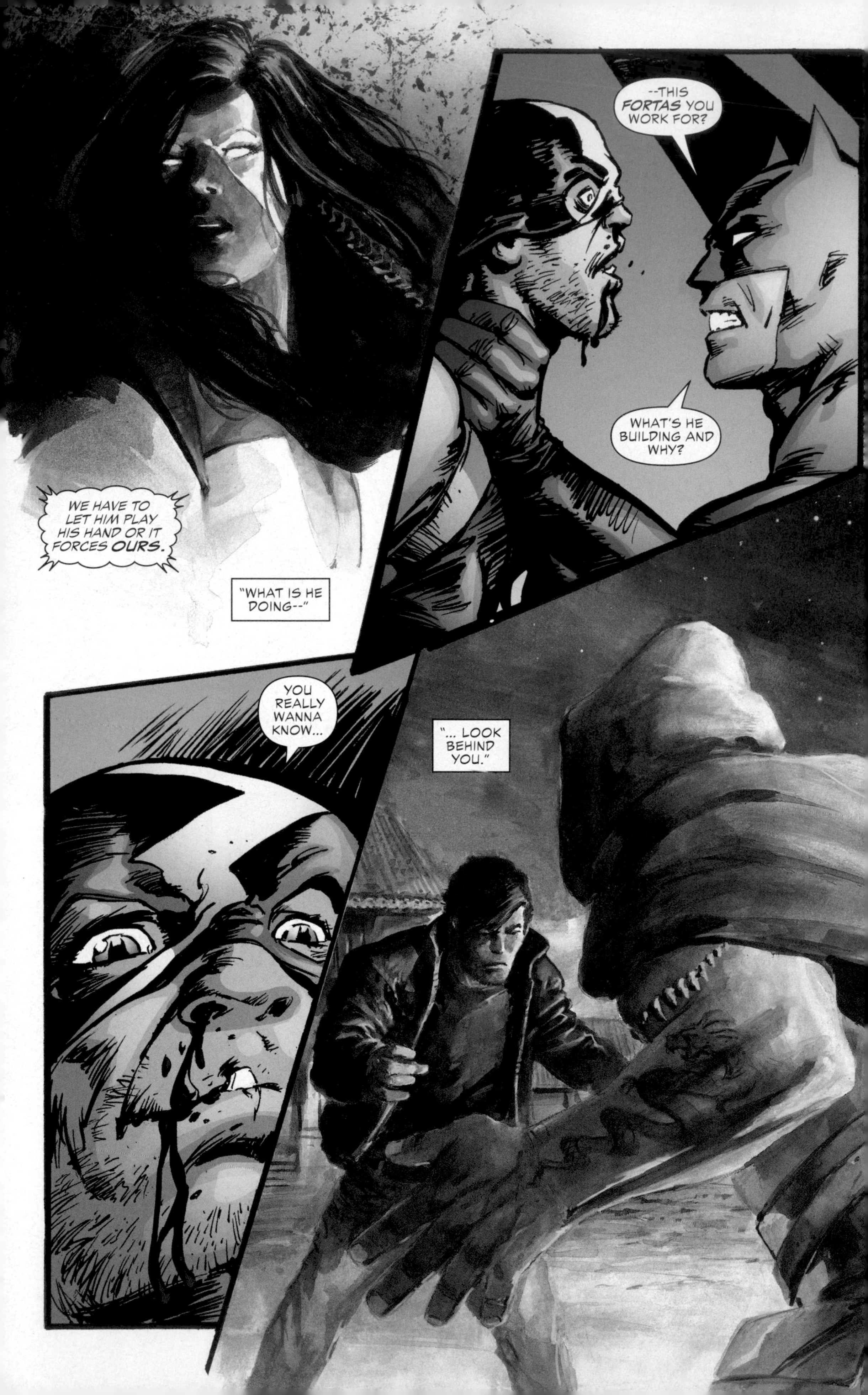

WE HAVE TO LET HIM PLAY HIS HAND OR IT FORCES OURS.
"WHAT IS HE DOING--"
--THIS FORTAS YOU WORK FOR?
WHAT'S HE BUILDING AND WHY?
YOU REALLY WANNA KNOW...
"... LOOK BEHIND YOU."

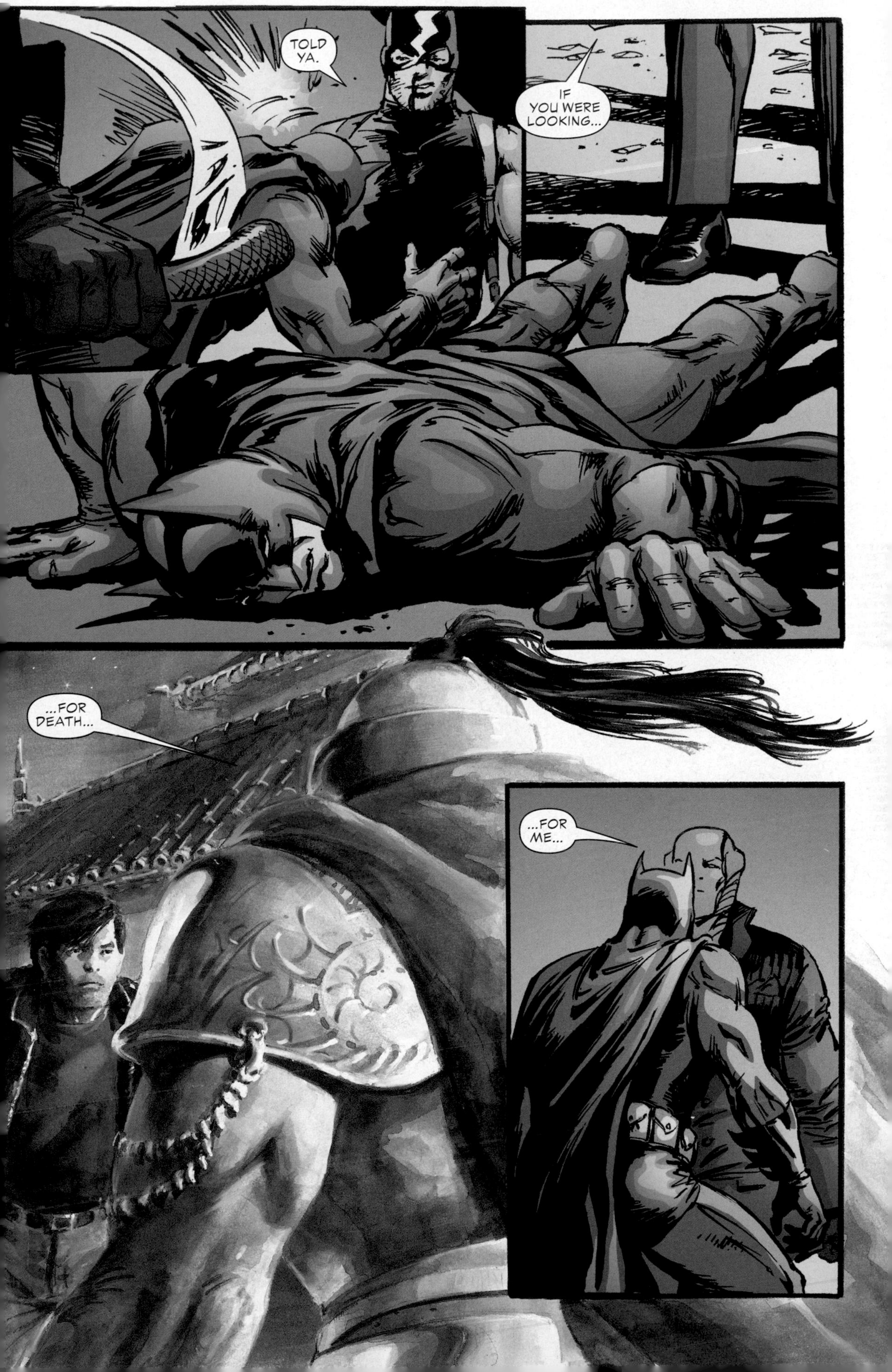
TOLD YA.
IF YOU WERE LOOKING...
...FOR DEATH...
...FOR ME...

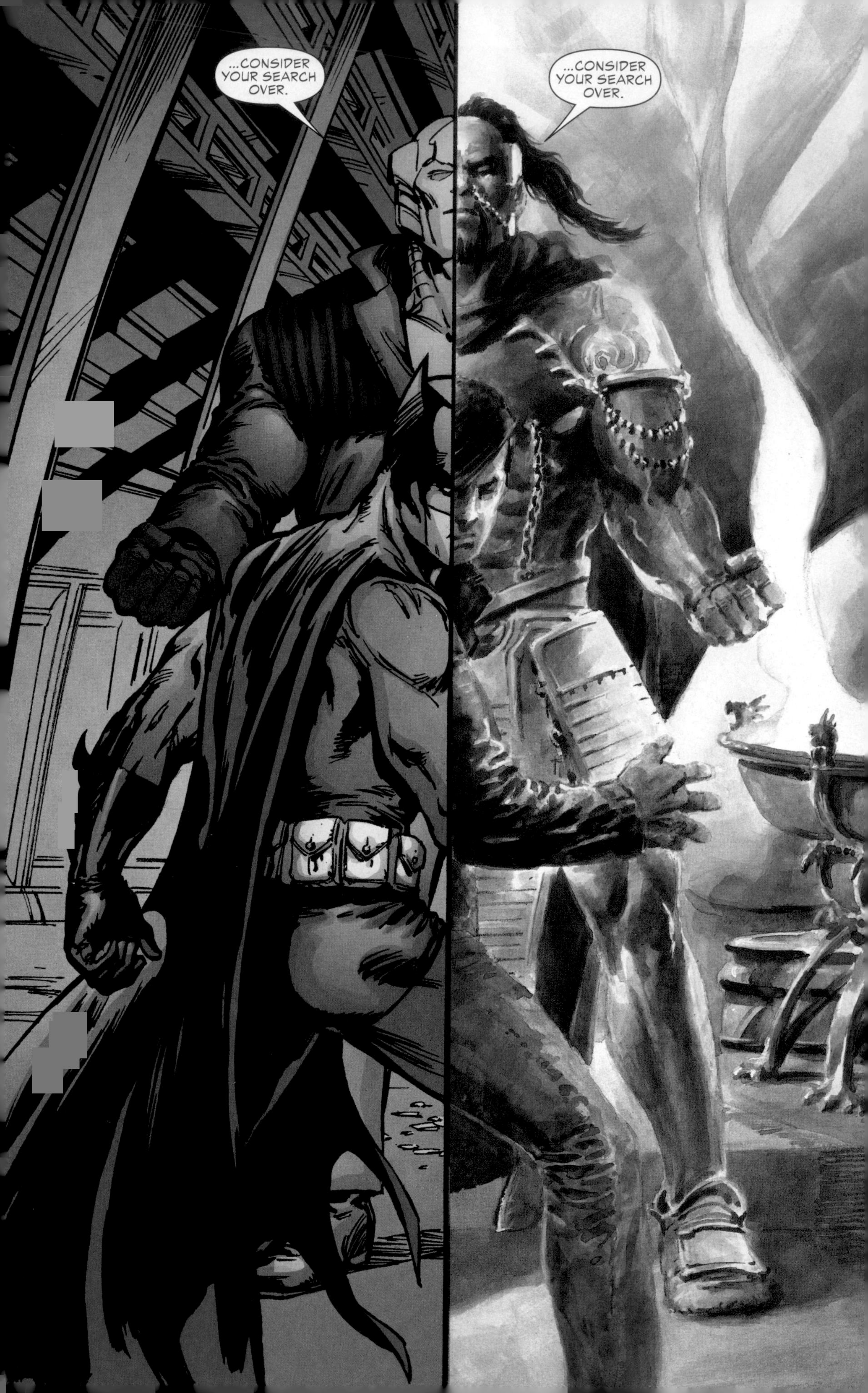
...CONSIDER YOUR SEARCH OVER.
...CONSIDER YOUR SEARCH OVER.

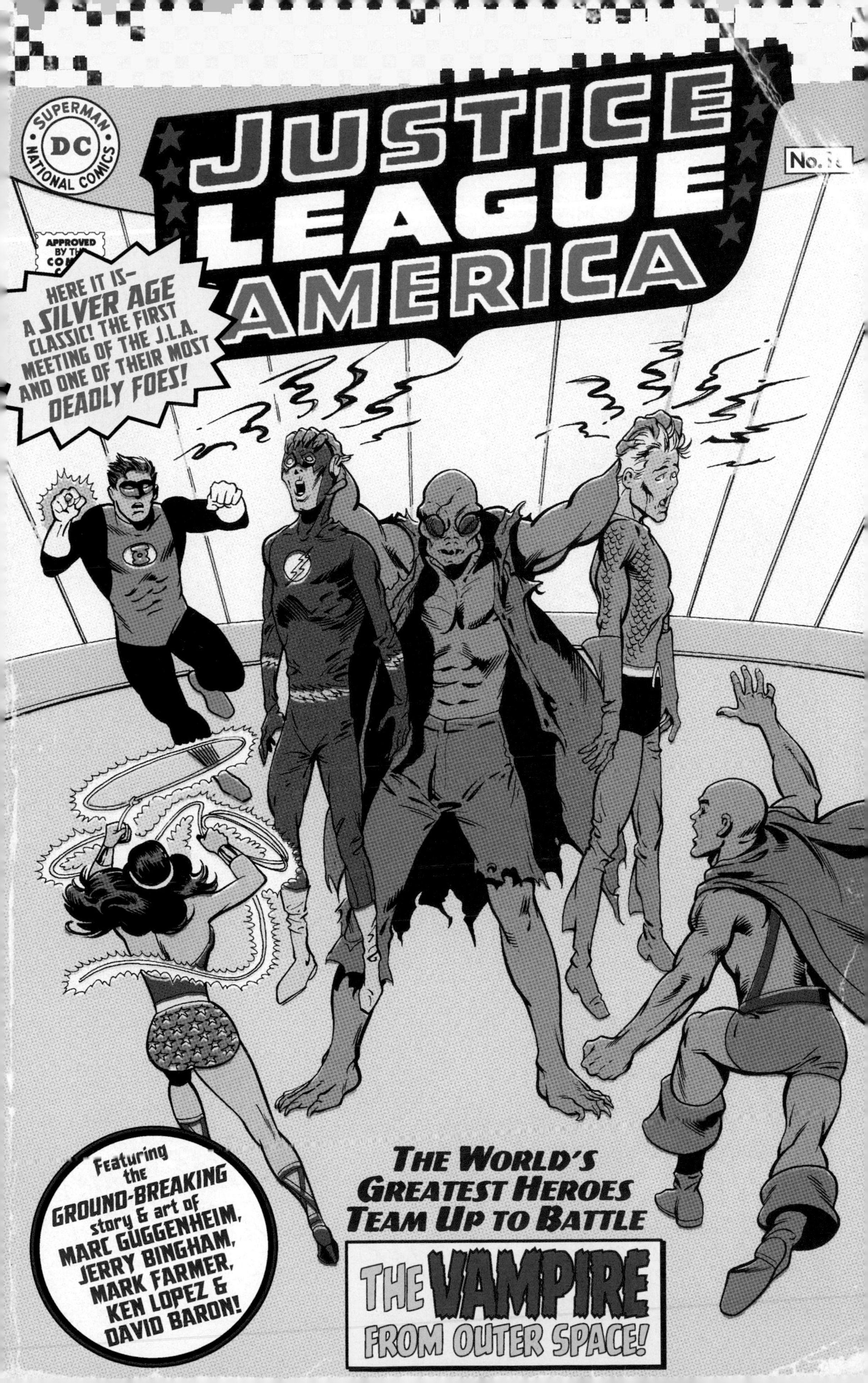
SUPERMAN DC NATIONAL COMICS
JUSTICE LEAGUE AMERICA
APPROVED
HERE IT IS— A SILVER AGE CLASSIC! THE FIRST MEETING OF THE J.L.A. AND ONE OF THEIR MOST DEADLY FOES!
THE WORLD'S GREATEST HEROES TEAM UP TO BATTLE
THE VAMPIRE FROM OUTER SPACE!
Featuring the GROUND-BREAKING story & art of MARC GUGGENHEIM, JERRY BINGHAM, MARK FARMER, KEN LOPEZ & DAVID BARON!

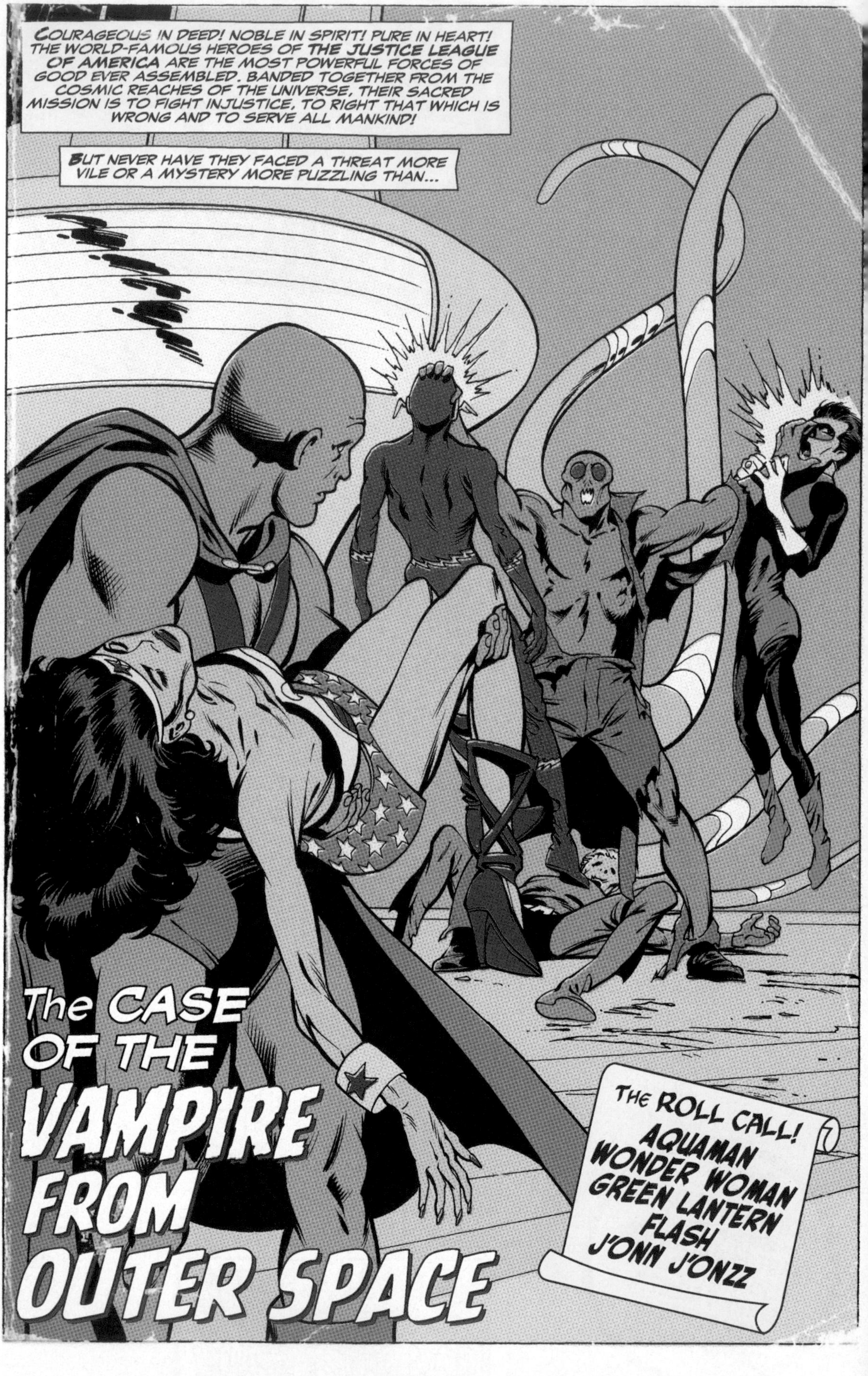
COURAGEOUS IN DEED! NOBLE IN SPIRIT! PURE IN HEART! THE WORLD-FAMOUS HEROES OF THE JUSTICE LEAGUE OF AMERICA ARE THE MOST POWERFUL FORCES OF GOOD EVER ASSEMBLED. BANDED TOGETHER FROM THE COSMIC REACHES OF THE UNIVERSE, THEIR SACRED MISSION IS TO FIGHT INJUSTICE, TO RIGHT THAT WHICH IS WRONG AND TO SERVE ALL MANKIND!
BUT NEVER HAVE THEY FACED A THREAT MORE VILE OR A MYSTERY MORE PUZZLING THAN...
The CASE OF THE VAMPIRE FROM OUTER SPACE
THE ROLL CALL! AQUAMAN WONDER WOMAN GREEN LANTERN FLASH J'ONN J'ONZZ

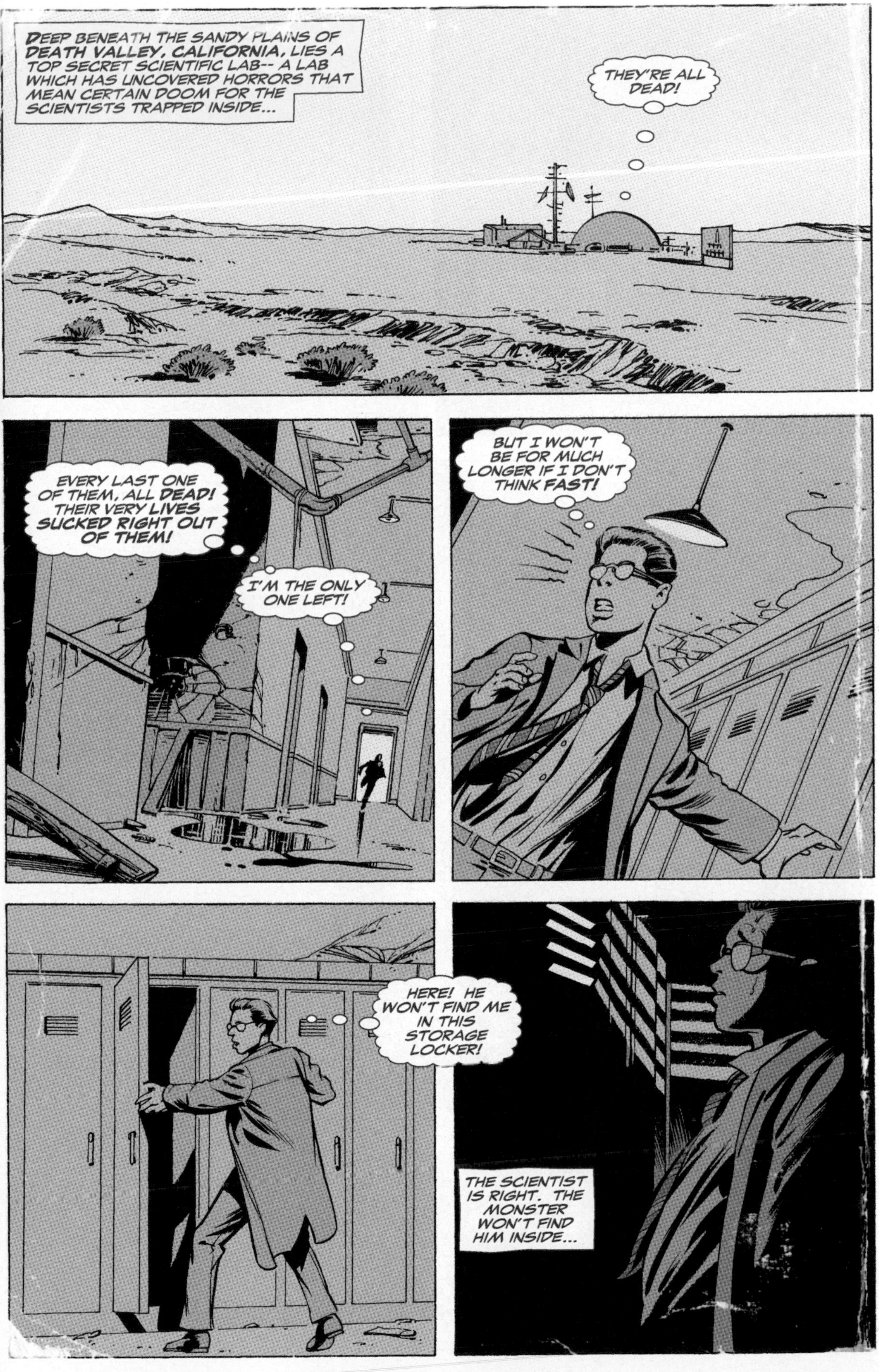
DEEP BENEATH THE SANDY PLAINS OF DEATH VALLEY, CALIFORNIA, LIES A TOP SECRET SCIENTIFIC LAB-- A LAB WHICH HAS UNCOVERED HORRORS THAT MEAN CERTAIN DOOM FOR THE SCIENTISTS TRAPPED INSIDE...
THEY'RE ALL DEAD!
EVERY LAST ONE OF THEM, ALL DEAD! THEIR VERY LIVES SUCKED RIGHT OUT OF THEM!
I'M THE ONLY ONE LEFT!
BUT I WON'T BE FOR MUCH LONGER IF I DON'T THINK FAST!
HERE! HE WON'T FIND ME IN THIS STORAGE LOCKER!
THE SCIENTIST IS RIGHT. THE MONSTER WON'T FIND HIM INSIDE...

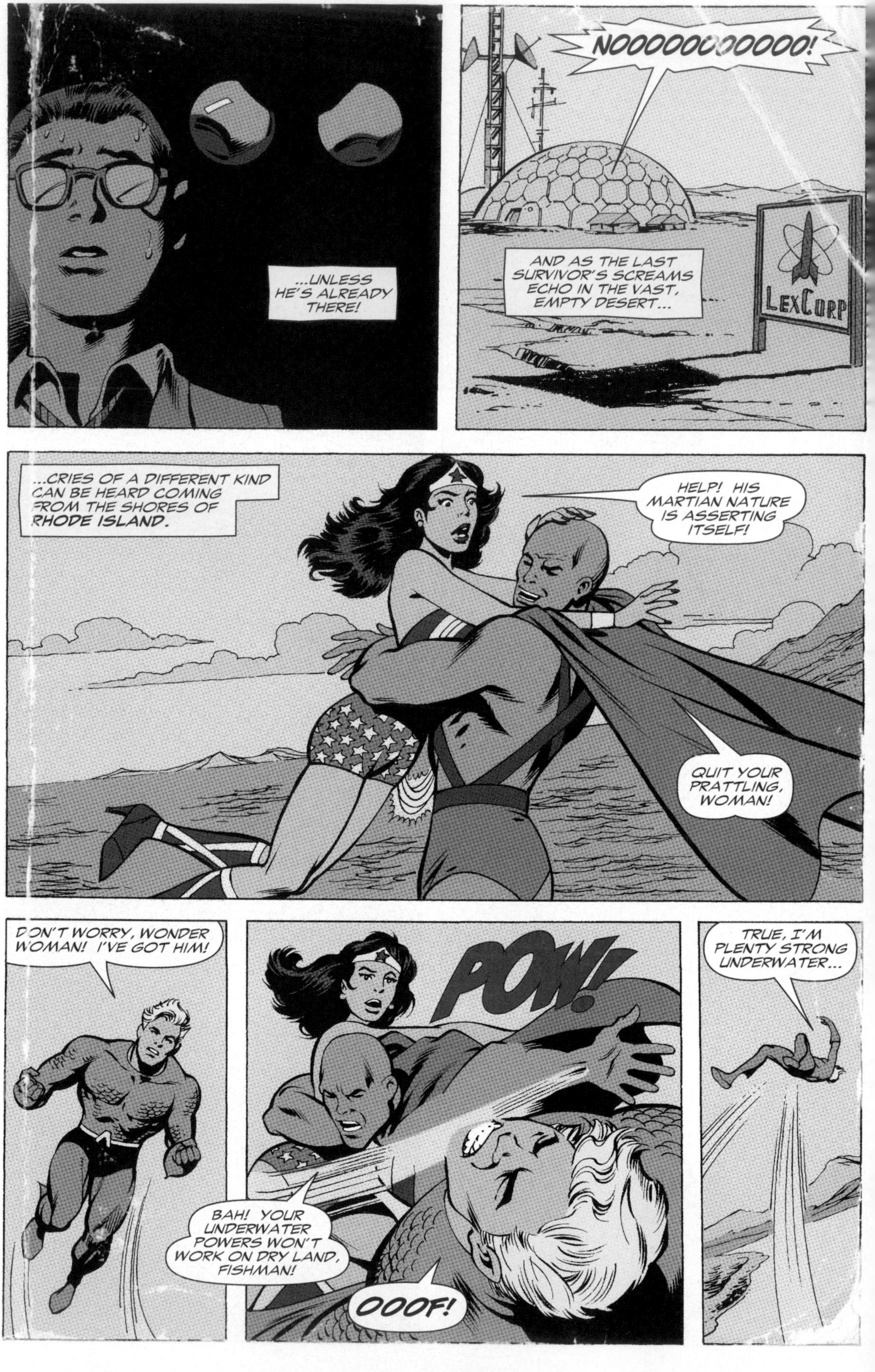
...UNLESS HE'S ALREADY THERE!
NOOOOOOOOOOO!
AND AS THE LAST SURVIVOR'S SCREAMS ECHO IN THE VAST, EMPTY DESERT...
LEXCORP
...CRIES OF A DIFFERENT KIND CAN BE HEARD COMING FROM THE SHORES OF RHODE ISLAND.
HELP! HIS MARTIAN NATURE IS ASSERTING ITSELF!
QUIT YOUR PRATTLING, WOMAN!
DON'T WORRY, WONDER WOMAN! I'VE GOT HIM!
POW!
BAH! YOUR UNDERWATER POWERS WON'T WORK ON DRY LAND, FISHMAN!
OOOF!
TRUE, I'M PLENTY STRONG UNDERWATER...

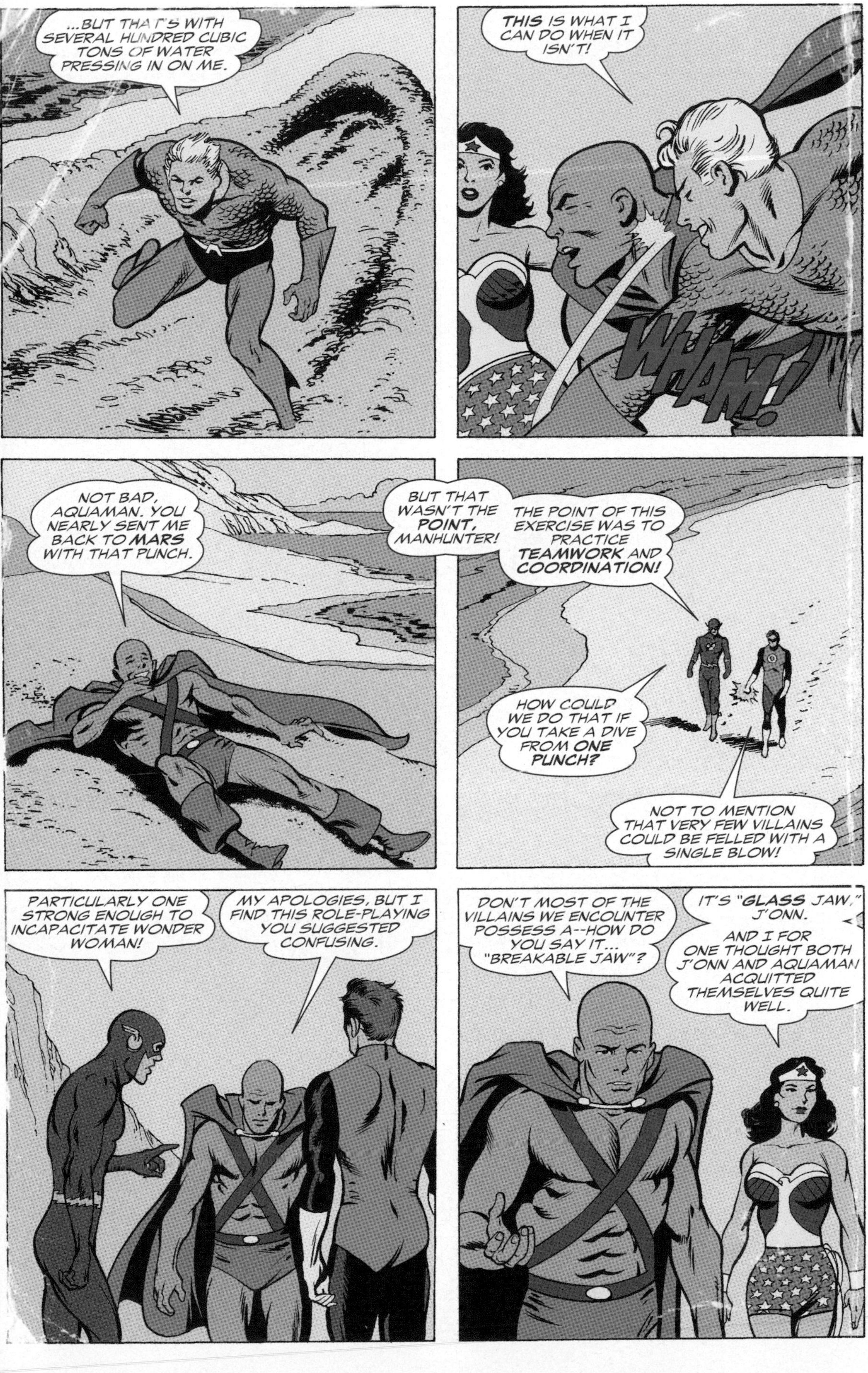
...BUT THAT'S WITH SEVERAL HUNDRED CUBIC TONS OF WATER PRESSING IN ON ME.
THIS IS WHAT I CAN DO WHEN IT ISN'T!
WHAM!
NOT BAD, AQUAMAN. YOU NEARLY SENT ME BACK TO MARS WITH THAT PUNCH.
BUT THAT WASN'T THE POINT, MANHUNTER!
THE POINT OF THIS EXERCISE WAS TO PRACTICE TEAMWORK AND COORDINATION!
HOW COULD WE DO THAT IF YOU TAKE A DIVE FROM ONE PUNCH?
NOT TO MENTION THAT VERY FEW VILLAINS COULD BE FELLED WITH A SINGLE BLOW!
PARTICULARLY ONE STRONG ENOUGH TO INCAPACITATE WONDER WOMAN!
MY APOLOGIES, BUT I FIND THIS ROLE-PLAYING YOU SUGGESTED CONFUSING.
DON'T MOST OF THE VILLAINS WE ENCOUNTER POSSESS A--HOW DO YOU SAY IT... "BREAKABLE JAW"?
IT'S "GLASS JAW," J'ONN.
AND I FOR ONE THOUGHT BOTH J'ONN AND AQUAMAN ACQUITTED THEMSELVES QUITE WELL.

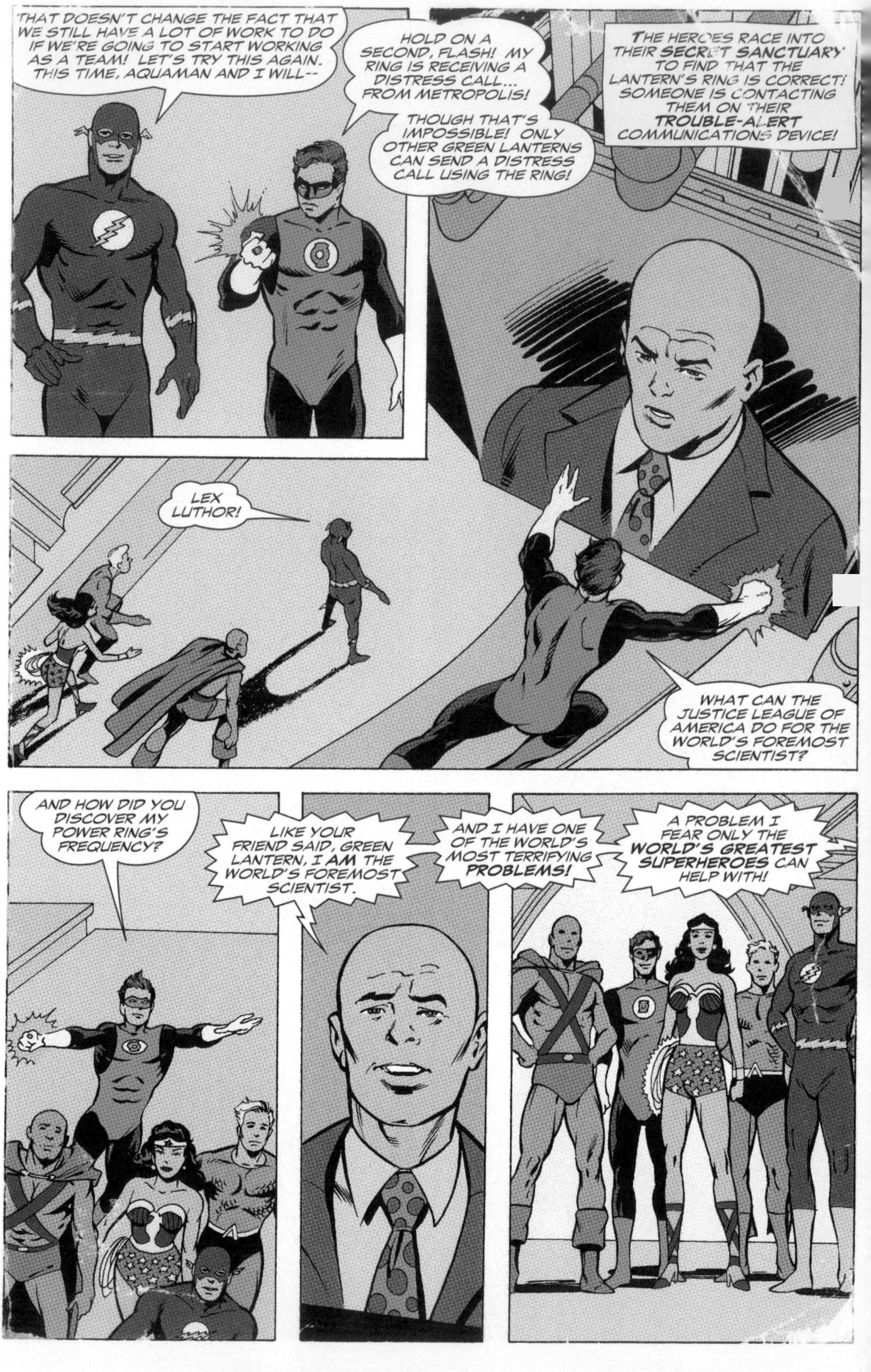
THAT DOESN'T CHANGE THE FACT THAT WE STILL HAVE A LOT OF WORK TO DO IF WE'RE GOING TO START WORKING AS A TEAM! LET'S TRY THIS AGAIN. THIS TIME, AQUAMAN AND I WILL--
HOLD ON A SECOND, FLASH! MY RING IS RECEIVING A DISTRESS CALL... FROM METROPOLIS!
THOUGH THAT'S IMPOSSIBLE! ONLY OTHER GREEN LANTERNS CAN SEND A DISTRESS CALL USING THE RING!
THE HEROES RACE INTO THEIR SECRET SANCTUARY TO FIND THAT THE LANTERN'S RING IS CORRECT! SOMEONE IS CONTACTING THEM ON THEIR TROUBLE-ALERT COMMUNICATIONS DEVICE!
LEX LUTHOR!
WHAT CAN THE JUSTICE LEAGUE OF AMERICA DO FOR THE WORLD'S FOREMOST SCIENTIST?
AND HOW DID YOU DISCOVER MY POWER RING'S FREQUENCY?
LIKE YOUR FRIEND SAID, GREEN LANTERN, I AM THE WORLD'S FOREMOST SCIENTIST.
AND I HAVE ONE OF THE WORLD'S MOST TERRIFYING PROBLEMS!
A PROBLEM I FEAR ONLY THE WORLD'S GREATEST SUPERHEROES CAN HELP WITH!

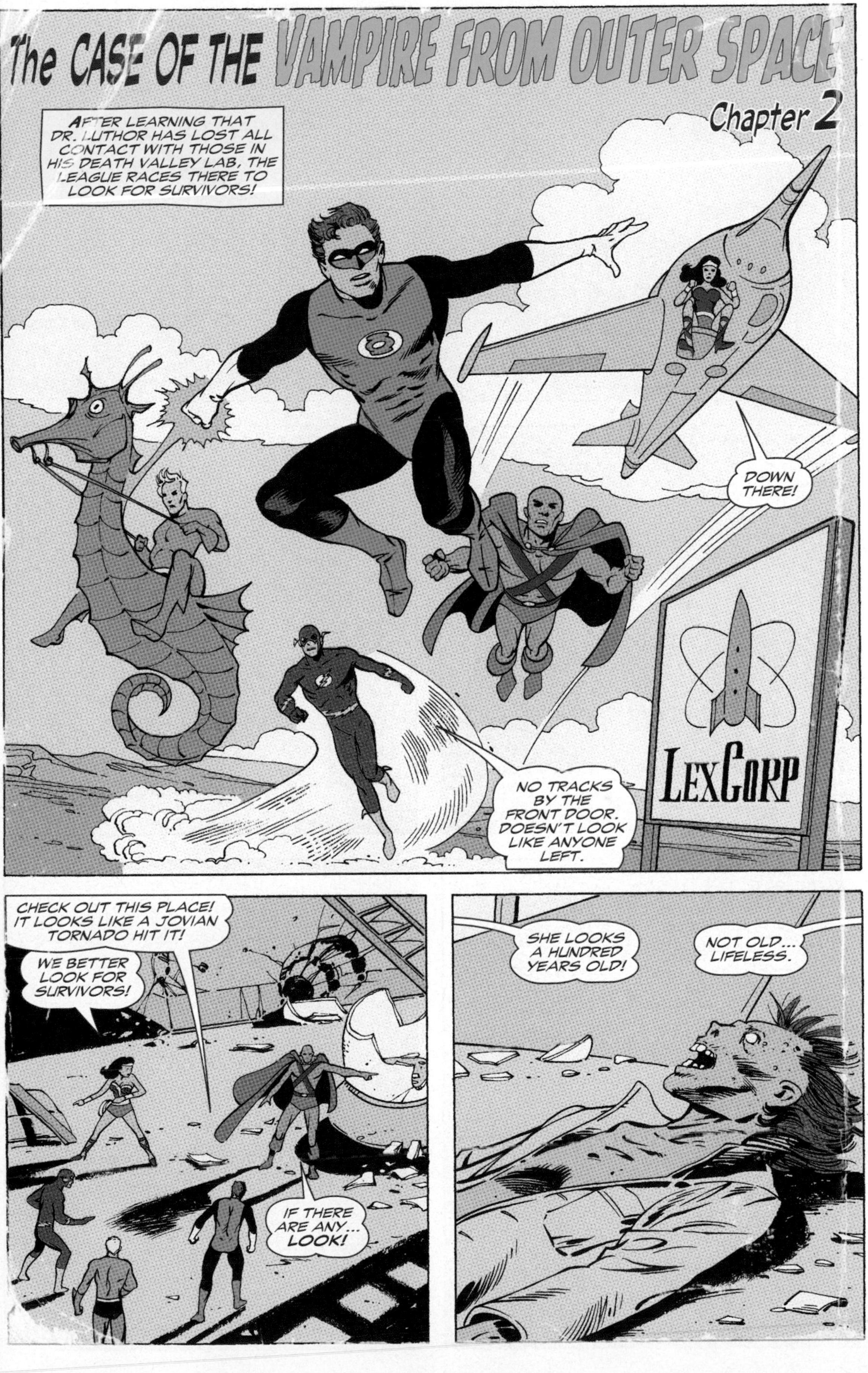
The CASE OF THE VAMPIRE FROM OUTER SPACE
Chapter 2
AFTER LEARNING THAT DR. LUTHOR HAS LOST ALL CONTACT WITH THOSE IN HIS DEATH VALLEY LAB, THE LEAGUE RACES THERE TO LOOK FOR SURVIVORS!
DOWN THERE!
LEXCORP
NO TRACKS BY THE FRONT DOOR. DOESN'T LOOK LIKE ANYONE LEFT.
CHECK OUT THIS PLACE! IT LOOKS LIKE A JOVIAN TORNADO HIT IT!
WE BETTER LOOK FOR SURVIVORS!
IF THERE ARE ANY... LOOK!
SHE LOOKS A HUNDRED YEARS OLD!
NOT OLD... LIFELESS.

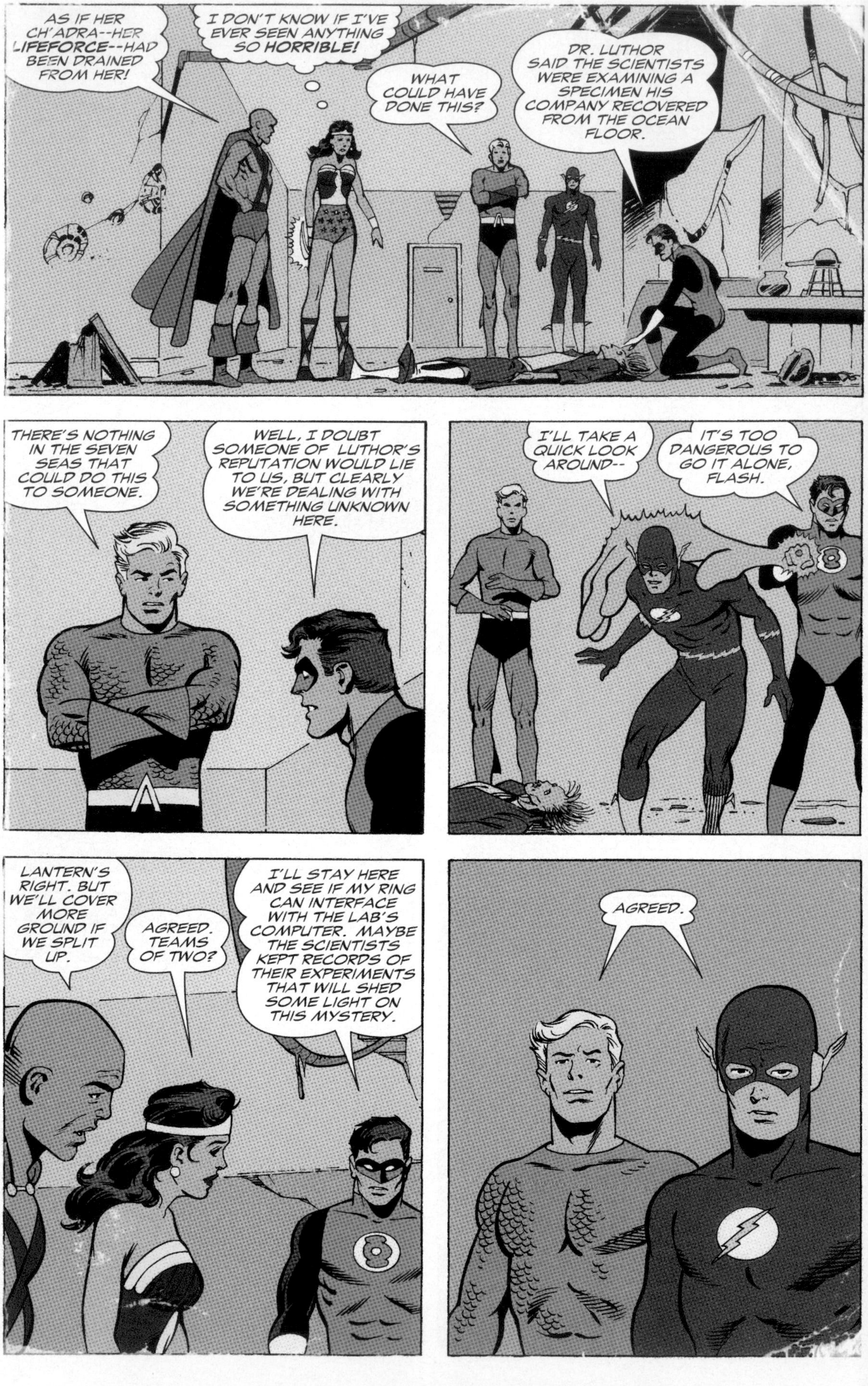
AS IF HER CH'ADRA--HER LIFEFORCE--HAD BEEN DRAINED FROM HER!
I DON'T KNOW IF I'VE EVER SEEN ANYTHING SO HORRIBLE!
WHAT COULD HAVE DONE THIS?
DR. LUTHOR SAID THE SCIENTISTS WERE EXAMINING A SPECIMEN HIS COMPANY RECOVERED FROM THE OCEAN FLOOR.
THERE'S NOTHING IN THE SEVEN SEAS THAT COULD DO THIS TO SOMEONE.
WELL, I DOUBT SOMEONE OF LUTHOR'S REPUTATION WOULD LIE TO US, BUT CLEARLY WE'RE DEALING WITH SOMETHING UNKNOWN HERE.
I'LL TAKE A QUICK LOOK AROUND--
IT'S TOO DANGEROUS TO GO IT ALONE, FLASH.
LANTERN'S RIGHT. BUT WE'LL COVER MORE GROUND IF WE SPLIT UP.
AGREED. TEAMS OF TWO?
I'LL STAY HERE AND SEE IF MY RING CAN INTERFACE WITH THE LAB'S COMPUTER. MAYBE THE SCIENTISTS KEPT RECORDS OF THEIR EXPERIMENTS THAT WILL SHED SOME LIGHT ON THIS MYSTERY.
AGREED.

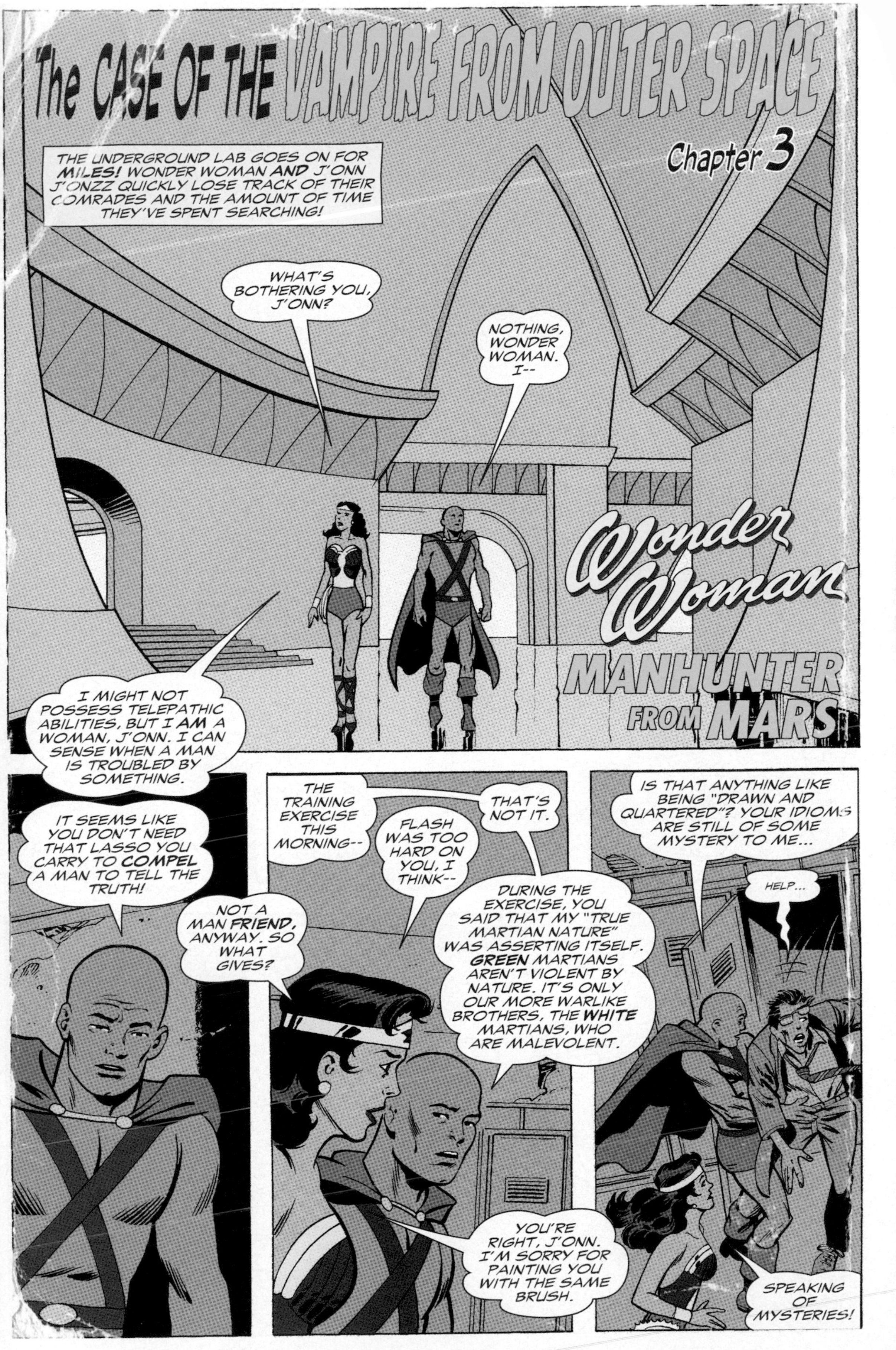

The CASE OF THE VAMPIRE FROM OUTER SPACE
Chapter 3
THE UNDERGROUND LAB GOES ON FOR MILES! WONDER WOMAN AND J'ONN J'ONZZ QUICKLY LOSE TRACK OF THEIR COMRADES AND THE AMOUNT OF TIME THEY'VE SPENT SEARCHING!
WHAT'S BOTHERING YOU, J'ONN?
NOTHING, WONDER WOMAN. I--
Wonder Woman
MANHUNTER FROM MARS
I MIGHT NOT POSSESS TELEPATHIC ABILITIES, BUT I AM A WOMAN, J'ONN. I CAN SENSE WHEN A MAN IS TROUBLED BY SOMETHING.
IT SEEMS LIKE YOU DON'T NEED THAT LASSO YOU CARRY TO COMPEL A MAN TO TELL THE TRUTH!
NOT A MAN FRIEND, ANYWAY. SO WHAT GIVES?
THE TRAINING EXERCISE THIS MORNING--
THAT'S NOT IT.
FLASH WAS TOO HARD ON YOU, I THINK--
DURING THE EXERCISE, YOU SAID THAT MY "TRUE MARTIAN NATURE" WAS ASSERTING ITSELF. GREEN MARTIANS AREN'T VIOLENT BY NATURE. IT'S ONLY OUR MORE WARLIKE BROTHERS, THE WHITE MARTIANS, WHO ARE MALEVOLENT.
YOU'RE RIGHT, J'ONN. I'M SORRY FOR PAINTING YOU WITH THE SAME BRUSH.
IS THAT ANYTHING LIKE BEING "DRAWN AND QUARTERED"? YOUR IDIOMS ARE STILL OF SOME MYSTERY TO ME...
HELP...
SPEAKING OF MYSTERIES!

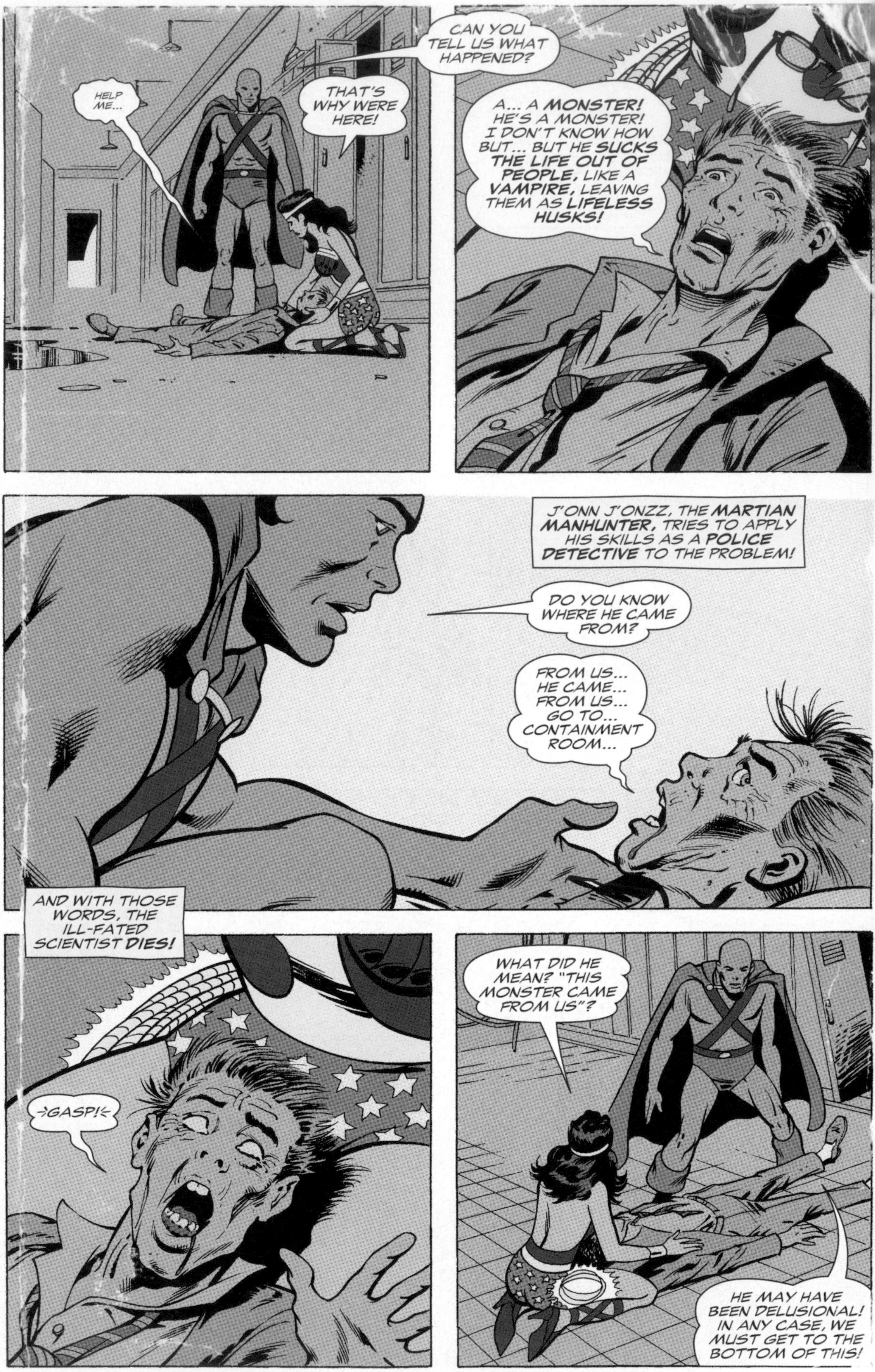
CAN YOU TELL US WHAT HAPPENED?
HELP ME...
THAT'S WHY WERE HERE!
A... A MONSTER! HE'S A MONSTER! I DON'T KNOW HOW BUT... BUT HE SUCKS THE LIFE OUT OF PEOPLE, LIKE A VAMPIRE, LEAVING THEM AS LIFELESS HUSKS!
J'ONN J'ONZZ, THE MARTIAN MANHUNTER, TRIES TO APPLY HIS SKILLS AS A POLICE DETECTIVE TO THE PROBLEM!
DO YOU KNOW WHERE HE CAME FROM?
FROM US... HE CAME... FROM US... GO TO... CONTAINMENT ROOM...
AND WITH THOSE WORDS, THE ILL-FATED SCIENTIST DIES!
GASP!
WHAT DID HE MEAN? "THIS MONSTER CAME FROM US"?
HE MAY HAVE BEEN DELUSIONAL! IN ANY CASE, WE MUST GET TO THE BOTTOM OF THIS!

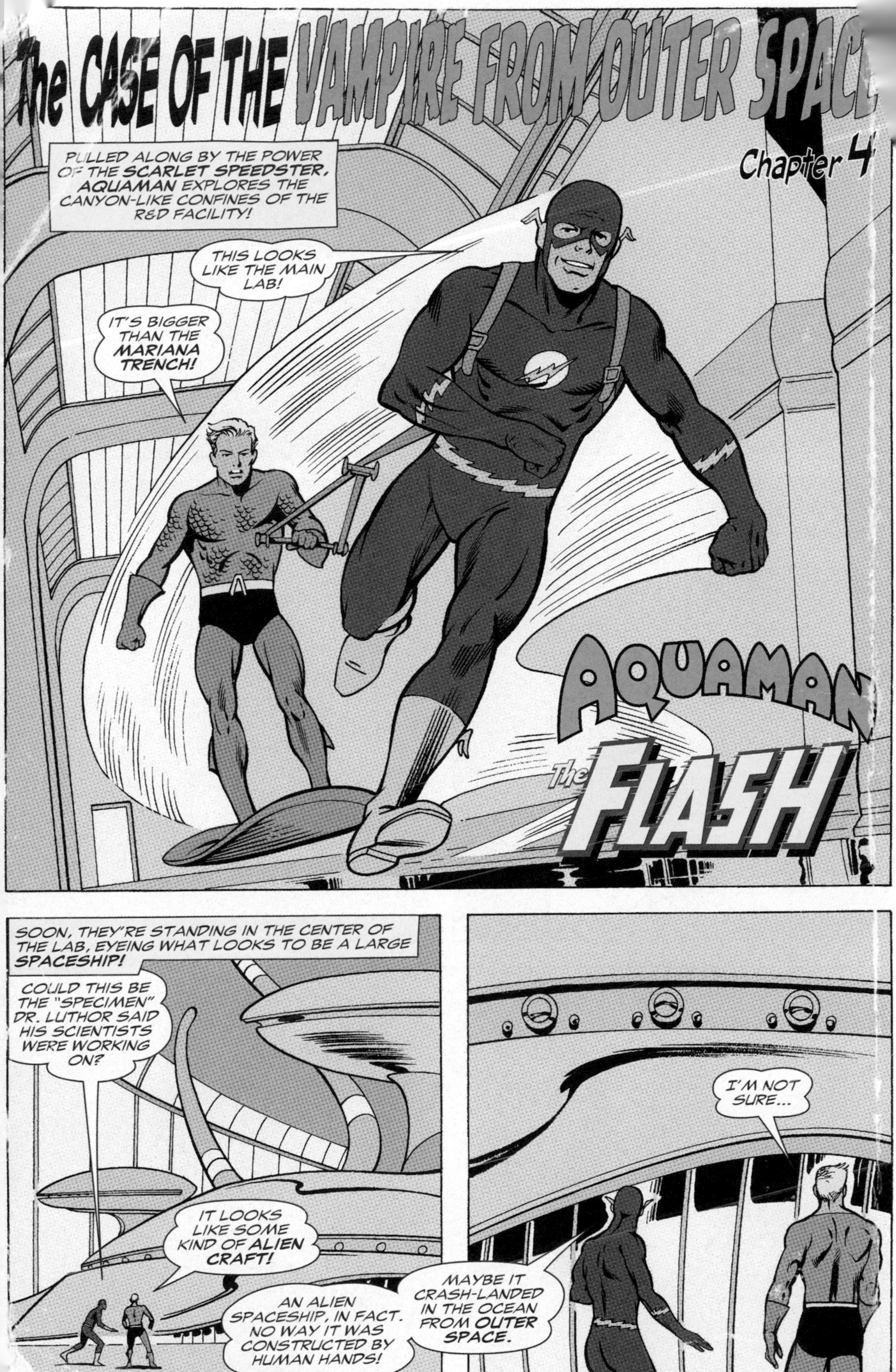
The CASE OF THE VAMPIRE FROM OUTER SPACE
Chapter 4
PULLED ALONG BY THE POWER OF THE SCARLET SPEEDSTER, AQUAMAN EXPLORES THE CANYON-LIKE CONFINES OF THE R&D FACILITY!
THIS LOOKS LIKE THE MAIN LAB!
IT'S BIGGER THAN THE MARIANA TRENCH!
AQUAMAN
The FLASH
SOON, THEY'RE STANDING IN THE CENTER OF THE LAB, EYEING WHAT LOOKS TO BE A LARGE SPACESHIP!
COULD THIS BE THE "SPECIMEN" DR. LUTHOR SAID HIS SCIENTISTS WERE WORKING ON?
IT LOOKS LIKE SOME KIND OF ALIEN CRAFT!
AN ALIEN SPACESHIP, IN FACT. NO WAY IT WAS CONSTRUCTED BY HUMAN HANDS!
MAYBE IT CRASH-LANDED IN THE OCEAN FROM OUTER SPACE.
I'M NOT SURE...

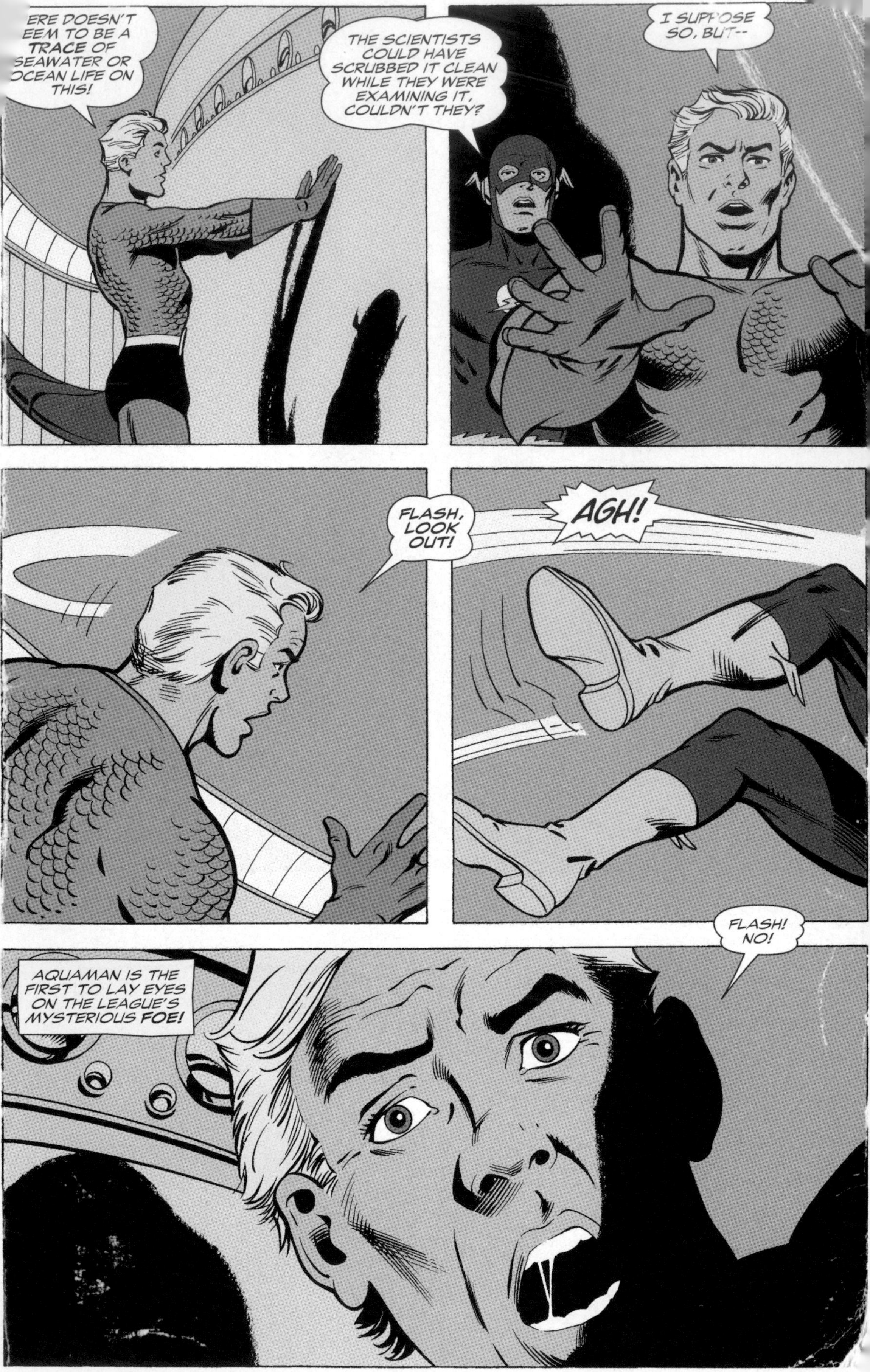
ERE DOESN'T EEM TO BE A TRACE OF SEAWATER OR OCEAN LIFE ON THIS!
THE SCIENTISTS COULD HAVE SCRUBBED IT CLEAN WHILE THEY WERE EXAMINING IT, COULDN'T THEY?
I SUPPOSE SO, BUT--
FLASH, LOOK OUT!
AGH!
AQUAMAN IS THE FIRST TO LAY EYES ON THE LEAGUE'S MYSTERIOUS FOE!
FLASH! NO!

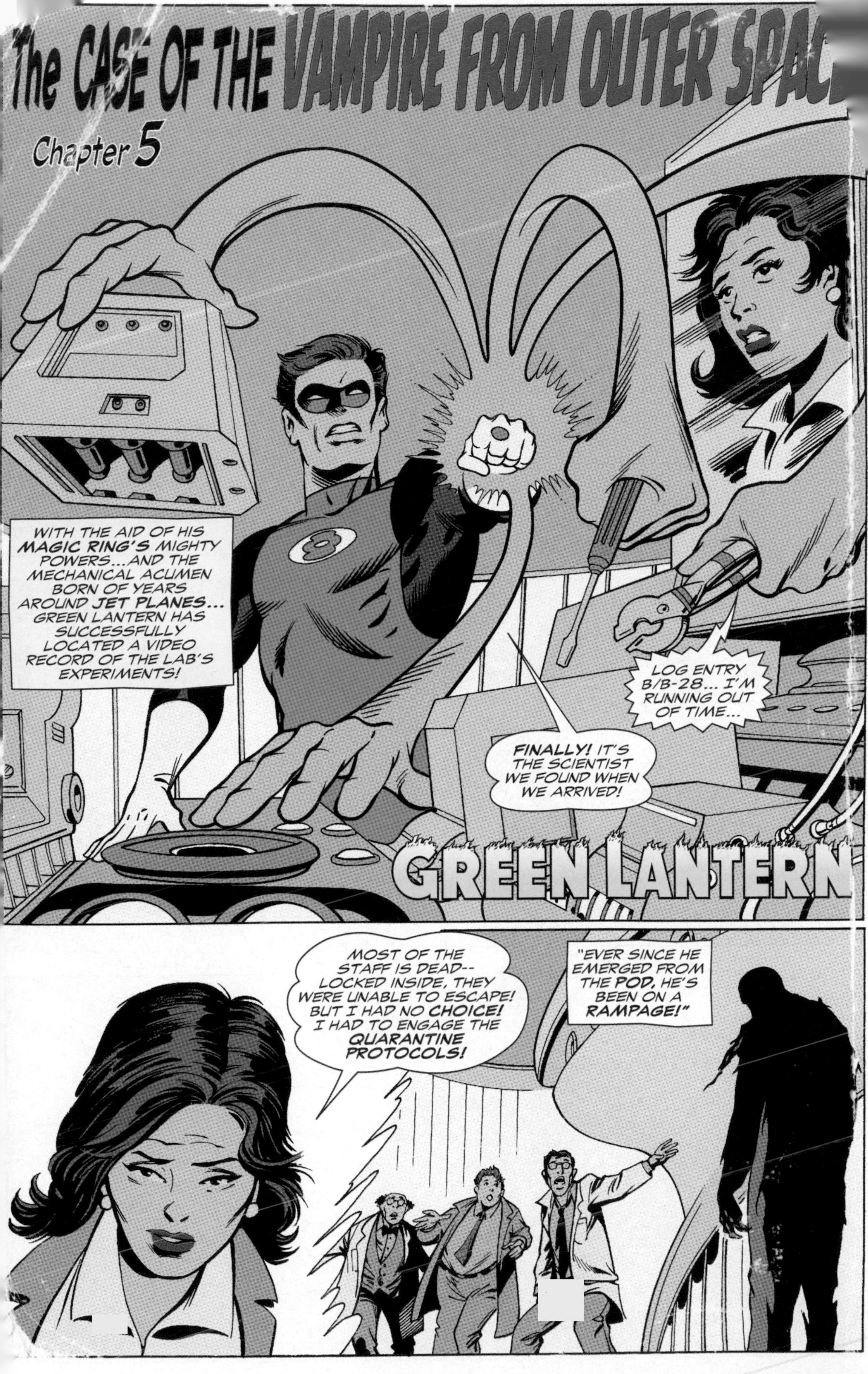
The CASE OF THE VAMPIRE FROM OUTER SPACE
Chapter 5
WITH THE AID OF HIS MAGIC RING'S MIGHTY POWERS...AND THE MECHANICAL ACUMEN BORN OF YEARS AROUND JET PLANES... GREEN LANTERN HAS SUCCESSFULLY LOCATED A VIDEO RECORD OF THE LAB'S EXPERIMENTS!
LOG ENTRY B/B-28... I'M RUNNING OUT OF TIME...
FINALLY! IT'S THE SCIENTIST WE FOUND WHEN WE ARRIVED!
GREEN LANTERN
MOST OF THE STAFF IS DEAD-- LOCKED INSIDE, THEY WERE UNABLE TO ESCAPE! BUT I HAD NO CHOICE! I HAD TO ENGAGE THE QUARANTINE PROTOCOLS!
"EVER SINCE HE EMERGED FROM THE POD, HE'S BEEN ON A RAMPAGE!"

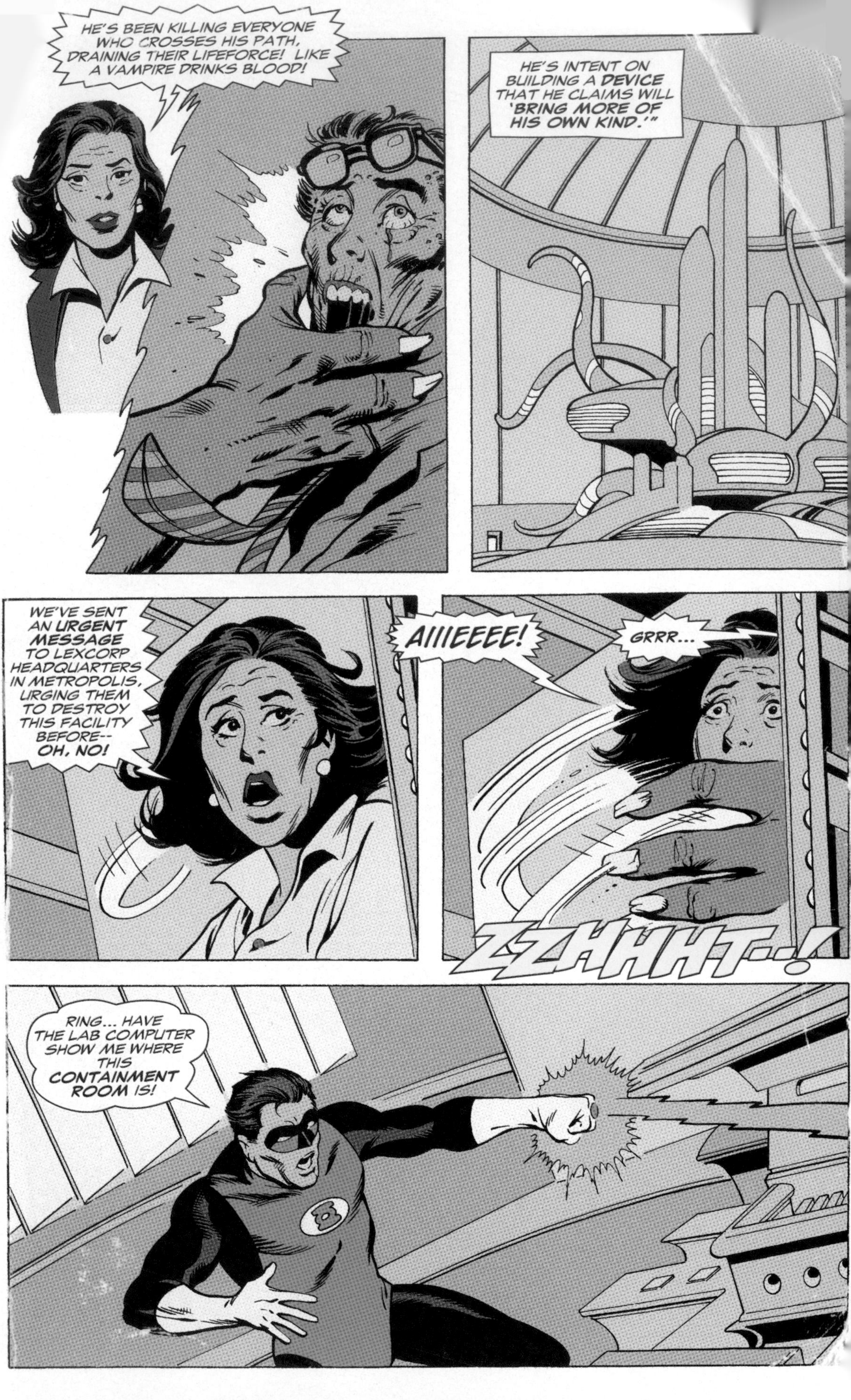
HE'S BEEN KILLING EVERYONE WHO CROSSES HIS PATH, DRAINING THEIR LIFEFORCE! LIKE A VAMPIRE DRINKS BLOOD!
HE'S INTENT ON BUILDING A DEVICE THAT HE CLAIMS WILL 'BRING MORE OF HIS OWN KIND.'"
WE'VE SENT AN URGENT MESSAGE TO LEXCORP HEADQUARTERS IN METROPOLIS, URGING THEM TO DESTROY THIS FACILITY BEFORE-- OH, NO!
AIIIEEEE!
GRRR...
ZZHHHT..!
RING... HAVE THE LAB COMPUTER SHOW ME WHERE THIS CONTAINMENT ROOM IS!

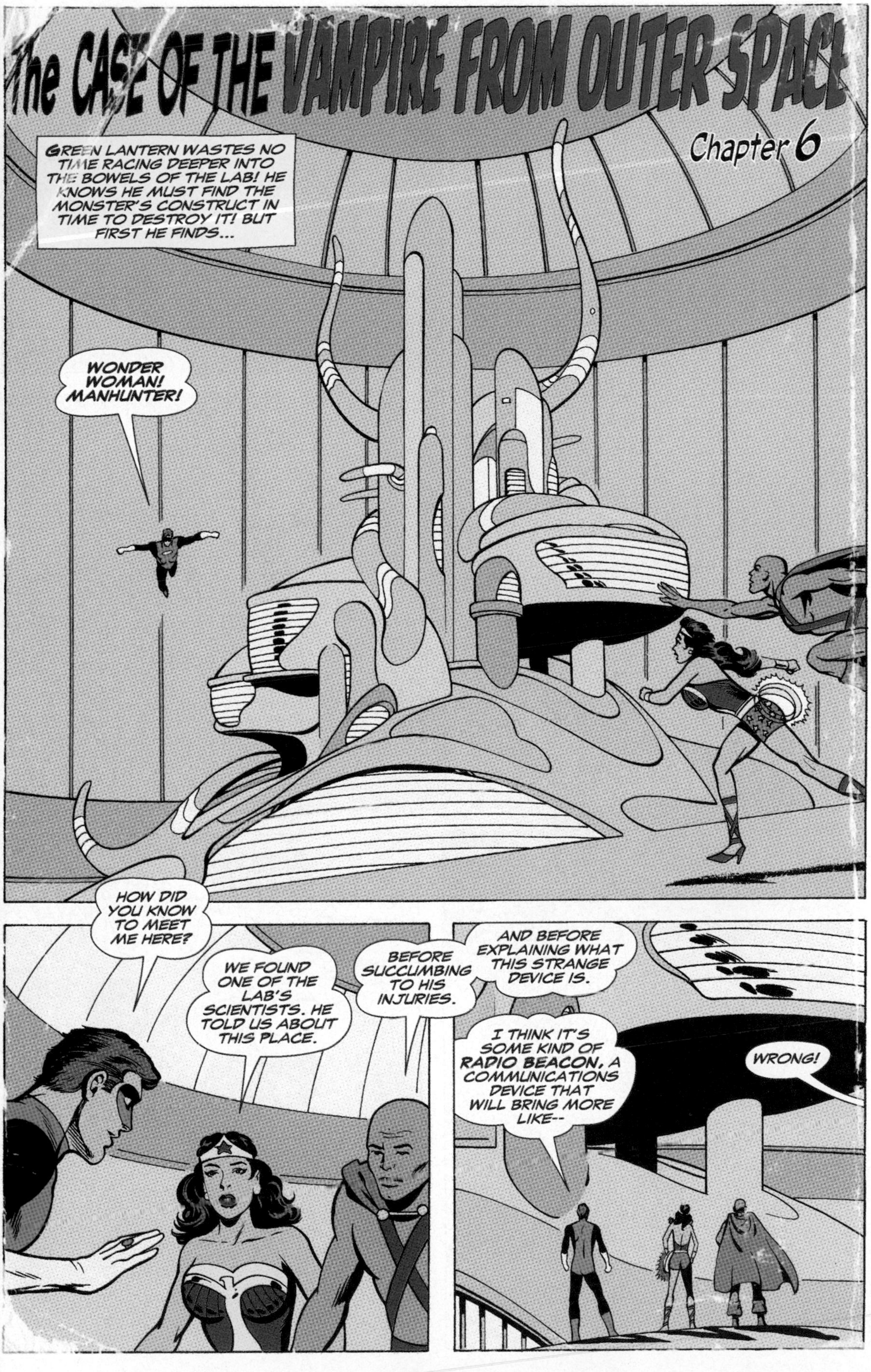
The CASE OF THE VAMPIRE FROM OUTER SPACE
Chapter 6
GREEN LANTERN WASTES NO TIME RACING DEEPER INTO THE BOWELS OF THE LAB! HE KNOWS HE MUST FIND THE MONSTER'S CONSTRUCT IN TIME TO DESTROY IT! BUT FIRST HE FINDS...
WONDER WOMAN! MANHUNTER!
HOW DID YOU KNOW TO MEET ME HERE?
WE FOUND ONE OF THE LAB'S SCIENTISTS. HE TOLD US ABOUT THIS PLACE.
BEFORE SUCCUMBING TO HIS INJURIES.
AND BEFORE EXPLAINING WHAT THIS STRANGE DEVICE IS.
I THINK IT'S SOME KIND OF RADIO BEACON, A COMMUNICATIONS DEVICE THAT WILL BRING MORE LIKE--
WRONG!

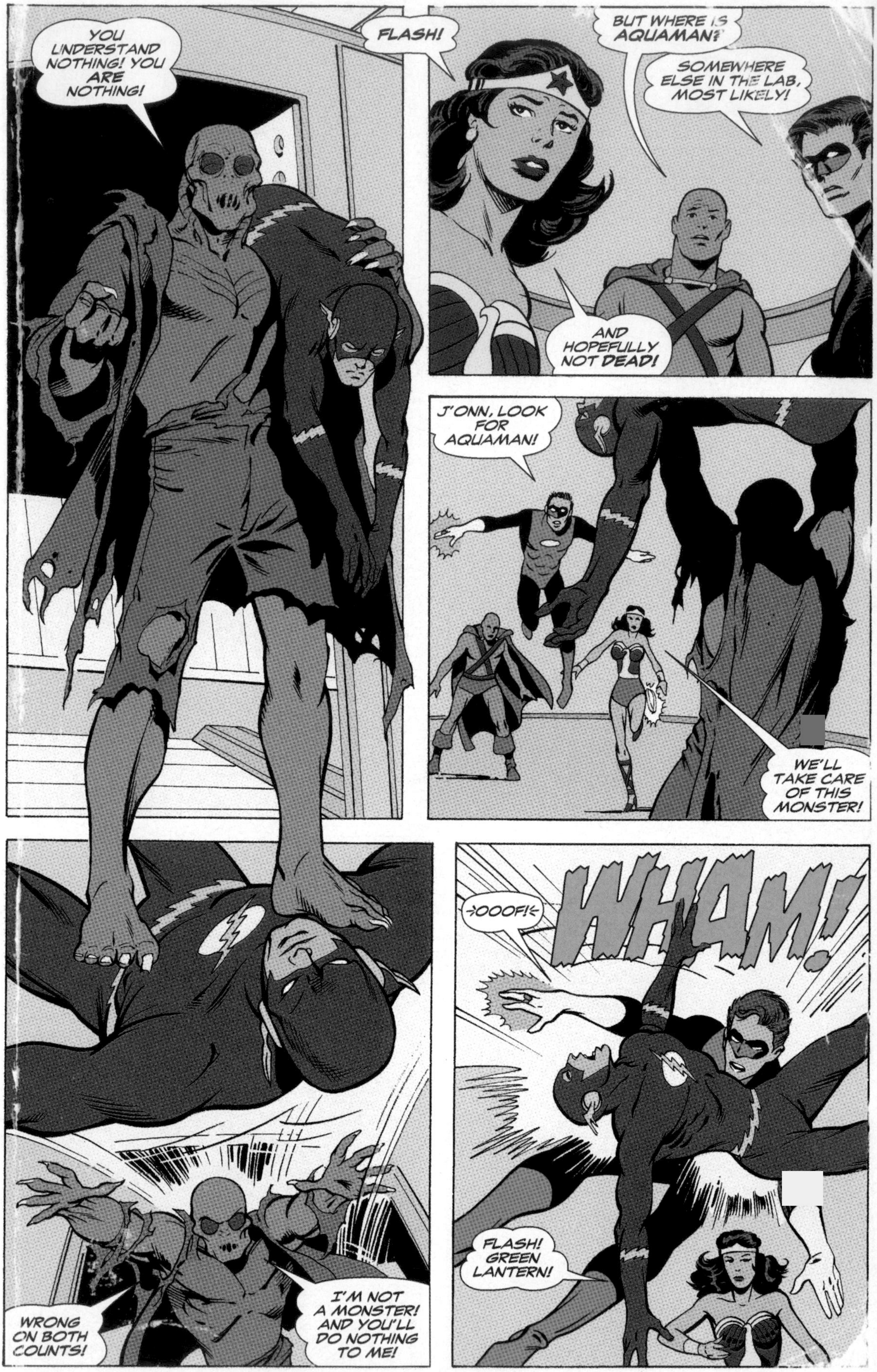
YOU UNDERSTAND NOTHING! YOU ARE NOTHING!
FLASH!
BUT WHERE IS AQUAMAN?
SOMEWHERE ELSE IN THE LAB, MOST LIKELY!
AND HOPEFULLY NOT DEAD!
J'ONN, LOOK FOR AQUAMAN!
WE'LL TAKE CARE OF THIS MONSTER!
WRONG ON BOTH COUNTS!
I'M NOT A MONSTER! AND YOU'LL DO NOTHING TO ME!
WHAM!
OOOF!
FLASH! GREEN LANTERN!

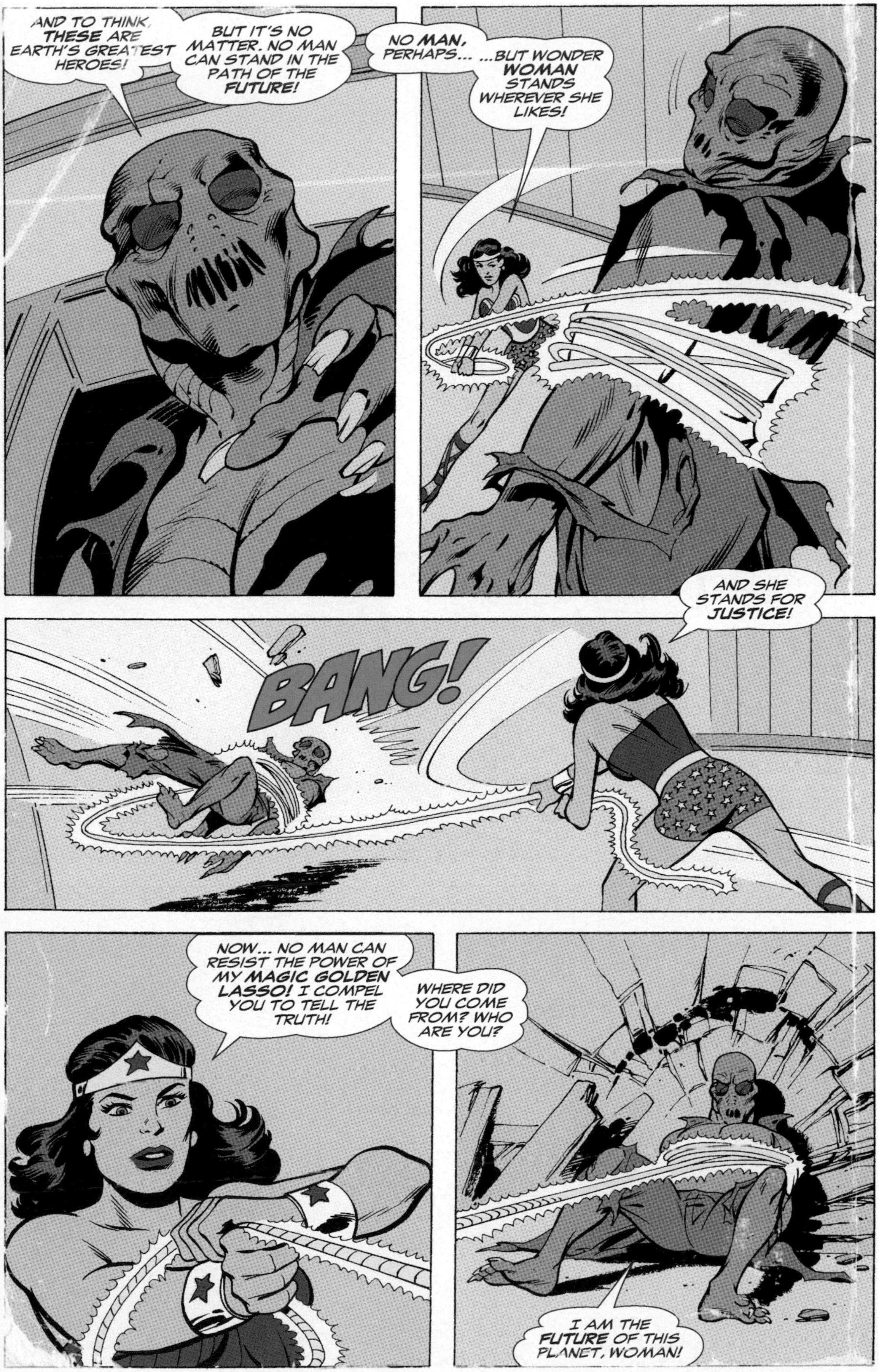
AND TO THINK, THESE ARE EARTH'S GREATEST HEROES!
BUT IT'S NO MATTER. NO MAN CAN STAND IN THE PATH OF THE FUTURE!
NO MAN, PERHAPS...
...BUT WONDER WOMAN STANDS WHEREVER SHE LIKES!
AND SHE STANDS FOR JUSTICE!
BANG!
NOW... NO MAN CAN RESIST THE POWER OF MY MAGIC GOLDEN LASSO! I COMPEL YOU TO TELL THE TRUTH!
WHERE DID YOU COME FROM? WHO ARE YOU?
I AM THE FUTURE OF THIS PLANET, WOMAN!

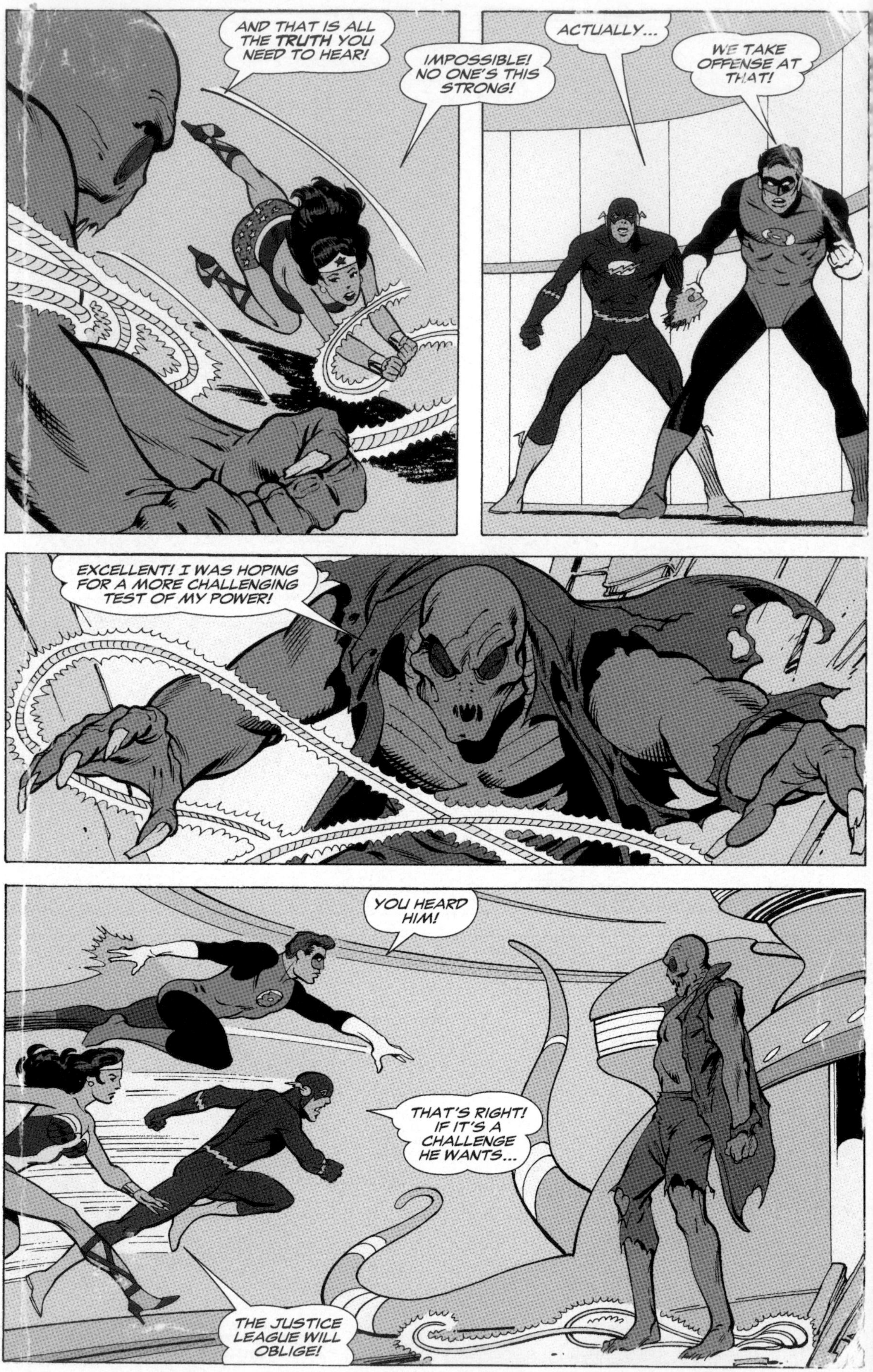
AND THAT IS ALL THE TRUTH YOU NEED TO HEAR!
IMPOSSIBLE! NO ONE'S THIS STRONG!
ACTUALLY...
WE TAKE OFFENSE AT THAT!
EXCELLENT! I WAS HOPING FOR A MORE CHALLENGING TEST OF MY POWER!
YOU HEARD HIM!
THAT'S RIGHT! IF IT'S A CHALLENGE HE WANTS...
THE JUSTICE LEAGUE WILL OBLIGE!

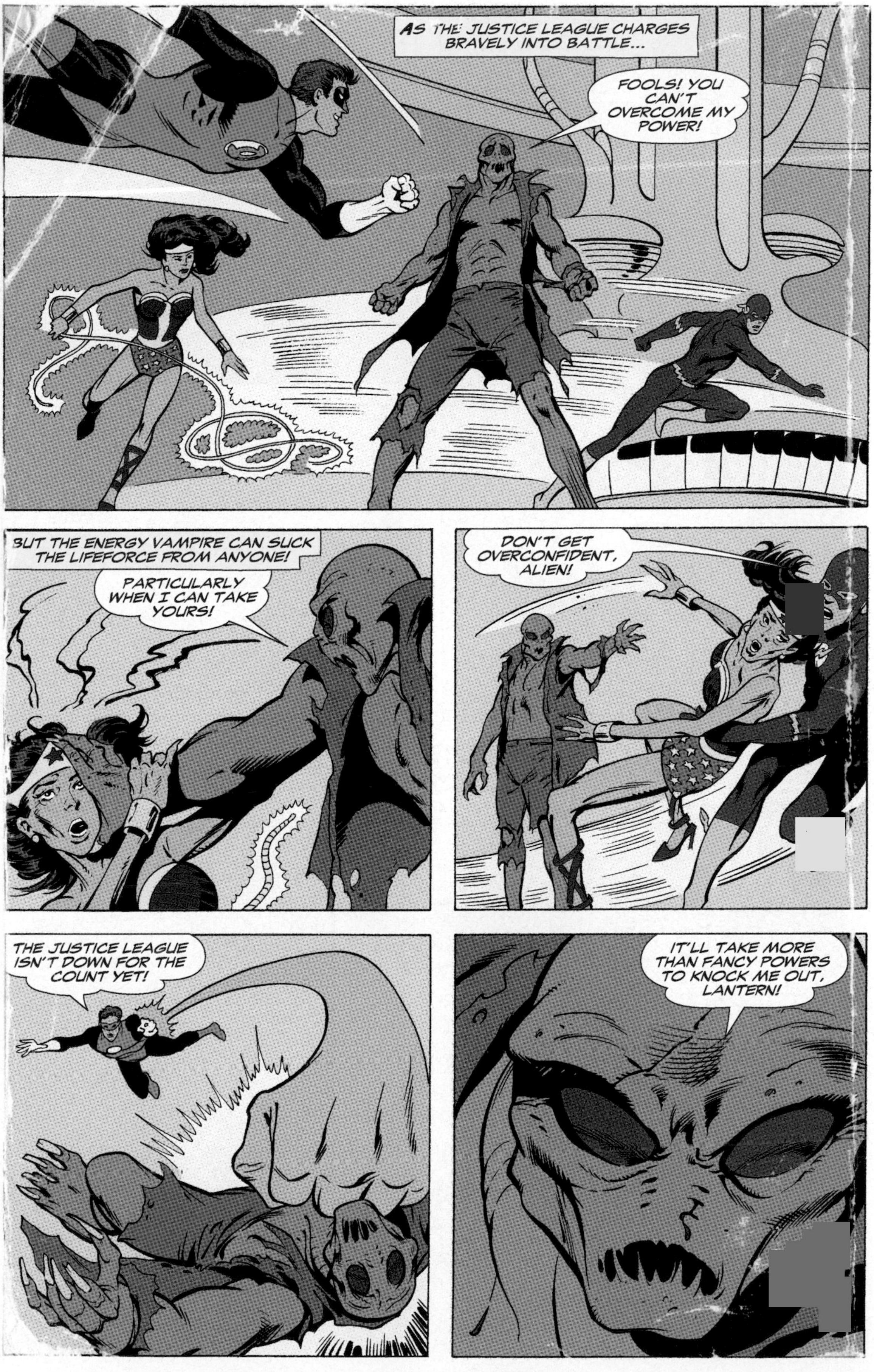
AS THE JUSTICE LEAGUE CHARGES BRAVELY INTO BATTLE...
FOOLS! YOU CAN'T OVERCOME MY POWER!
BUT THE ENERGY VAMPIRE CAN SUCK THE LIFEFORCE FROM ANYONE!
PARTICULARLY WHEN I CAN TAKE YOURS!
DON'T GET OVERCONFIDENT, ALIEN!
THE JUSTICE LEAGUE ISN'T DOWN FOR THE COUNT YET!
IT'LL TAKE MORE THAN FANCY POWERS TO KNOCK ME OUT, LANTERN!

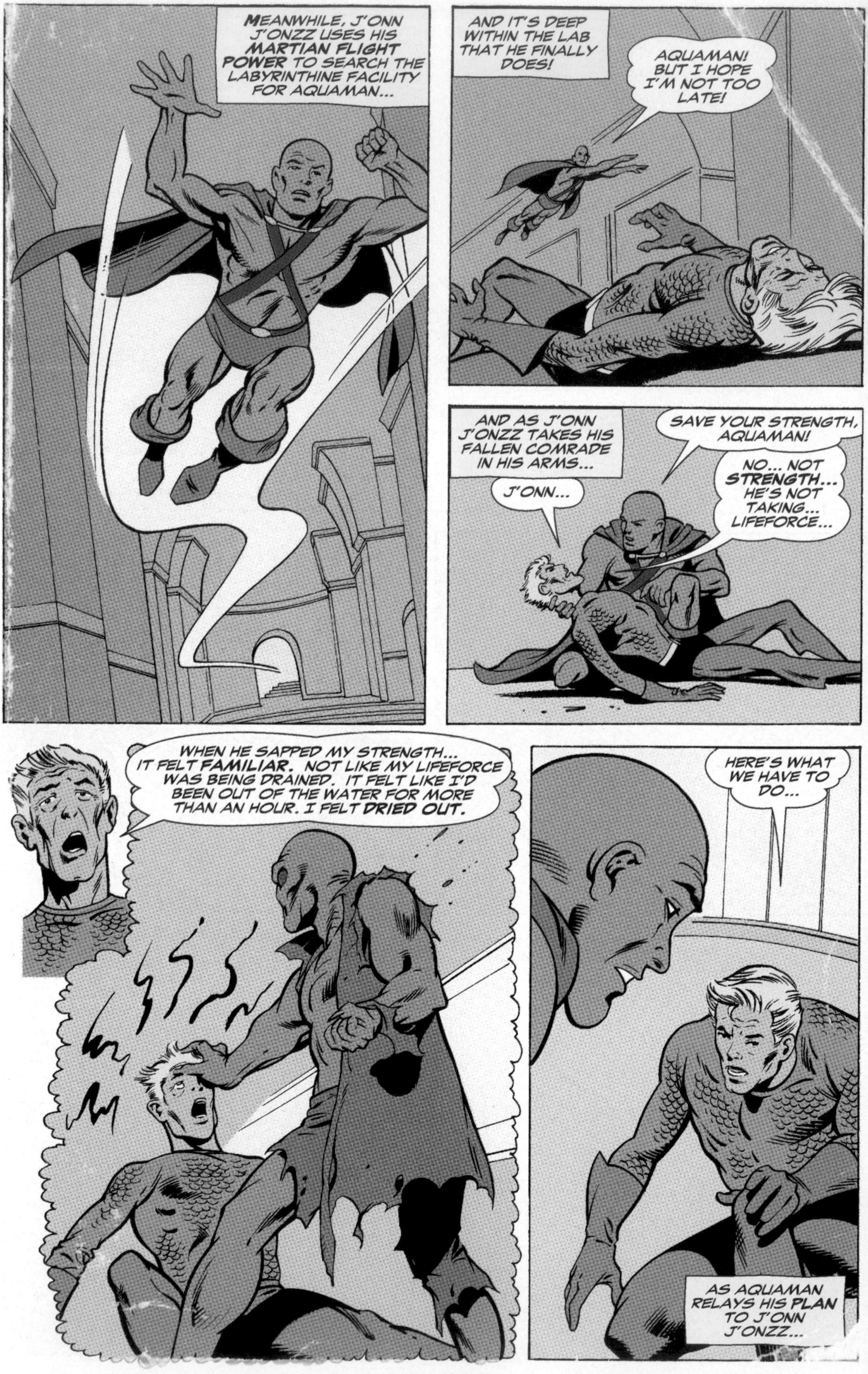

MEANWHILE, J'ONN J'ONZZ USES HIS MARTIAN FLIGHT POWER TO SEARCH THE LABYRINTHINE FACILITY FOR AQUAMAN...
AND IT'S DEEP WITHIN THE LAB THAT HE FINALLY DOES!
AQUAMAN! BUT I HOPE I'M NOT TOO LATE!
AND AS J'ONN J'ONZZ TAKES HIS FALLEN COMRADE IN HIS ARMS...
SAVE YOUR STRENGTH, AQUAMAN!
J'ONN...
NO... NOT STRENGTH... HE'S NOT TAKING... LIFEFORCE...
WHEN HE SAPPED MY STRENGTH... IT FELT FAMILIAR. NOT LIKE MY LIFEFORCE WAS BEING DRAINED. IT FELT LIKE I'D BEEN OUT OF THE WATER FOR MORE THAN AN HOUR. I FELT DRIED OUT.
HERE'S WHAT WE HAVE TO DO...
AS AQUAMAN RELAYS HIS PLAN TO J'ONN J'ONZZ...

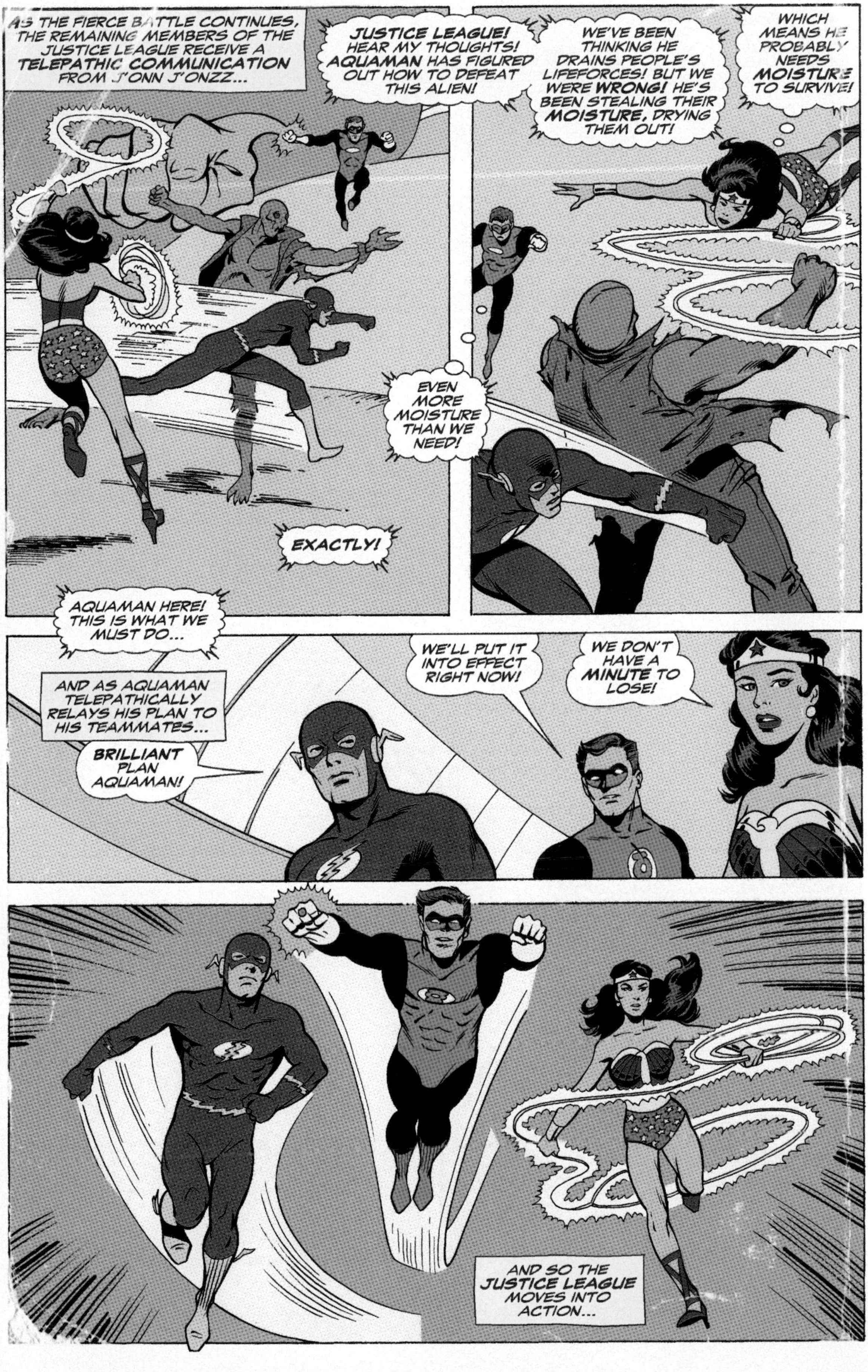
AS THE FIERCE BATTLE CONTINUES, THE REMAINING MEMBERS OF THE JUSTICE LEAGUE RECEIVE A TELEPATHIC COMMUNICATION FROM J'ONN J'ONZZ...
JUSTICE LEAGUE! HEAR MY THOUGHTS! AQUAMAN HAS FIGURED OUT HOW TO DEFEAT THIS ALIEN!
EXACTLY!
WE'VE BEEN THINKING HE DRAINS PEOPLE'S LIFEFORCES! BUT WE WERE WRONG! HE'S BEEN STEALING THEIR MOISTURE, DRYING THEM OUT!
WHICH MEANS HE PROBABLY NEEDS MOISTURE TO SURVIVE!
EVEN MORE MOISTURE THAN WE NEED!
AQUAMAN HERE! THIS IS WHAT WE MUST DO...
AND AS AQUAMAN TELEPATHICALLY RELAYS HIS PLAN TO HIS TEAMMATES...
BRILLIANT PLAN AQUAMAN!
WE'LL PUT IT INTO EFFECT RIGHT NOW!
WE DON'T HAVE A MINUTE TO LOSE!
AND SO THE JUSTICE LEAGUE MOVES INTO ACTION...

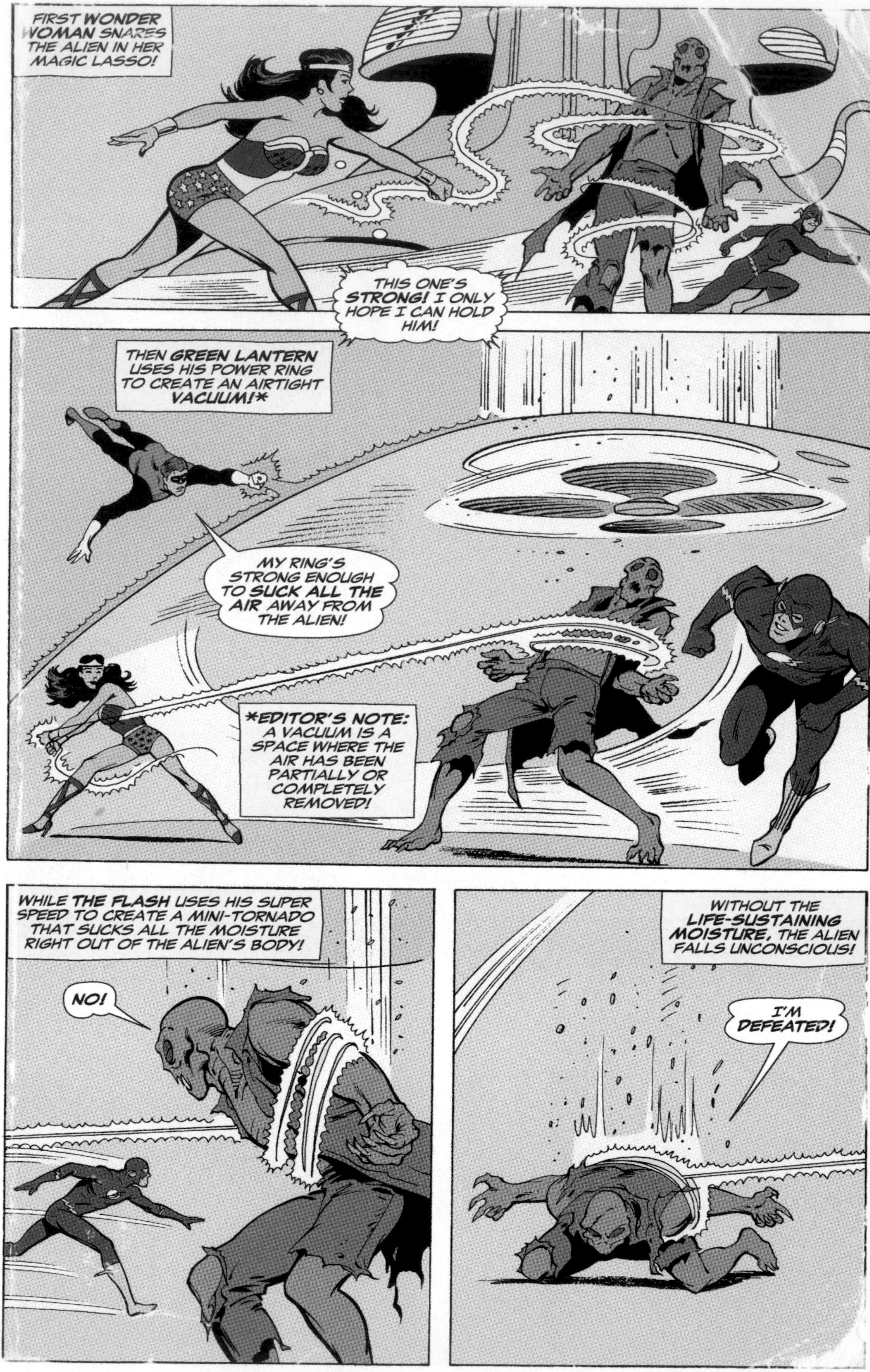
FIRST WONDER WOMAN SNARES THE ALIEN IN HER MAGIC LASSO!
THIS ONE'S STRONG! I ONLY HOPE I CAN HOLD HIM!
THEN GREEN LANTERN USES HIS POWER RING TO CREATE AN AIRTIGHT VACUUM!*
MY RING'S STRONG ENOUGH TO SUCK ALL THE AIR AWAY FROM THE ALIEN!
*EDITOR'S NOTE: A VACUUM IS A SPACE WHERE THE AIR HAS BEEN PARTIALLY OR COMPLETELY REMOVED!
WHILE THE FLASH USES HIS SUPER SPEED TO CREATE A MINI-TORNADO THAT SUCKS ALL THE MOISTURE RIGHT OUT OF THE ALIEN'S BODY!
NO!
WITHOUT THE LIFE-SUSTAINING MOISTURE, THE ALIEN FALLS UNCONSCIOUS!
I'M DEFEATED!

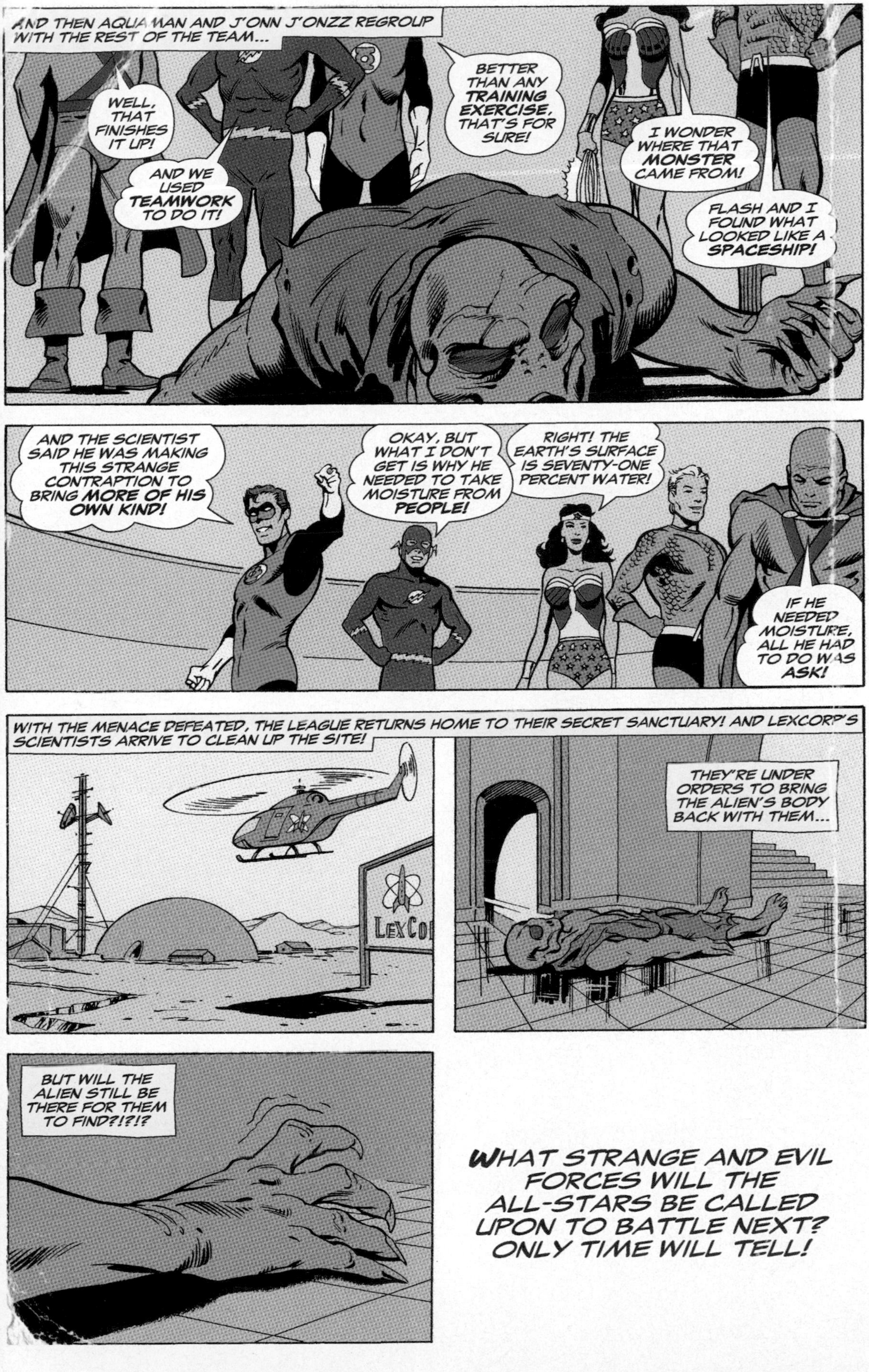
AND THEN AQUAMAN AND J'ONN J'ONZZ REGROUP WITH THE REST OF THE TEAM...
WELL, THAT FINISHES IT UP!
AND WE USED TEAMWORK TO DO IT!
BETTER THAN ANY TRAINING EXERCISE, THAT'S FOR SURE!
I WONDER WHERE THAT MONSTER CAME FROM!
FLASH AND I FOUND WHAT LOOKED LIKE A SPACESHIP!
AND THE SCIENTIST SAID HE WAS MAKING THIS STRANGE CONTRAPTION TO BRING MORE OF HIS OWN KIND!
OKAY, BUT WHAT I DON'T GET IS WHY HE NEEDED TO TAKE MOISTURE FROM PEOPLE!
RIGHT! THE EARTH'S SURFACE IS SEVENTY-ONE PERCENT WATER!
IF HE NEEDED MOISTURE, ALL HE HAD TO DO WAS ASK!
WITH THE MENACE DEFEATED, THE LEAGUE RETURNS HOME TO THEIR SECRET SANCTUARY! AND LEXCORP'S SCIENTISTS ARRIVE TO CLEAN UP THE SITE!
LEXCOR
THEY'RE UNDER ORDERS TO BRING THE ALIEN'S BODY BACK WITH THEM...
BUT WILL THE ALIEN STILL BE THERE FOR THEM TO FIND?!?!?

WHAT STRANGE AND EVIL FORCES WILL THE ALL-STARS BE CALLED UPON TO BATTLE NEXT? ONLY TIME WILL TELL!

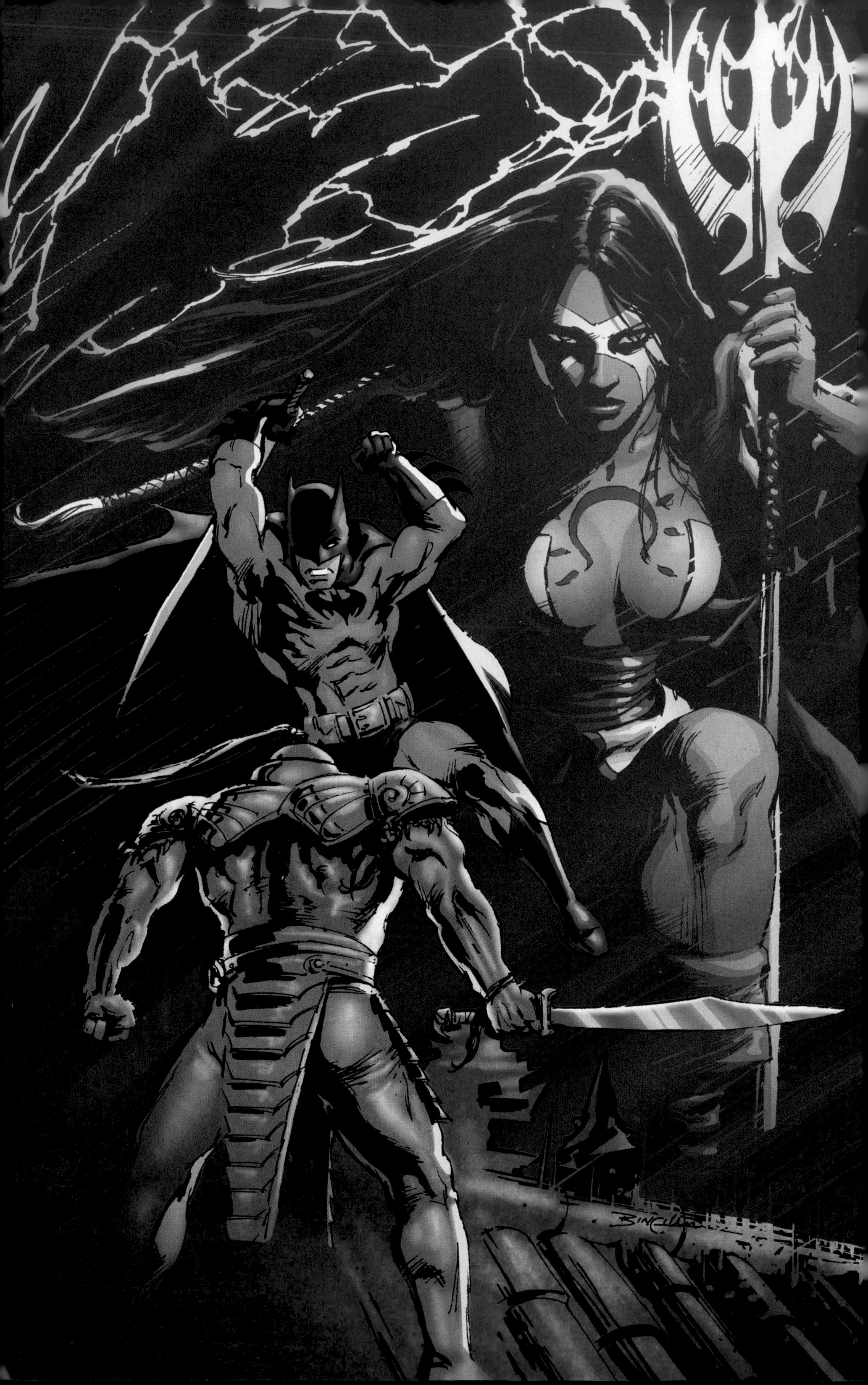

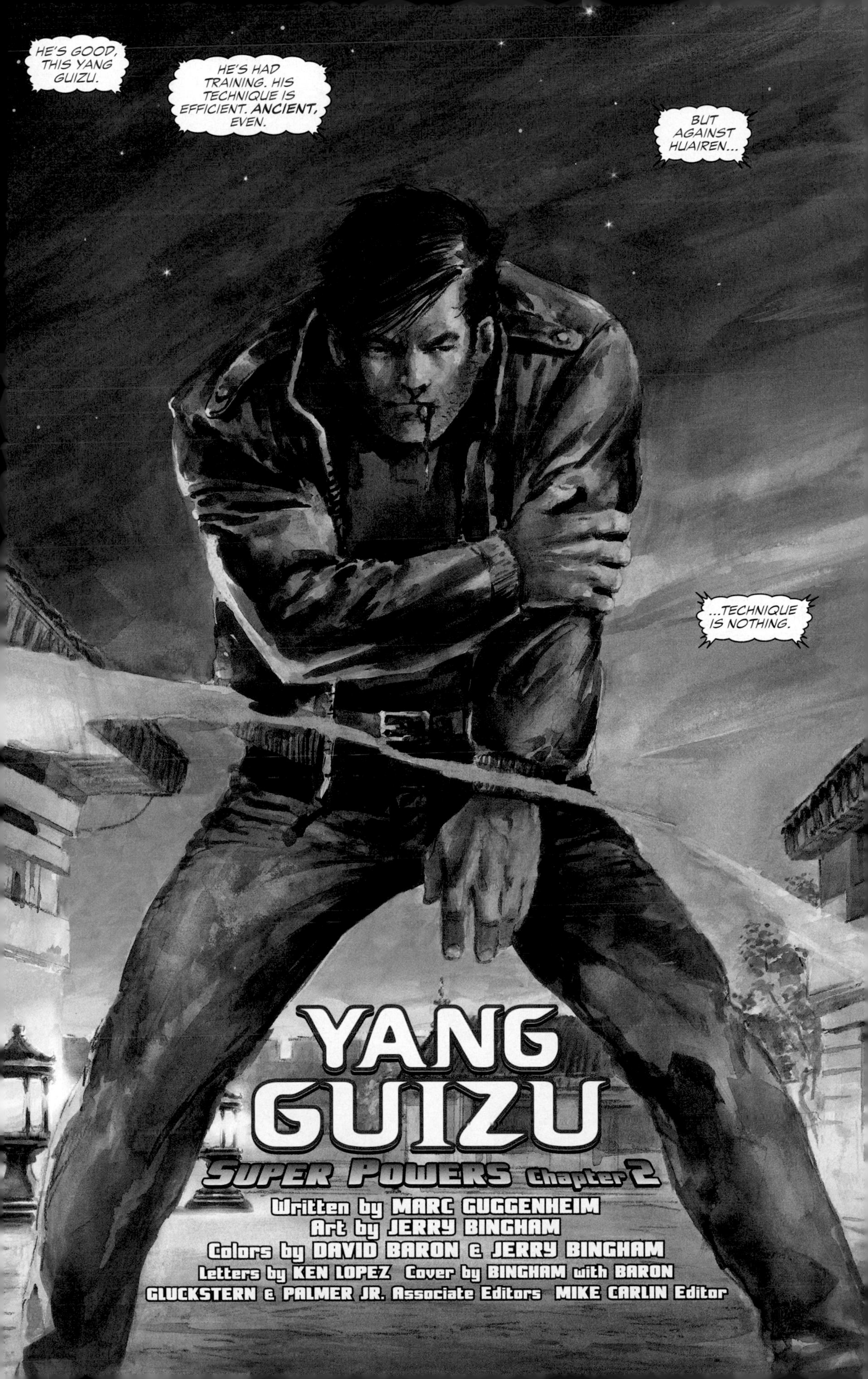
HE'S GOOD, THIS YANG GUIZU.
HE'S HAD TRAINING. HIS TECHNIQUE IS EFFICIENT. ANCIENT, EVEN.
BUT AGAINST HUAIREN...
...TECHNIQUE IS NOTHING.
YANG GUIZU
SUPER POWERS Chapter 2
Written by MARC GUGGENHEIM
Art by JERRY BINGHAM
Colors by DAVID BARON & JERRY BINGHAM
Letters by KEN LOPEZ Cover by BINGHAM with BARON
GLUCKSTERN & PALMER JR. Associate Editors MIKE CARLIN Editor

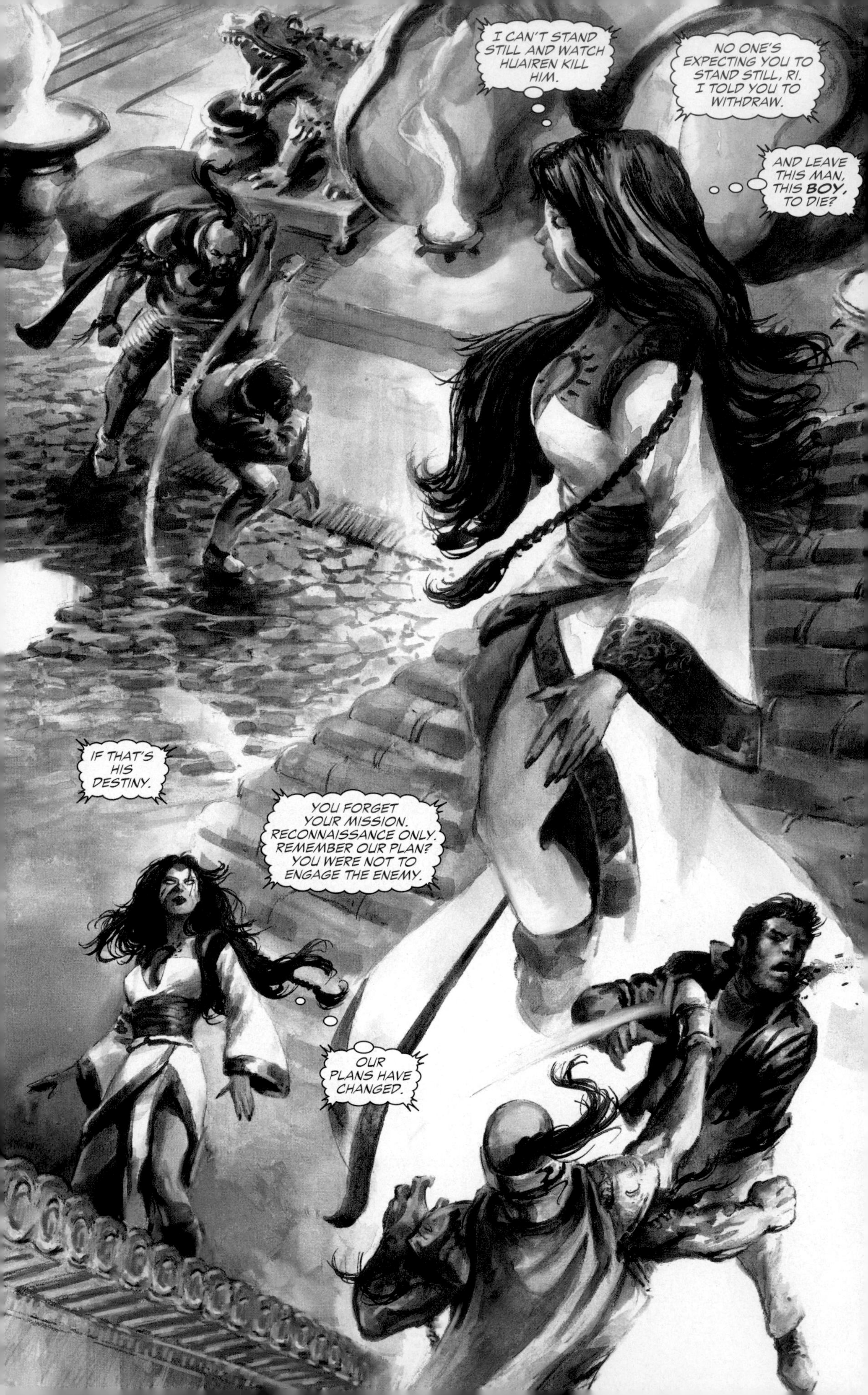
I CAN'T STAND STILL AND WATCH HUAIREN KILL HIM.
NO ONE'S EXPECTING YOU TO STAND STILL, RI. I TOLD YOU TO WITHDRAW.
AND LEAVE THIS MAN, THIS BOY, TO DIE?
IF THAT'S HIS DESTINY.
YOU FORGET YOUR MISSION. RECONNAISSANCE ONLY. REMEMBER OUR PLAN? YOU WERE NOT TO ENGAGE THE ENEMY.
OUR PLANS HAVE CHANGED.

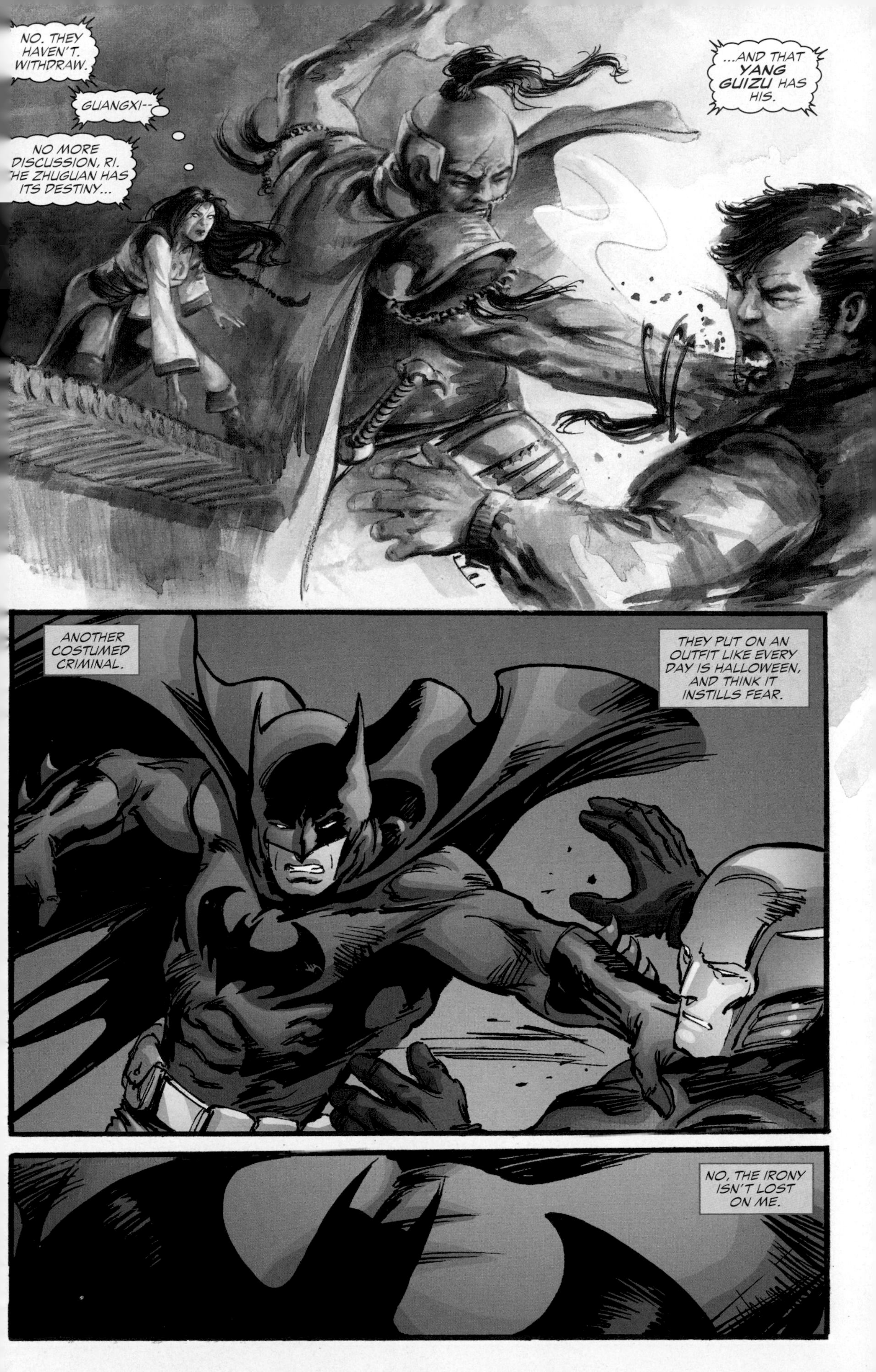
NO. THEY HAVEN'T. WITHDRAW.
GUANGXI--
NO MORE DISCUSSION, RI. THE ZHUGUAN HAS ITS DESTINY...
...AND THAT YANG GUIZU HAS HIS.
ANOTHER COSTUMED CRIMINAL.
THEY PUT ON AN OUTFIT LIKE EVERY DAY IS HALLOWEEN, AND THINK IT INSTILLS FEAR.
NO, THE IRONY ISN'T LOST ON ME.

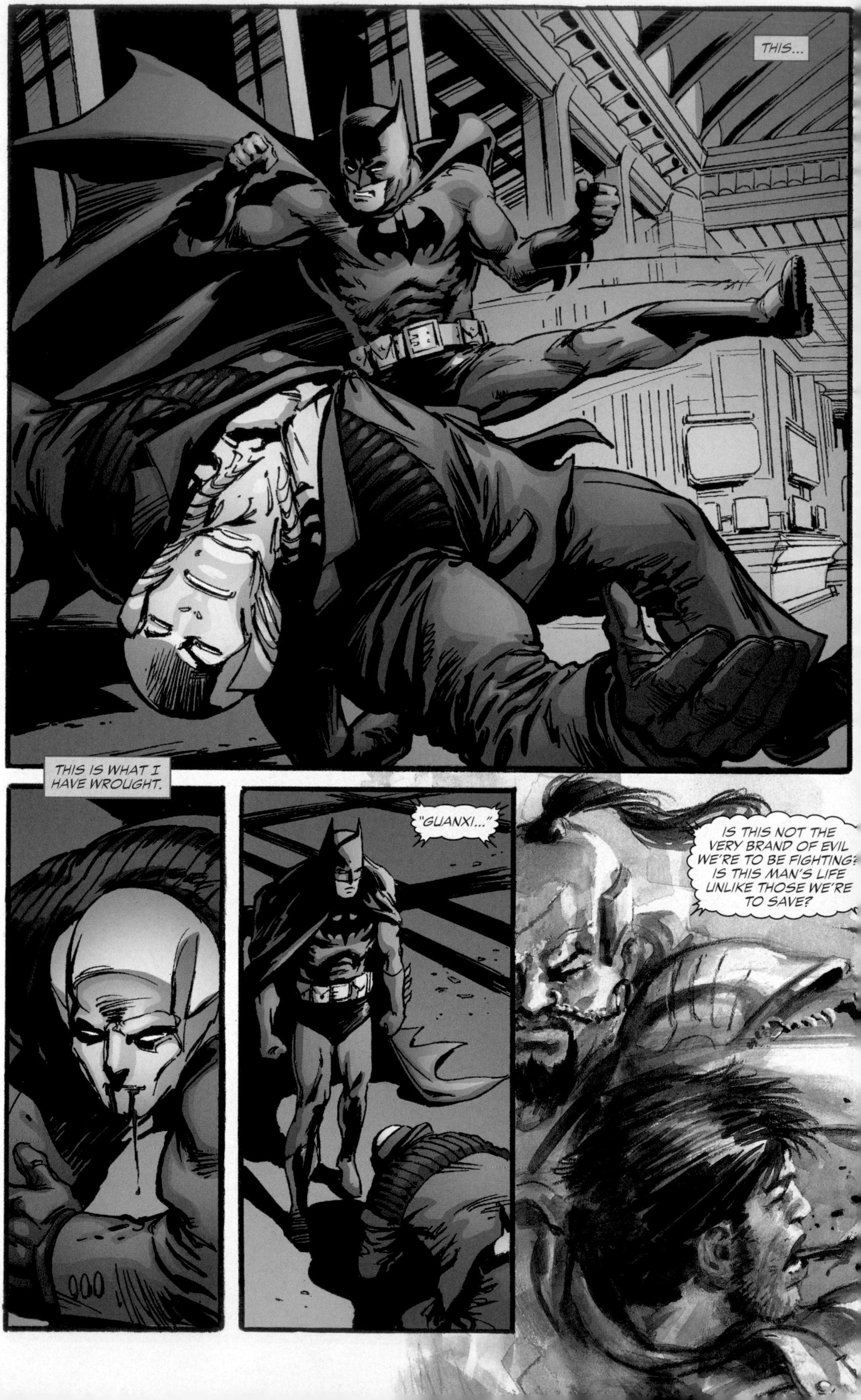
THIS...
THIS IS WHAT I HAVE WROUGHT.
"GUANXI..."
IS THIS NOT THE VERY BRAND OF EVIL WE'RE TO BE FIGHTING? IS THIS MAN'S LIFE UNLIKE THOSE WE'RE TO SAVE?

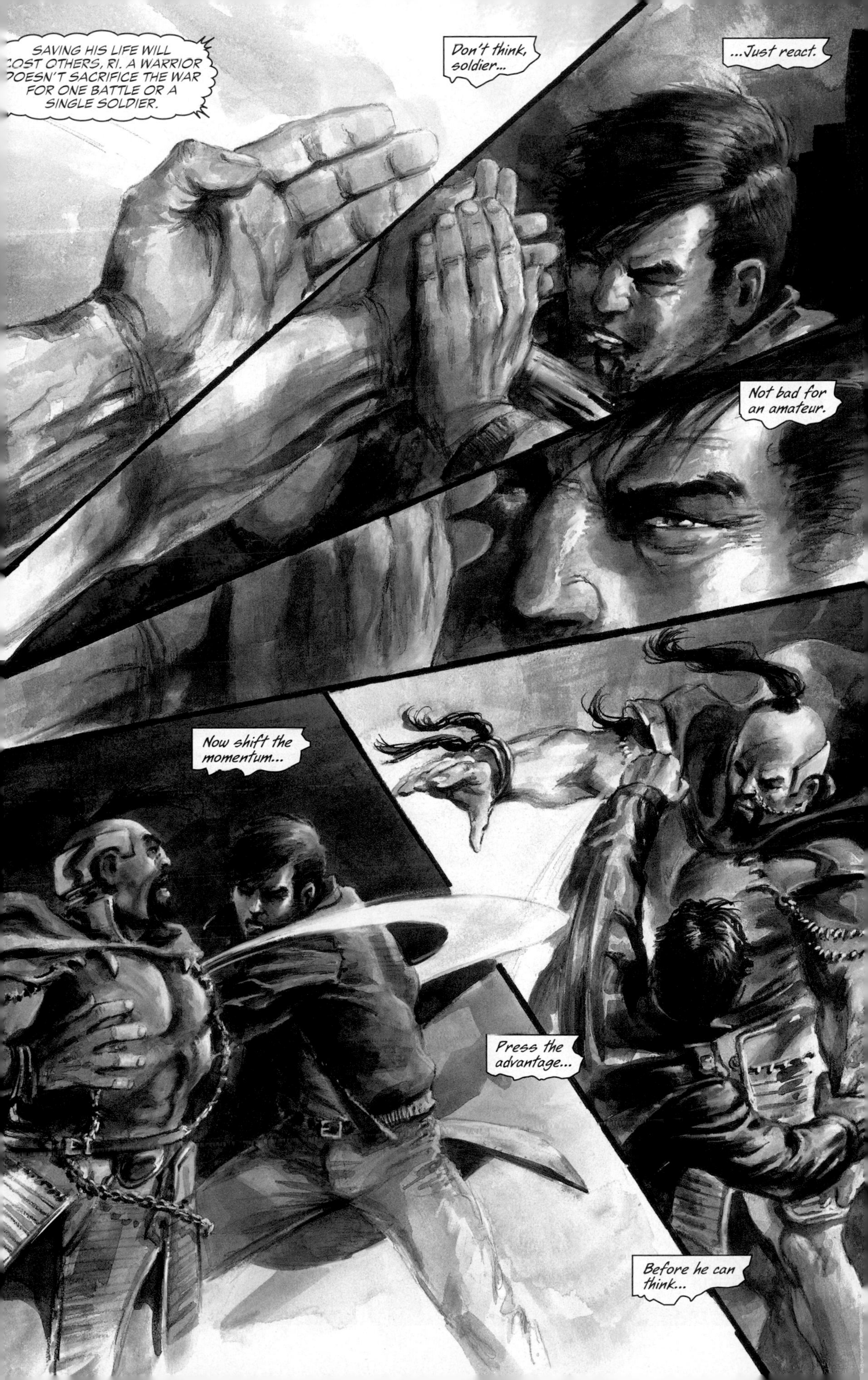
SAVING HIS LIFE WILL COST OTHERS, RI. A WARRIOR DOESN'T SACRIFICE THE WAR FOR ONE BATTLE OR A SINGLE SOLDIER.
Don't think, soldier...
...Just react.
Not bad for an amateur.
Now shift the momentum...
Press the advantage...
Before he can think...

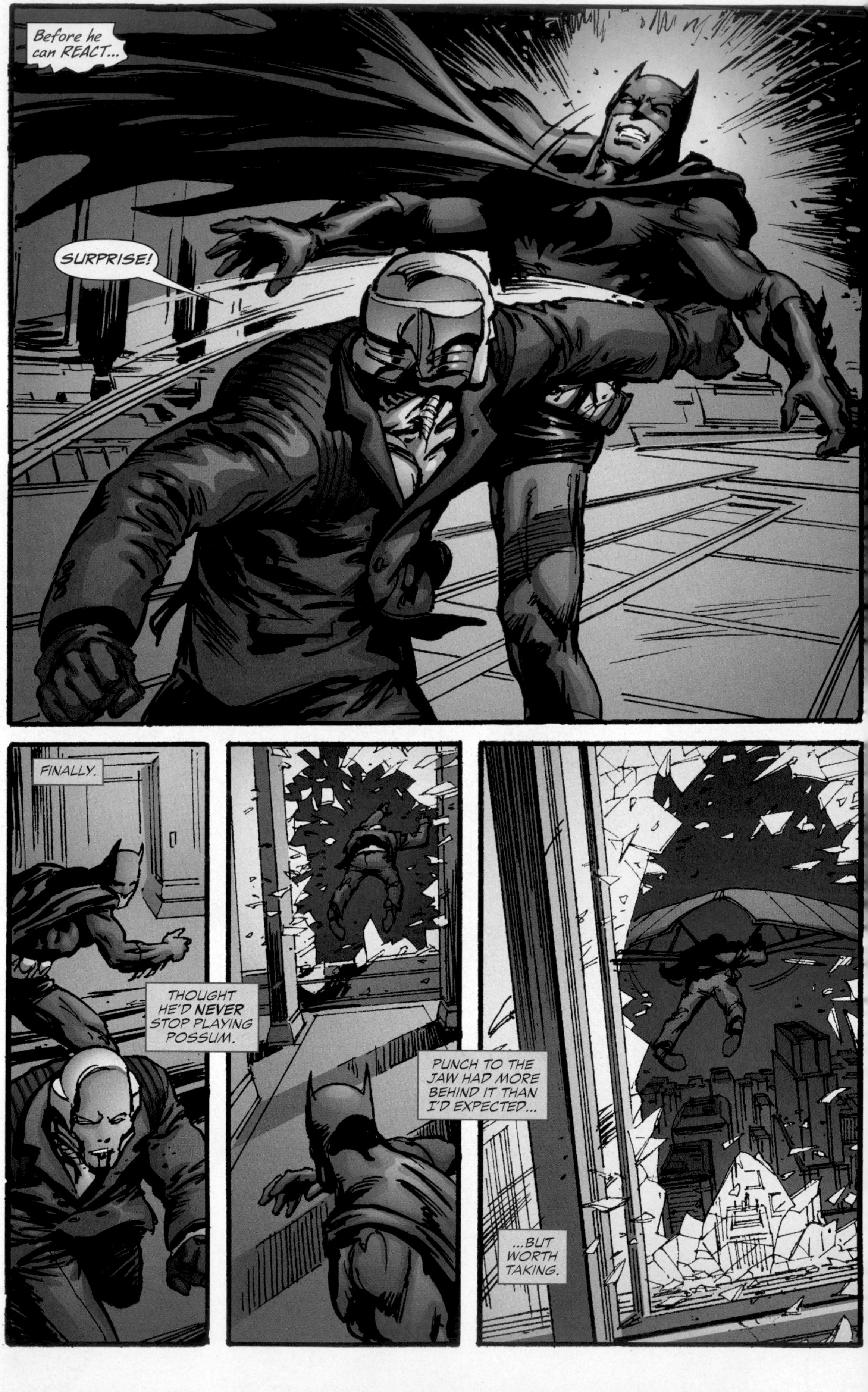
Before he can REACT...
SURPRISE!
FINALLY.
THOUGHT HE'D NEVER STOP PLAYING POSSUM.
PUNCH TO THE JAW HAD MORE BEHIND IT THAN I'D EXPECTED...
...BUT WORTH TAKING.

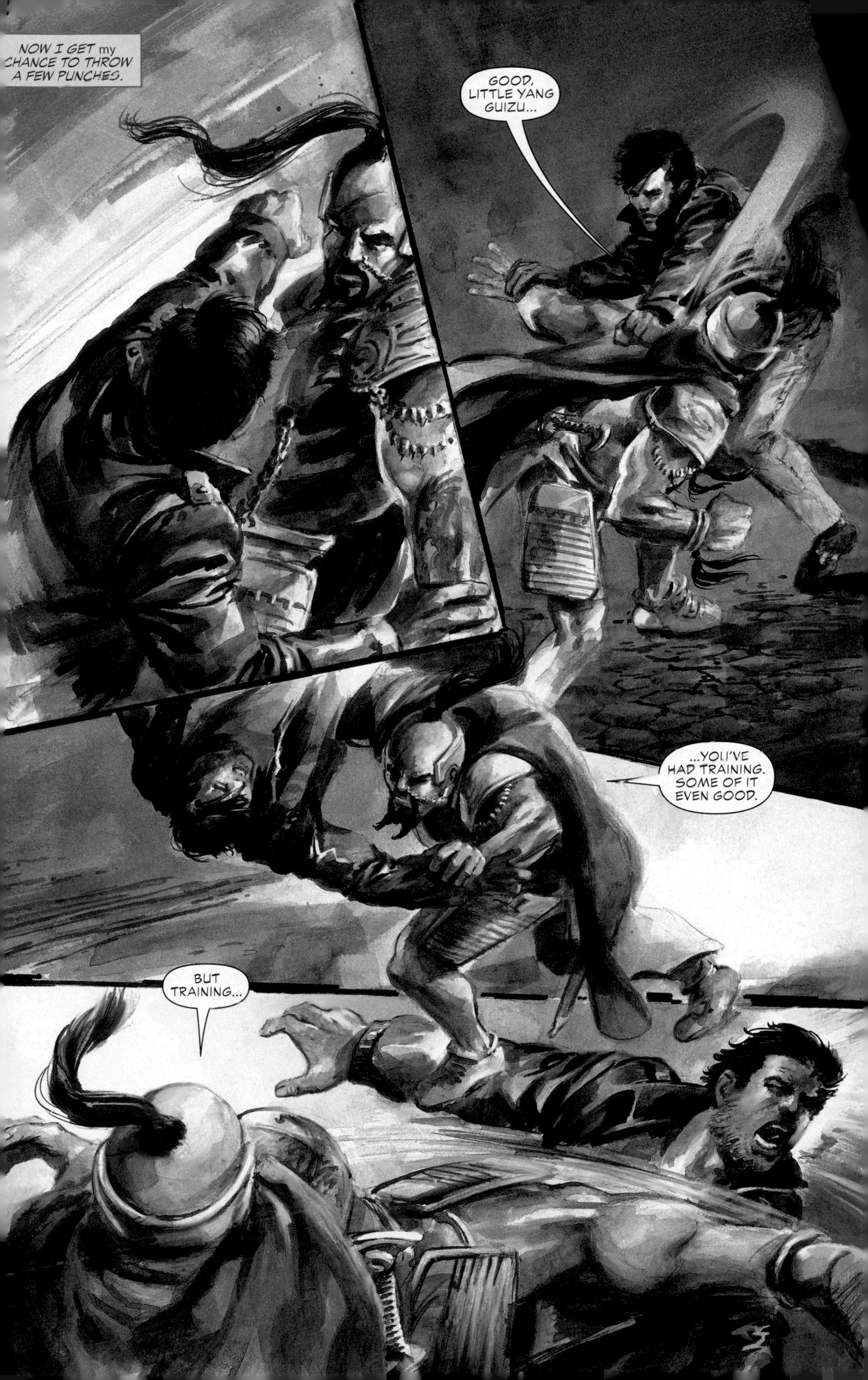
NOW I GET my CHANCE TO THROW A FEW PUNCHES.
GOOD, LITTLE YANG GUIZU...
...YOU'VE HAD TRAINING. SOME OF IT EVEN GOOD.
BUT TRAINING...

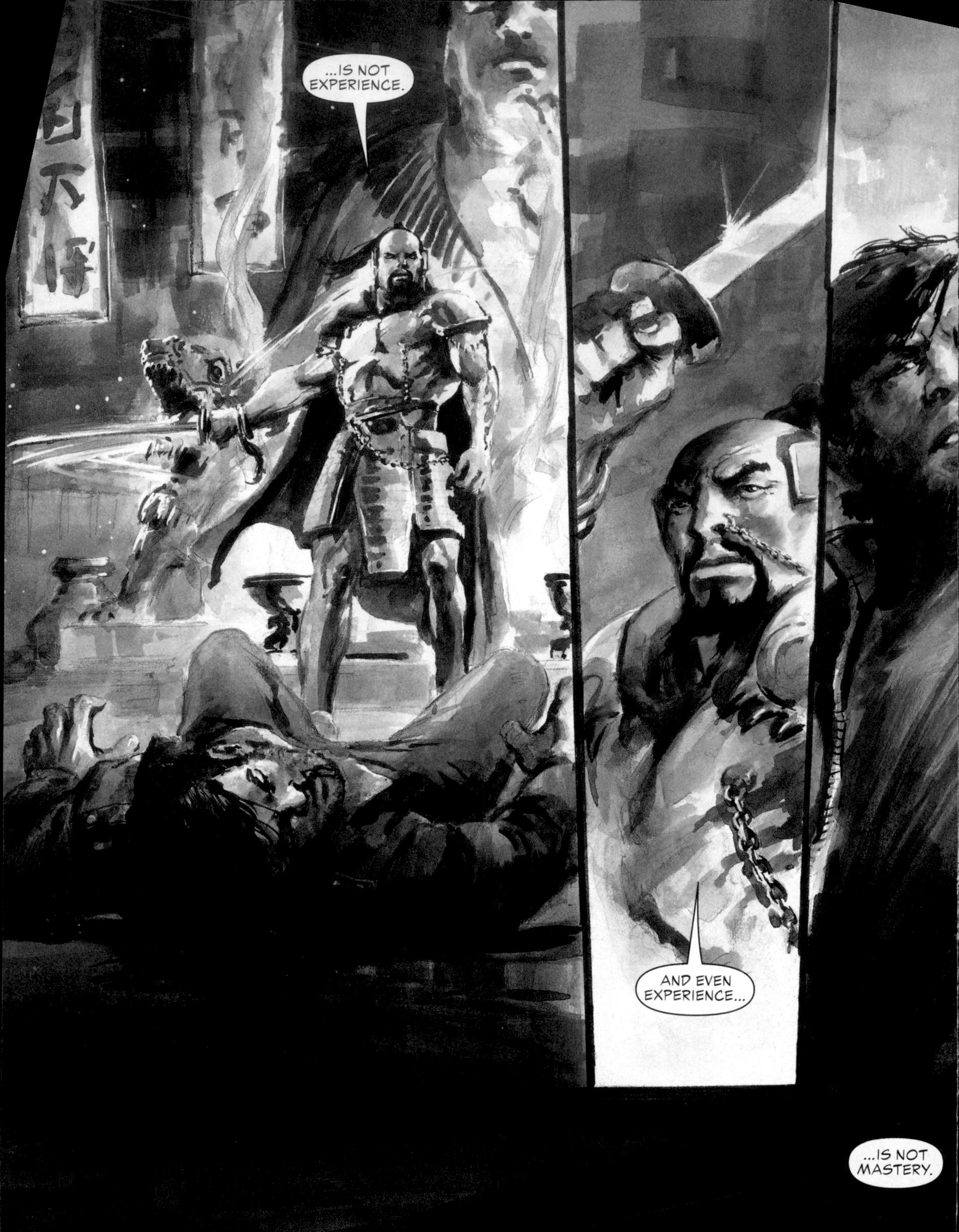
...IS NOT
EXPERIENCE.
AND EVEN
EXPERIENCE...
...IS NOT
MASTERY.

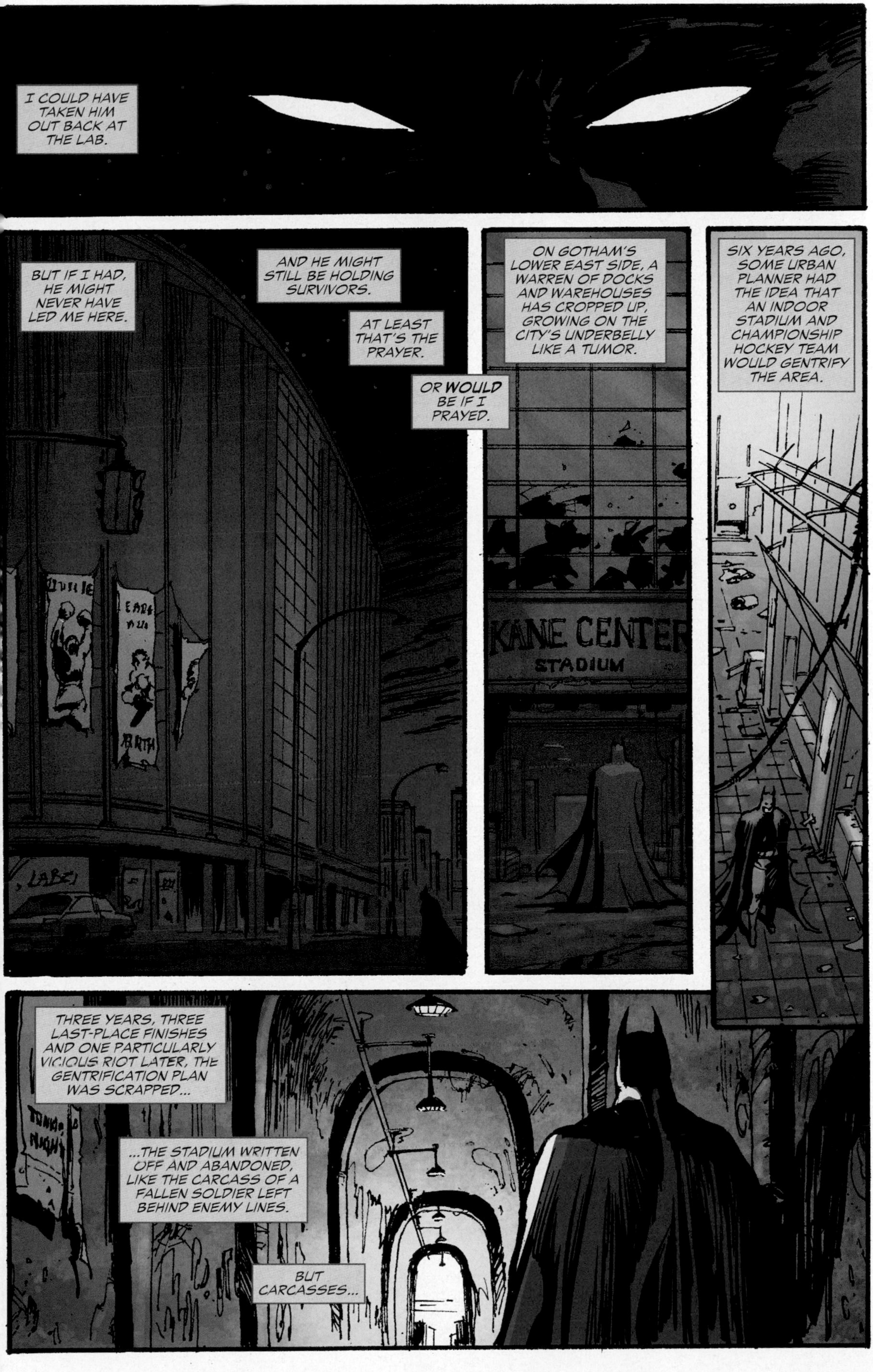
I COULD HAVE TAKEN HIM OUT BACK AT THE LAB.
BUT IF I HAD, HE MIGHT NEVER HAVE LED ME HERE.
AND HE MIGHT STILL BE HOLDING SURVIVORS.
AT LEAST THAT'S THE PRAYER.
OR **WOULD** BE IF I PRAYED.
ON GOTHAM'S LOWER EAST SIDE, A WARREN OF DOCKS AND WAREHOUSES HAS CROPPED UP, GROWING ON THE CITY'S UNDERBELLY LIKE A TUMOR.
KANE CENTER
STADIUM
SIX YEARS AGO, SOME URBAN PLANNER HAD THE IDEA THAT AN INDOOR STADIUM AND CHAMPIONSHIP HOCKEY TEAM WOULD GENTRIFY THE AREA.
THREE YEARS, THREE LAST-PLACE FINISHES AND ONE PARTICULARLY VICIOUS RIOT LATER, THE GENTRIFICATION PLAN WAS SCRAPPED...
...THE STADIUM WRITTEN OFF AND ABANDONED, LIKE THE CARCASS OF A FALLEN SOLDIER LEFT BEHIND ENEMY LINES.
BUT CARCASSES...

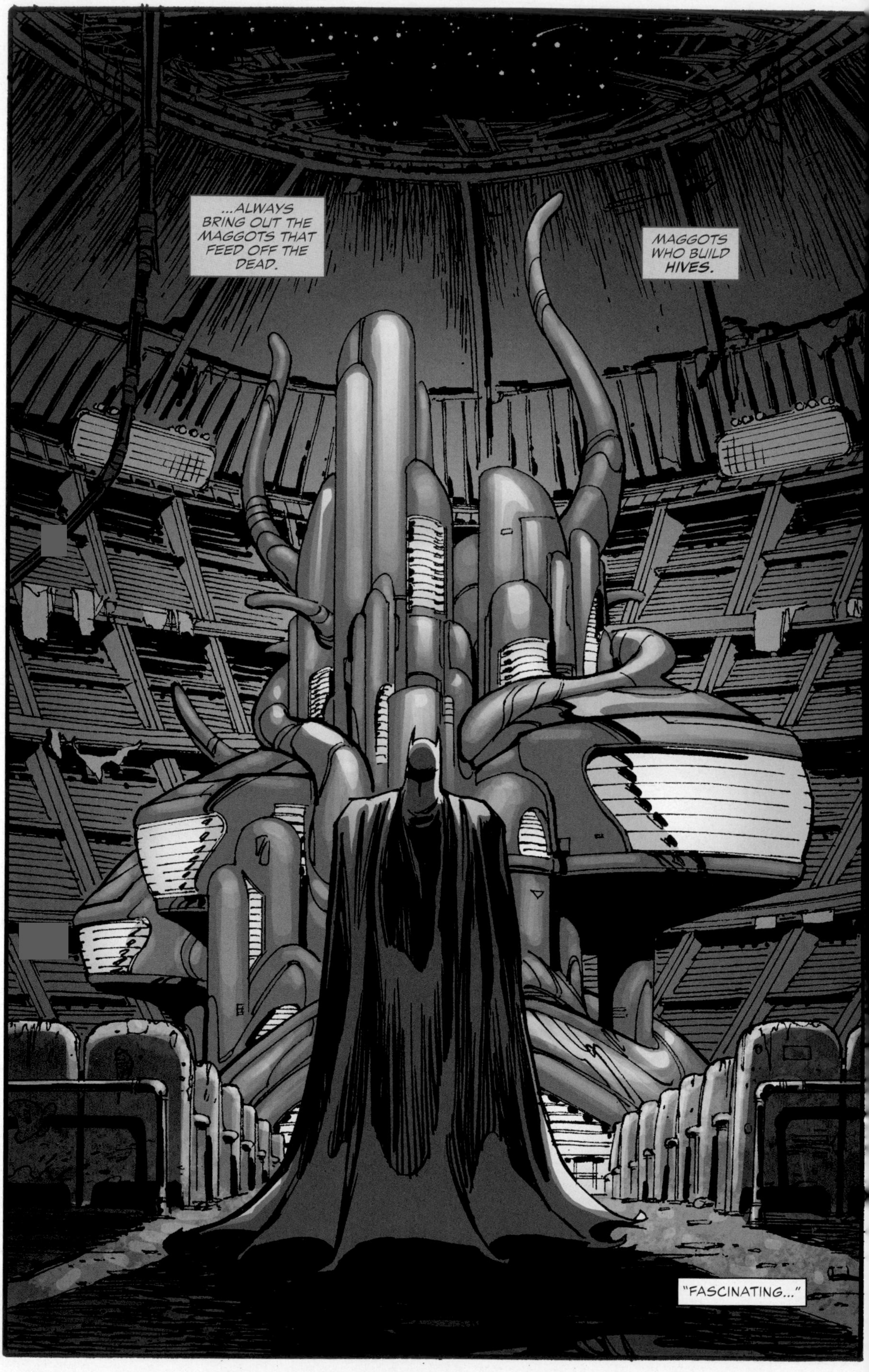
...ALWAYS BRING OUT THE MAGGOTS THAT FEED OFF THE DEAD.
MAGGOTS WHO BUILD HIVES.
"FASCINATING..."

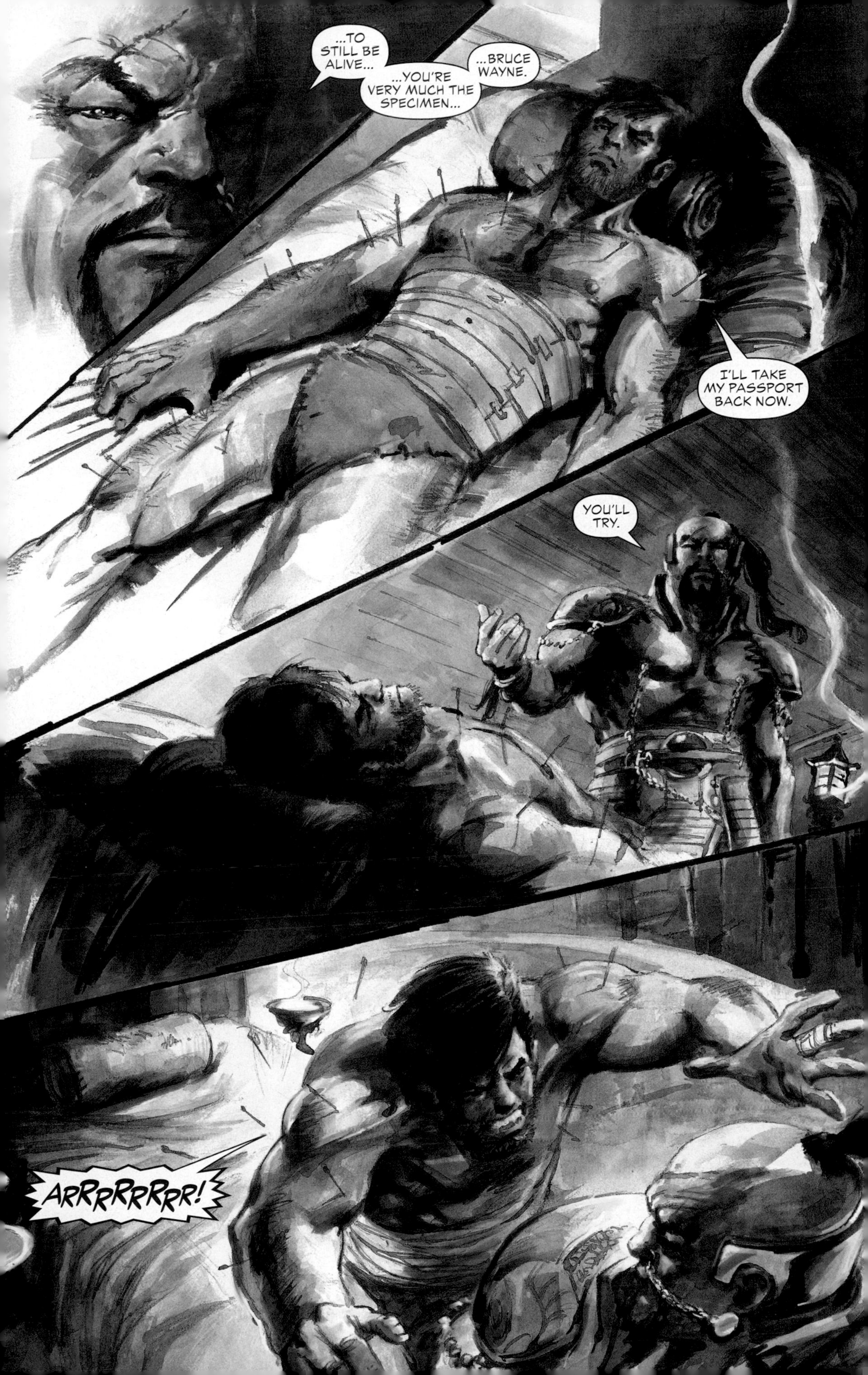
...TO STILL BE ALIVE...
...YOU'RE VERY MUCH THE SPECIMEN...
...BRUCE WAYNE.
I'LL TAKE MY PASSPORT BACK NOW.
YOU'LL TRY.
ARRRRRRRR!

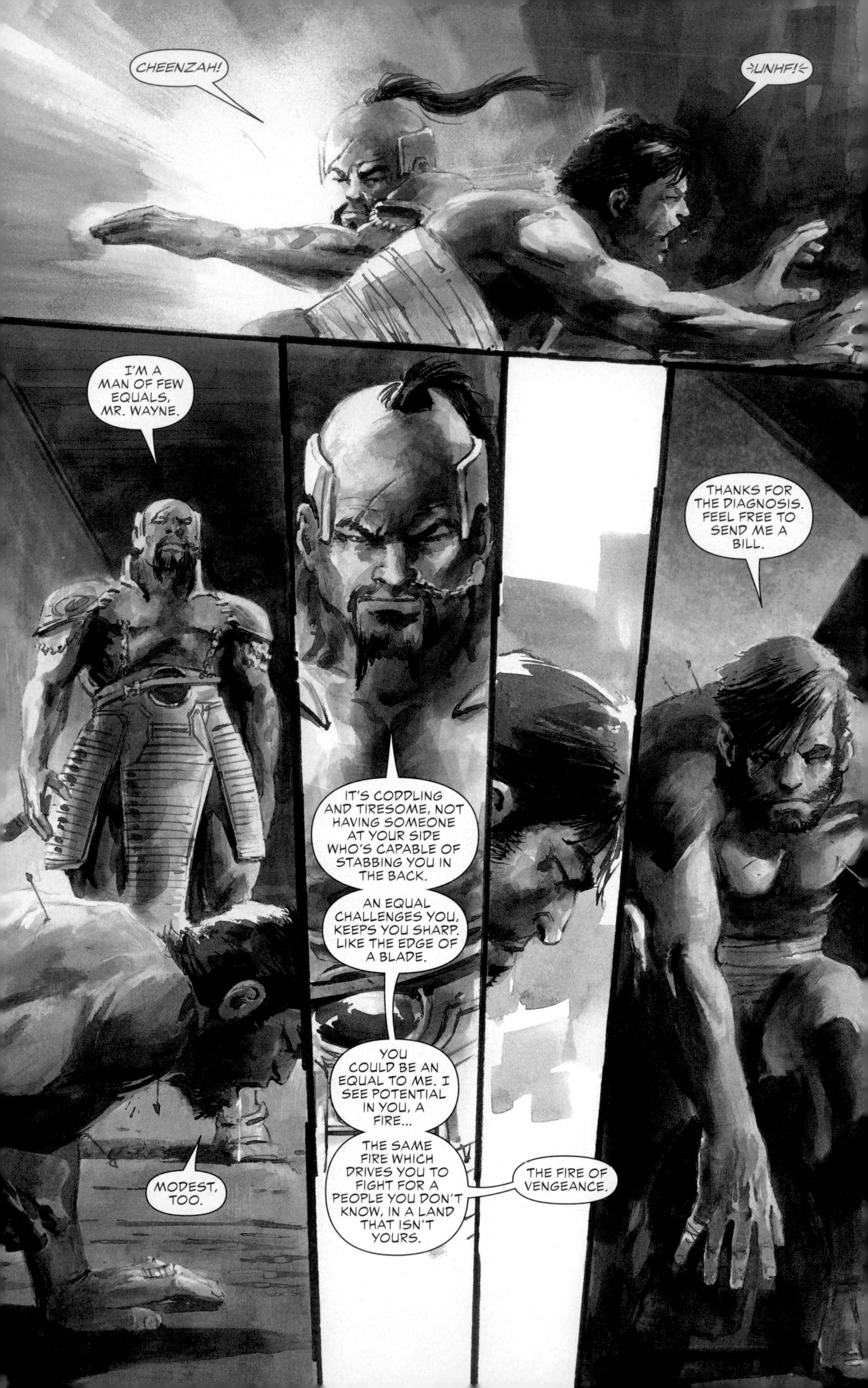
CHEENZAH!
UNHF!
I'M A MAN OF FEW EQUALS, MR. WAYNE.
MODEST, TOO.
IT'S CODDLING AND TIRESOME, NOT HAVING SOMEONE AT YOUR SIDE WHO'S CAPABLE OF STABBING YOU IN THE BACK.
AN EQUAL CHALLENGES YOU, KEEPS YOU SHARP. LIKE THE EDGE OF A BLADE.
YOU COULD BE AN EQUAL TO ME. I SEE POTENTIAL IN YOU, A FIRE...
THE SAME FIRE WHICH DRIVES YOU TO FIGHT FOR A PEOPLE YOU DON'T KNOW, IN A LAND THAT ISN'T YOURS.
THE FIRE OF VENGEANCE.
THANKS FOR THE DIAGNOSIS. FEEL FREE TO SEND ME A BILL.

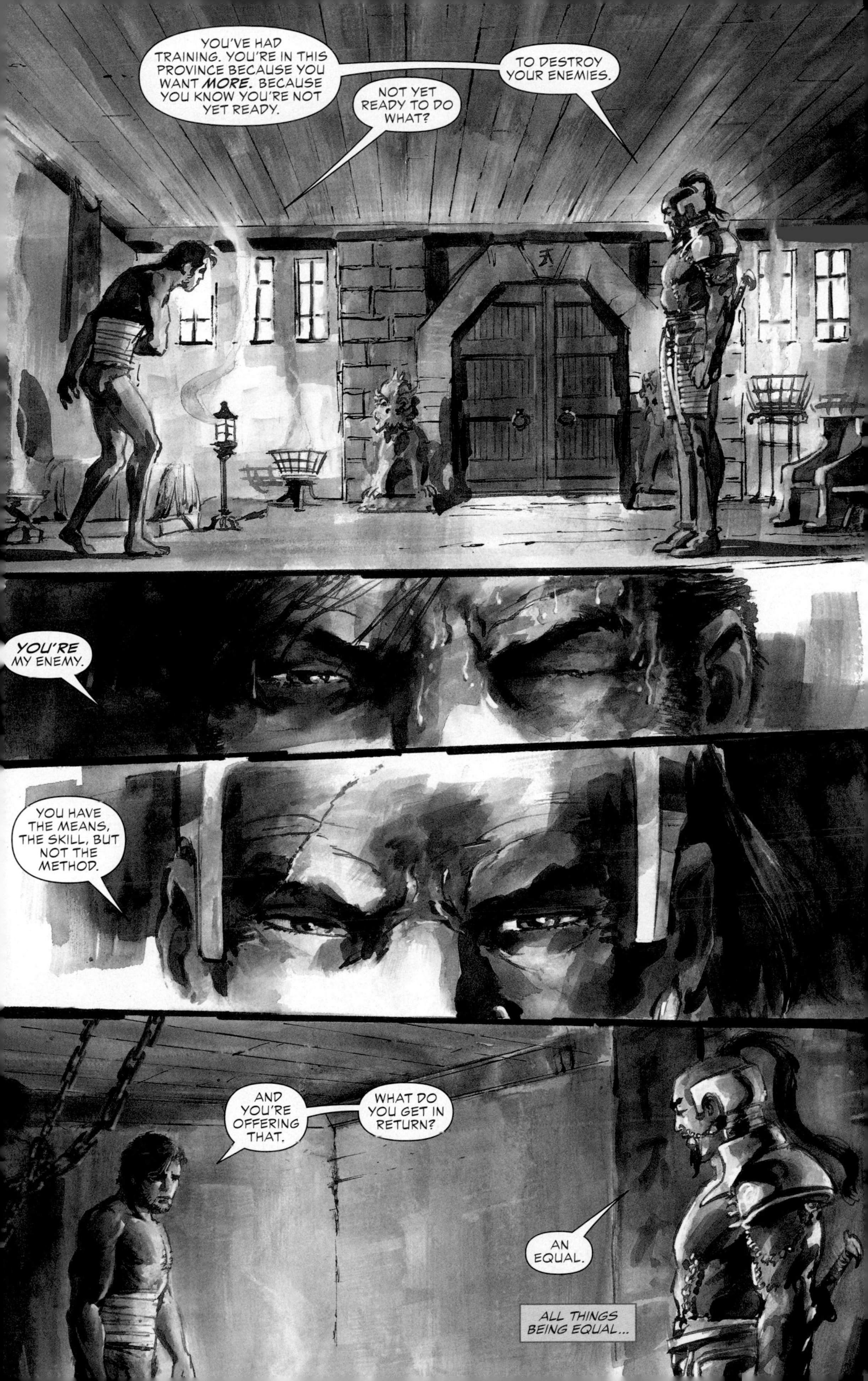
YOU'VE HAD TRAINING. YOU'RE IN THIS PROVINCE BECAUSE YOU WANT MORE. BECAUSE YOU KNOW YOU'RE NOT YET READY.
NOT YET READY TO DO WHAT?
TO DESTROY YOUR ENEMIES.
YOU'RE MY ENEMY.
YOU HAVE THE MEANS, THE SKILL, BUT NOT THE METHOD.
AND YOU'RE OFFERING THAT.
WHAT DO YOU GET IN RETURN?
AN EQUAL.
ALL THINGS BEING EQUAL...

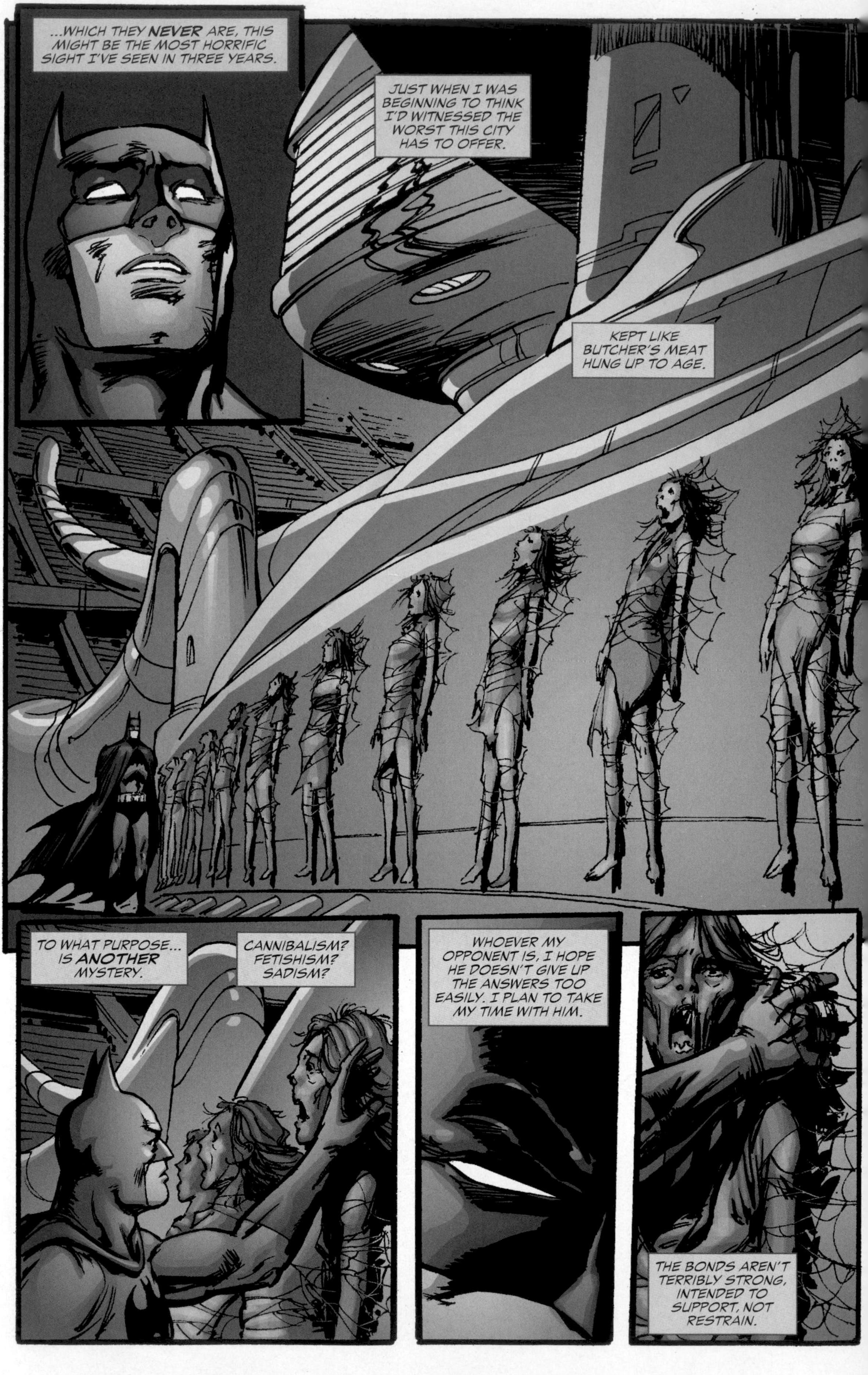
...WHICH THEY NEVER ARE, THIS MIGHT BE THE MOST HORRIFIC SIGHT I'VE SEEN IN THREE YEARS.
JUST WHEN I WAS BEGINNING TO THINK I'D WITNESSED THE WORST THIS CITY HAS TO OFFER.
KEPT LIKE BUTCHER'S MEAT HUNG UP TO AGE.
TO WHAT PURPOSE... IS ANOTHER MYSTERY.
CANNIBALISM? FETISHISM? SADISM?
WHOEVER MY OPPONENT IS, I HOPE HE DOESN'T GIVE UP THE ANSWERS TOO EASILY. I PLAN TO TAKE MY TIME WITH HIM.
THE BONDS AREN'T TERRIBLY STRONG, INTENDED TO SUPPORT, NOT RESTRAIN.

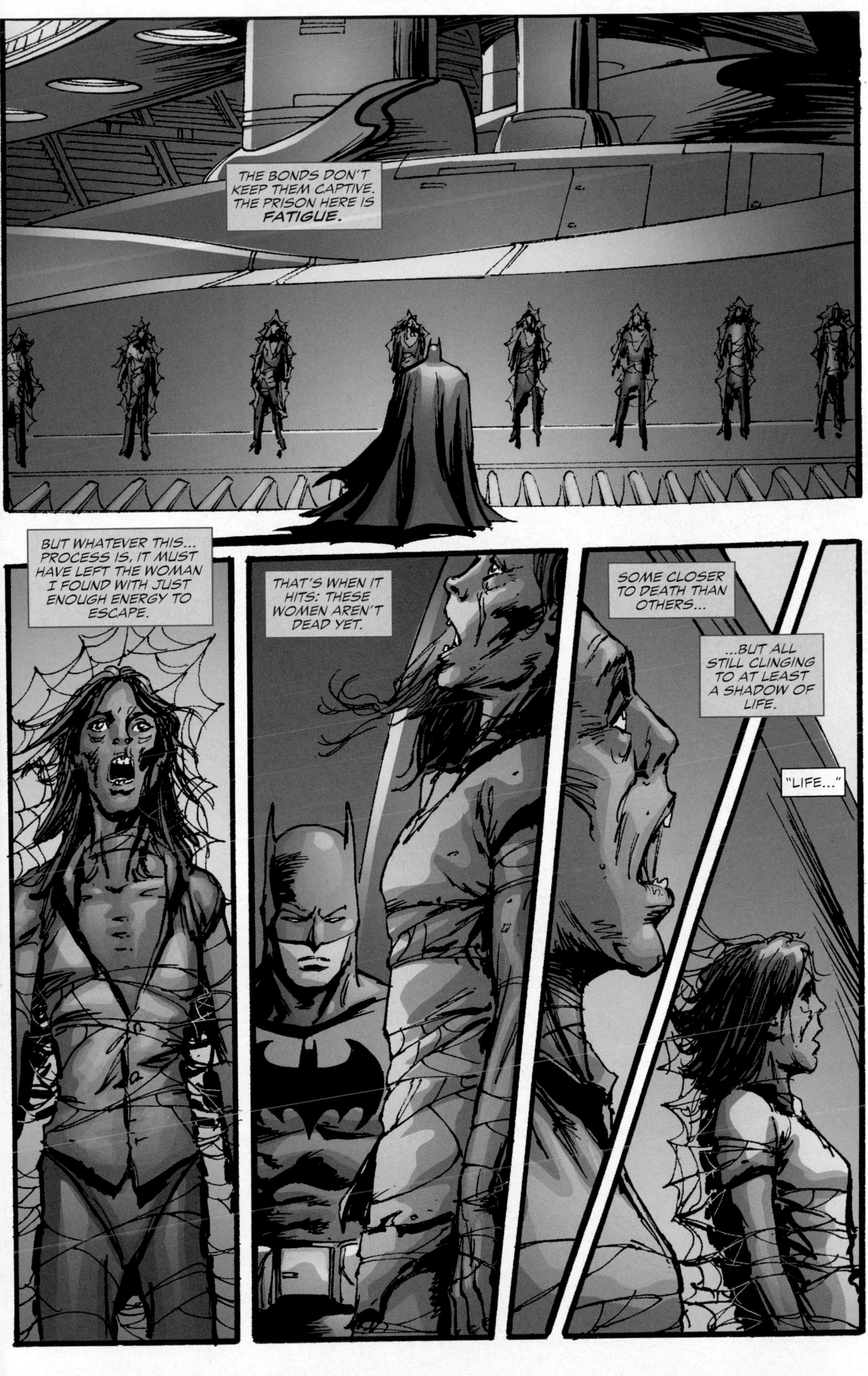
THE BONDS DON'T KEEP THEM CAPTIVE. THE PRISON HERE IS FATIGUE.
BUT WHATEVER THIS... PROCESS IS, IT MUST HAVE LEFT THE WOMAN I FOUND WITH JUST ENOUGH ENERGY TO ESCAPE.
THAT'S WHEN IT HITS: THESE WOMEN AREN'T DEAD YET.
SOME CLOSER TO DEATH THAN OTHERS...
...BUT ALL STILL CLINGING TO AT LEAST A SHADOW OF LIFE.
"LIFE..."

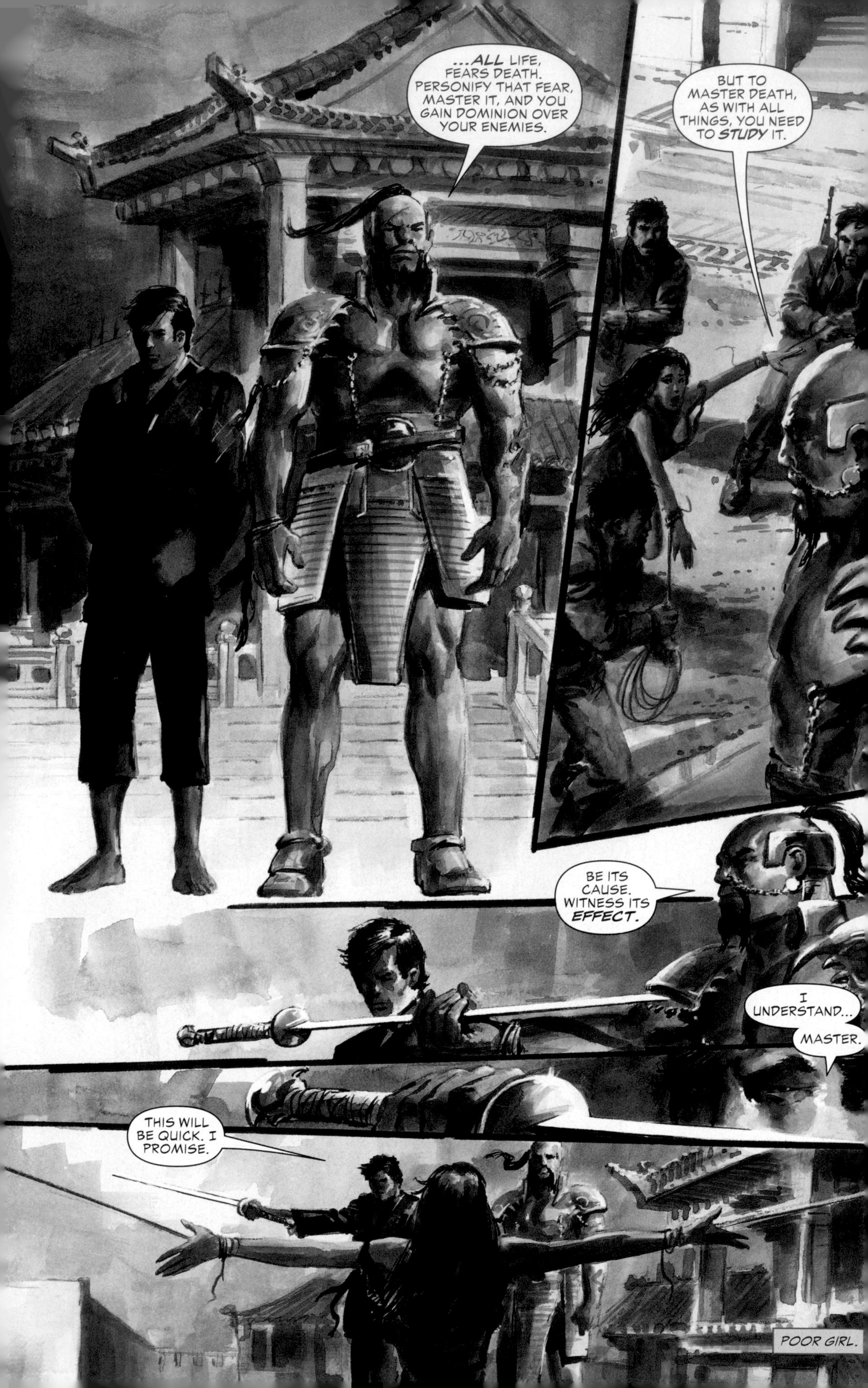
...ALL LIFE, FEARS DEATH. PERSONIFY THAT FEAR, MASTER IT, AND YOU GAIN DOMINION OVER YOUR ENEMIES.
BUT TO MASTER DEATH, AS WITH ALL THINGS, YOU NEED TO STUDY IT.
BE ITS CAUSE. WITNESS ITS EFFECT.
I UNDERSTAND...
MASTER.
THIS WILL BE QUICK. I PROMISE.
POOR GIRL.

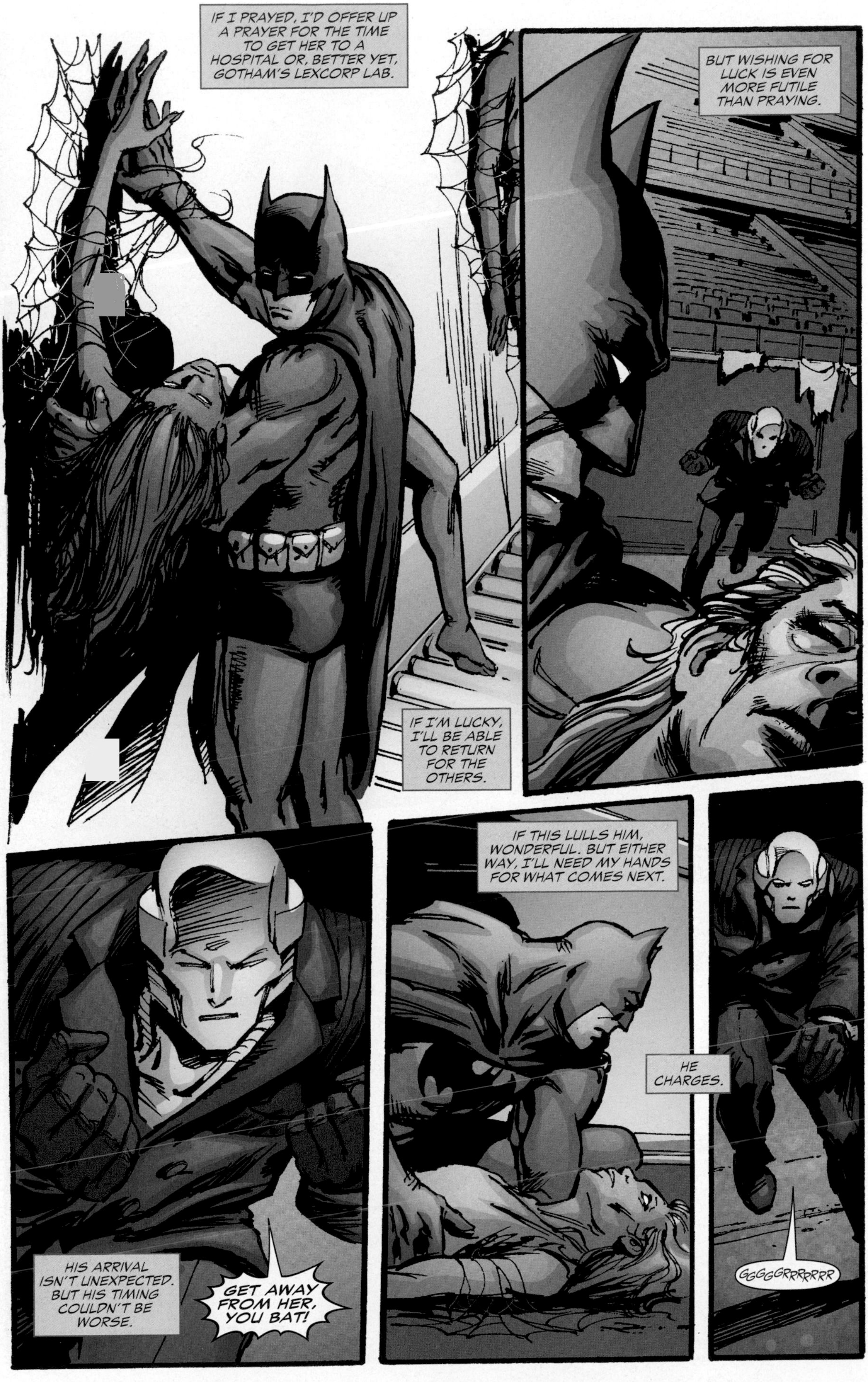
IF I PRAYED, I'D OFFER UP A PRAYER FOR THE TIME TO GET HER TO A HOSPITAL OR, BETTER YET, GOTHAM'S LEXCORP LAB.
IF I'M LUCKY, I'LL BE ABLE TO RETURN FOR THE OTHERS.
BUT WISHING FOR LUCK IS EVEN MORE FUTILE THAN PRAYING.
HIS ARRIVAL ISN'T UNEXPECTED. BUT HIS TIMING COULDN'T BE WORSE.
GET AWAY FROM HER, YOU BAT!
IF THIS LULLS HIM, WONDERFUL. BUT EITHER WAY, I'LL NEED MY HANDS FOR WHAT COMES NEXT.
HE CHARGES.
GGGGGRRRRRRR

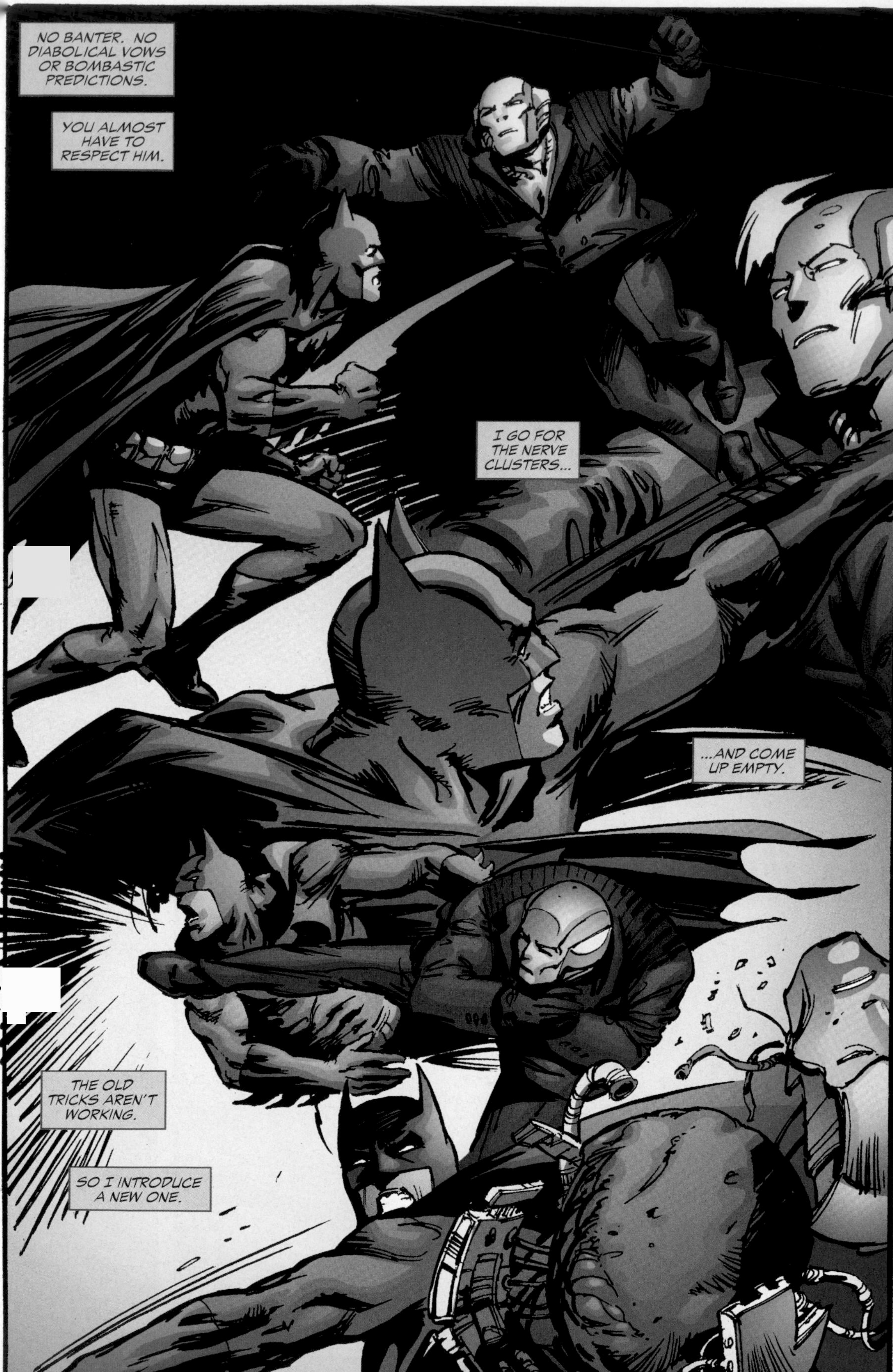
NO BANTER. NO DIABOLICAL VOWS OR BOMBASTIC PREDICTIONS.
YOU ALMOST HAVE TO RESPECT HIM.
I GO FOR THE NERVE CLUSTERS...
...AND COME UP EMPTY.
THE OLD TRICKS AREN'T WORKING.
SO I INTRODUCE A NEW ONE.

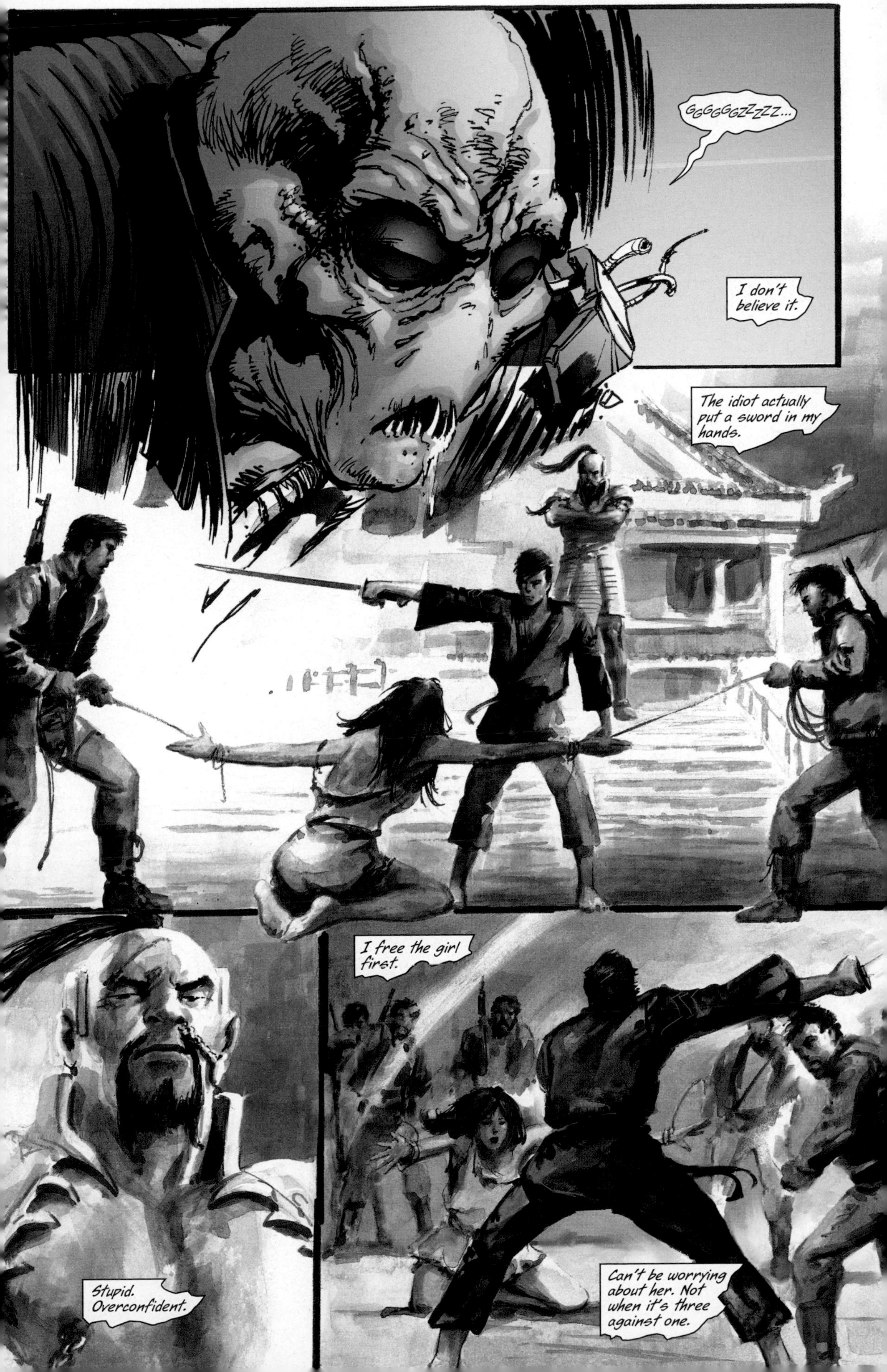
GGGGGGZZZZZ...
I don't believe it.
The idiot actually put a sword in my hands.
Stupid. Overconfident.
I free the girl first.
Can't be worrying about her. Not when it's three against one.

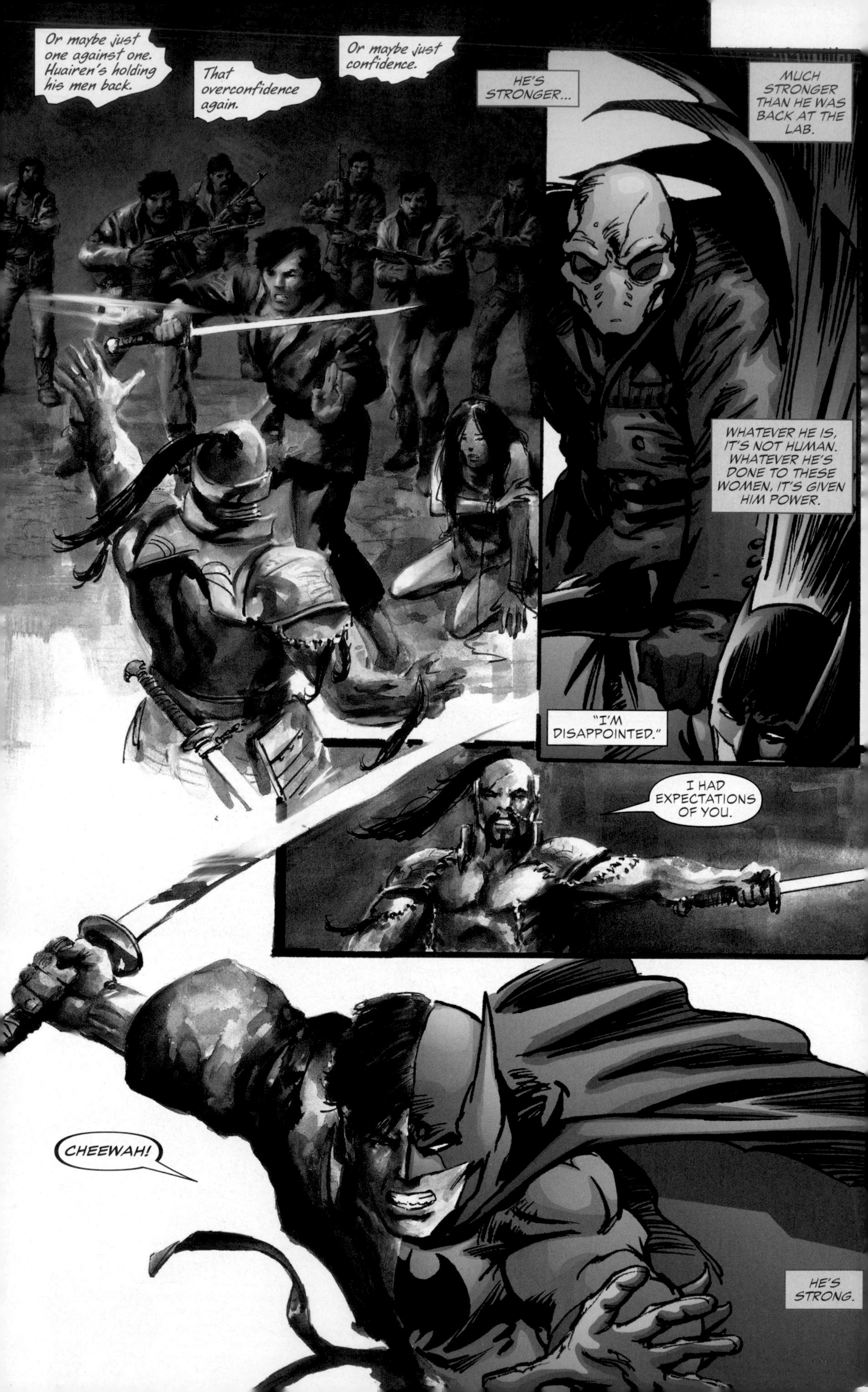
Or maybe just one against one. Huairen's holding his men back.
That overconfidence again.
Or maybe just confidence.
HE'S STRONGER...
MUCH STRONGER THAN HE WAS BACK AT THE LAB.
WHATEVER HE IS, IT'S NOT HUMAN. WHATEVER HE'S DONE TO THESE WOMEN, IT'S GIVEN HIM POWER.
"I'M DISAPPOINTED."
I HAD EXPECTATIONS OF YOU.
CHEEWAH!
HE'S STRONG.

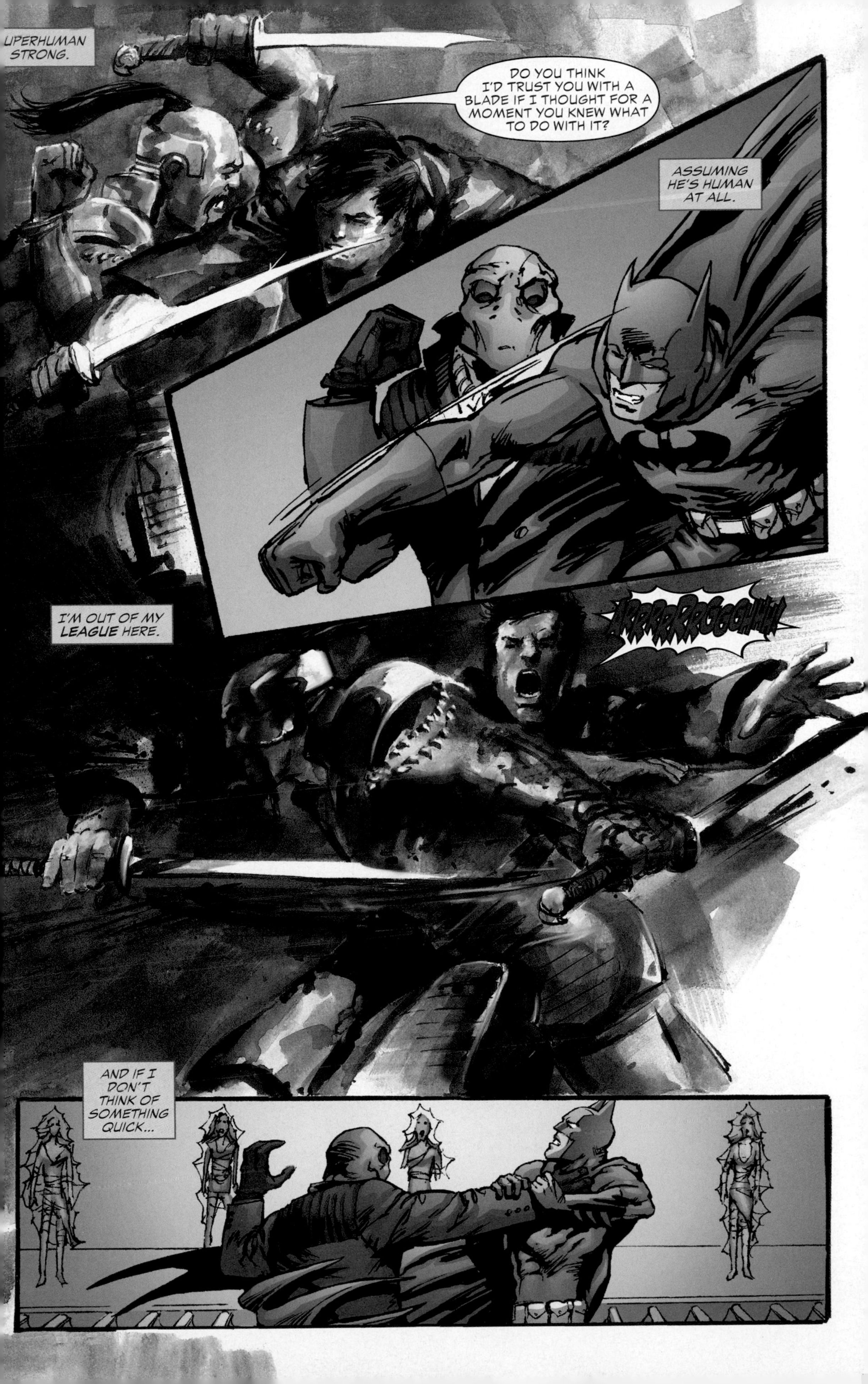
UPERHUMAN STRONG.
DO YOU THINK I'D TRUST YOU WITH A BLADE IF I THOUGHT FOR A MOMENT YOU KNEW WHAT TO DO WITH IT?
ASSUMING HE'S HUMAN AT ALL.
I'M OUT OF MY *LEAGUE* HERE.
AND IF I DON'T THINK OF SOMETHING QUICK...

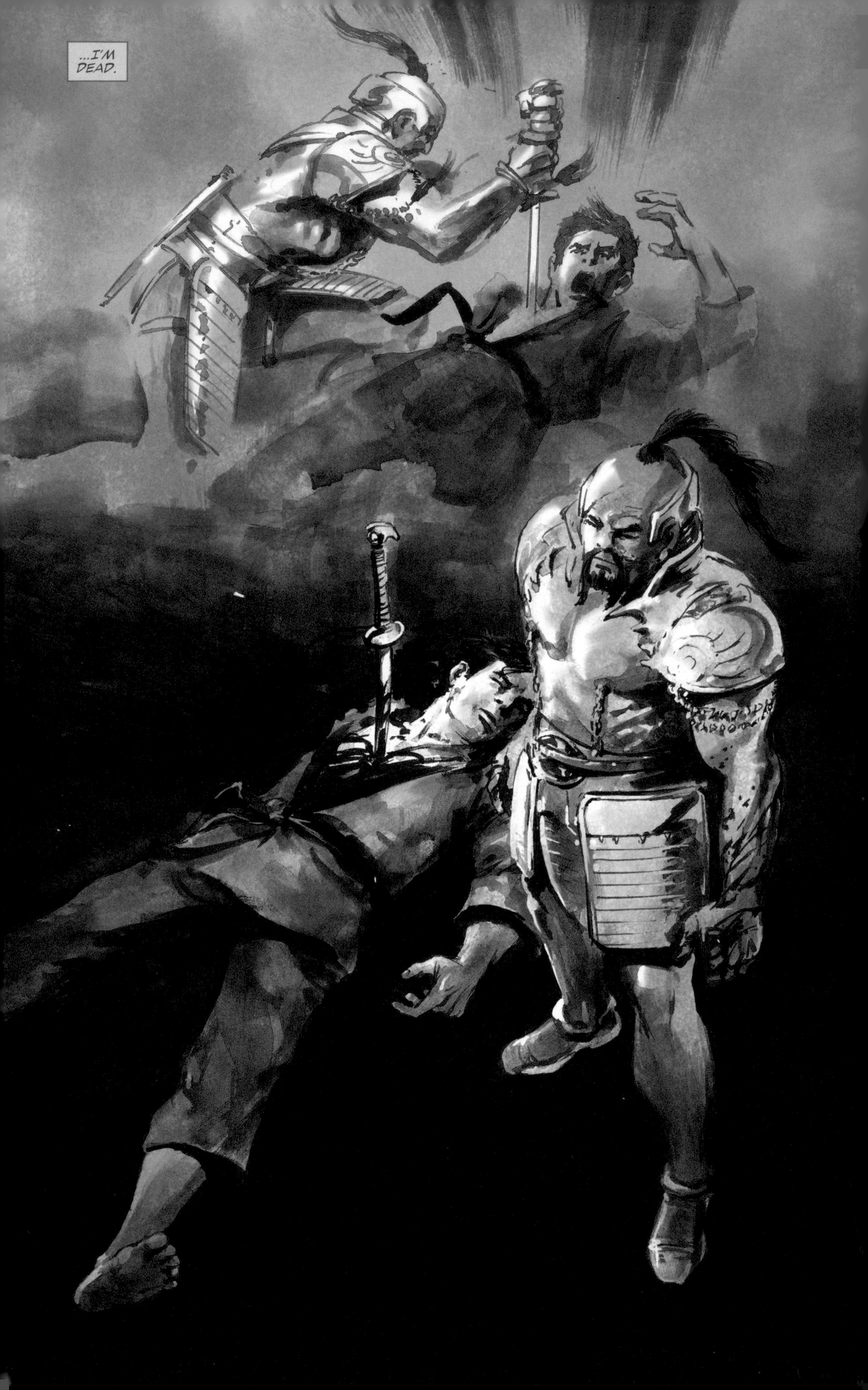
...I'M DEAD.

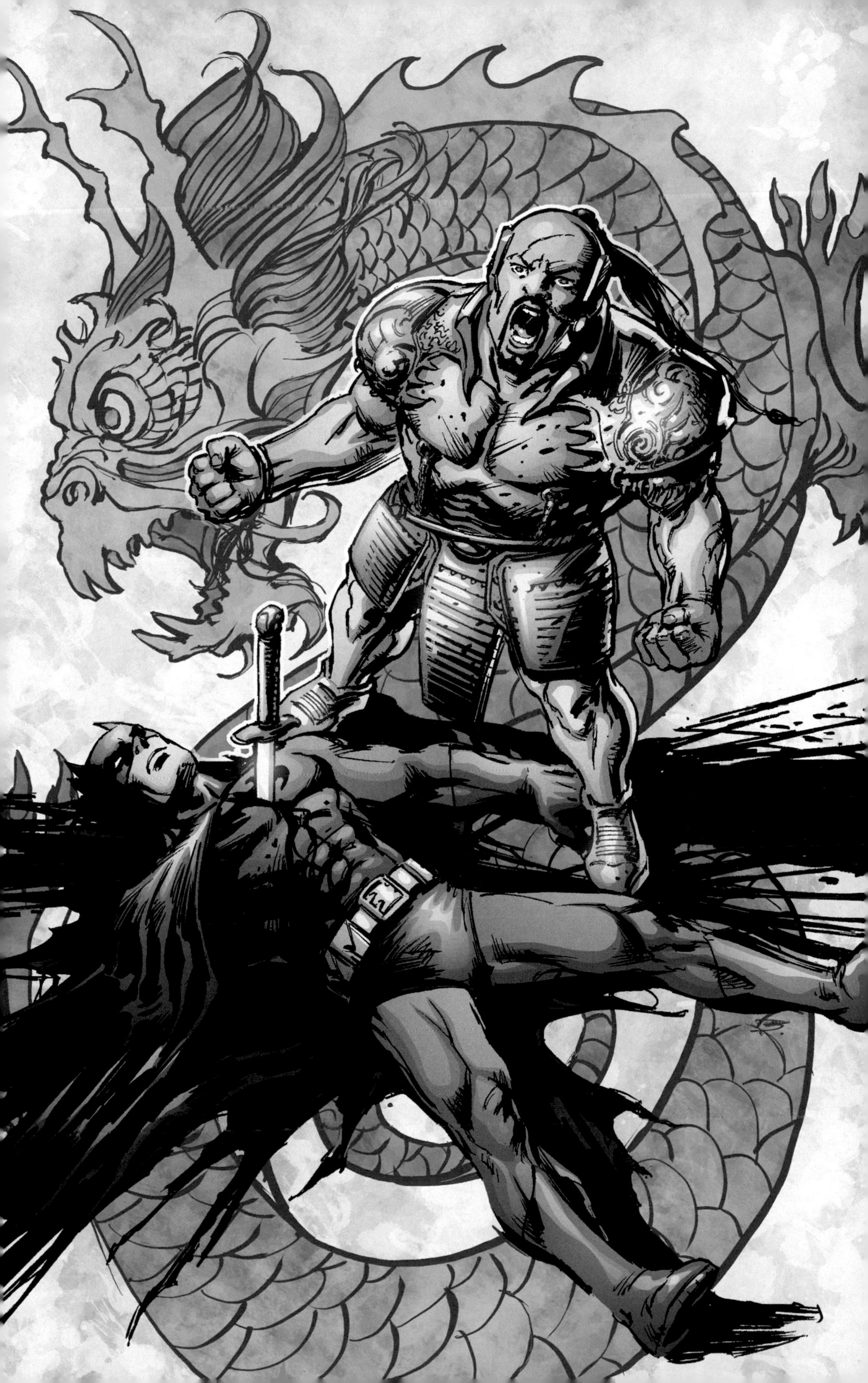

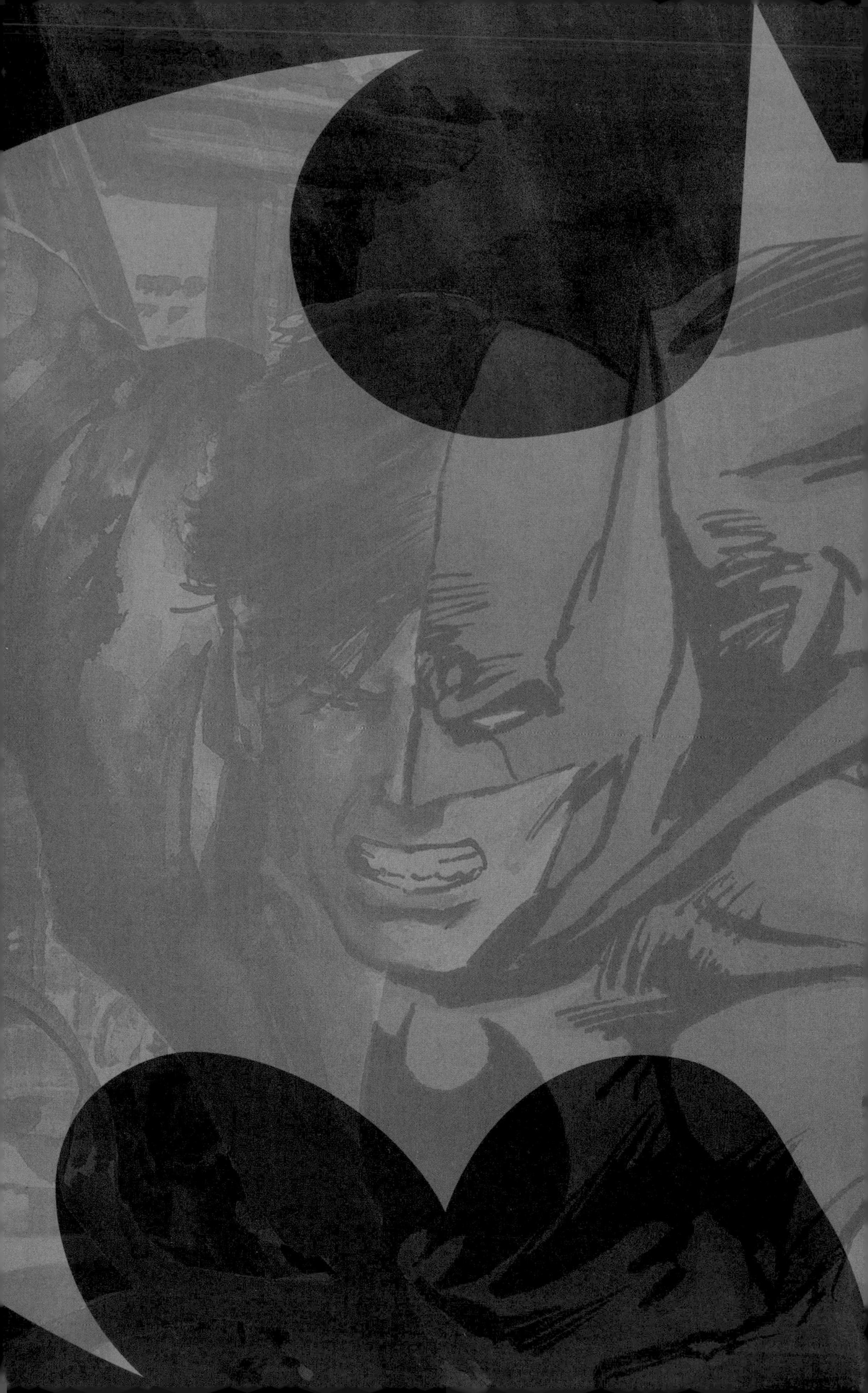

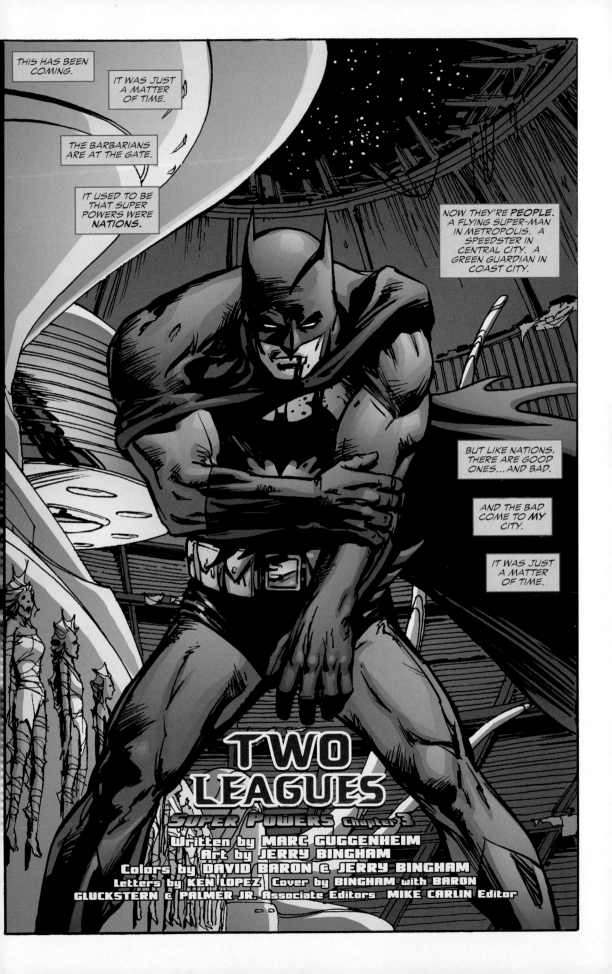

THIS HAS BEEN COMING.

IT WAS JUST A MATTER OF TIME.

THE BARBARIANS ARE AT THE GATE.

IT USED TO BE THAT SUPER POWERS WERE NATIONS.

NOW THEY'RE PEOPLE. A FLYING SUPER-MAN IN METROPOLIS. A SPEEDSTER IN CENTRAL CITY. A GREEN GUARDIAN IN COAST CITY.

BUT LIKE NATIONS, THERE ARE GOOD ONES...AND BAD.

AND THE BAD COME TO MY CITY.

IT WAS JUST A MATTER OF TIME.

TWO LEAGUES
SUPER POWERS Chapter 3
Written by MARC GUGGENHEIM
Art by JERRY BINGHAM
Colors by DAVID BARON & JERRY BINGHAM
Letters by KEN LOPEZ Cover by BINGHAM with BARON
GLUCKSTERN & PALMER JR. Associate Editors MIKE CARLIN Editor

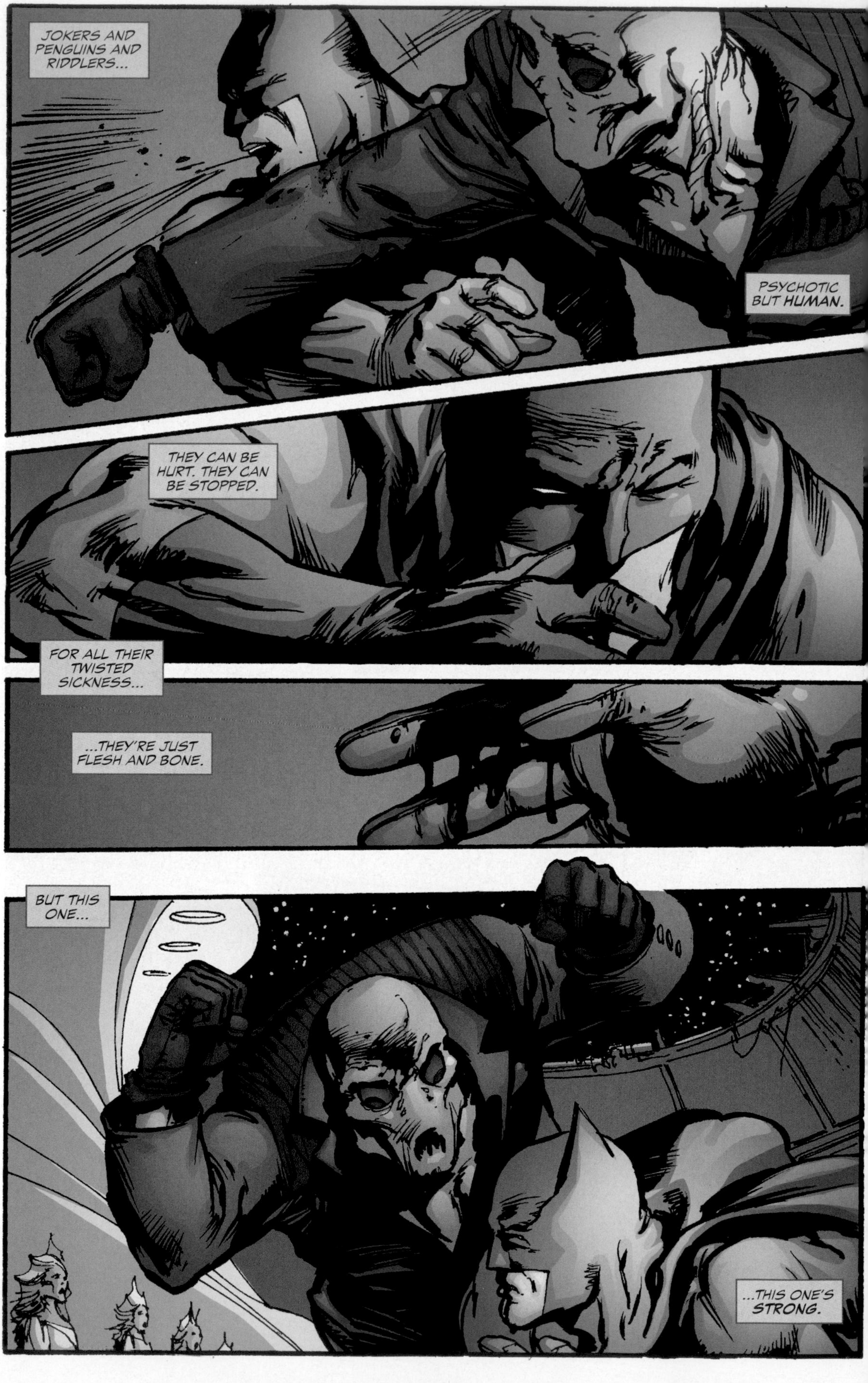
JOKERS AND PENGUINS AND RIDDLERS...
PSYCHOTIC BUT HUMAN.
THEY CAN BE HURT. THEY CAN BE STOPPED.
FOR ALL THEIR TWISTED SICKNESS...
...THEY'RE JUST FLESH AND BONE.
BUT THIS ONE...
...THIS ONE'S STRONG.

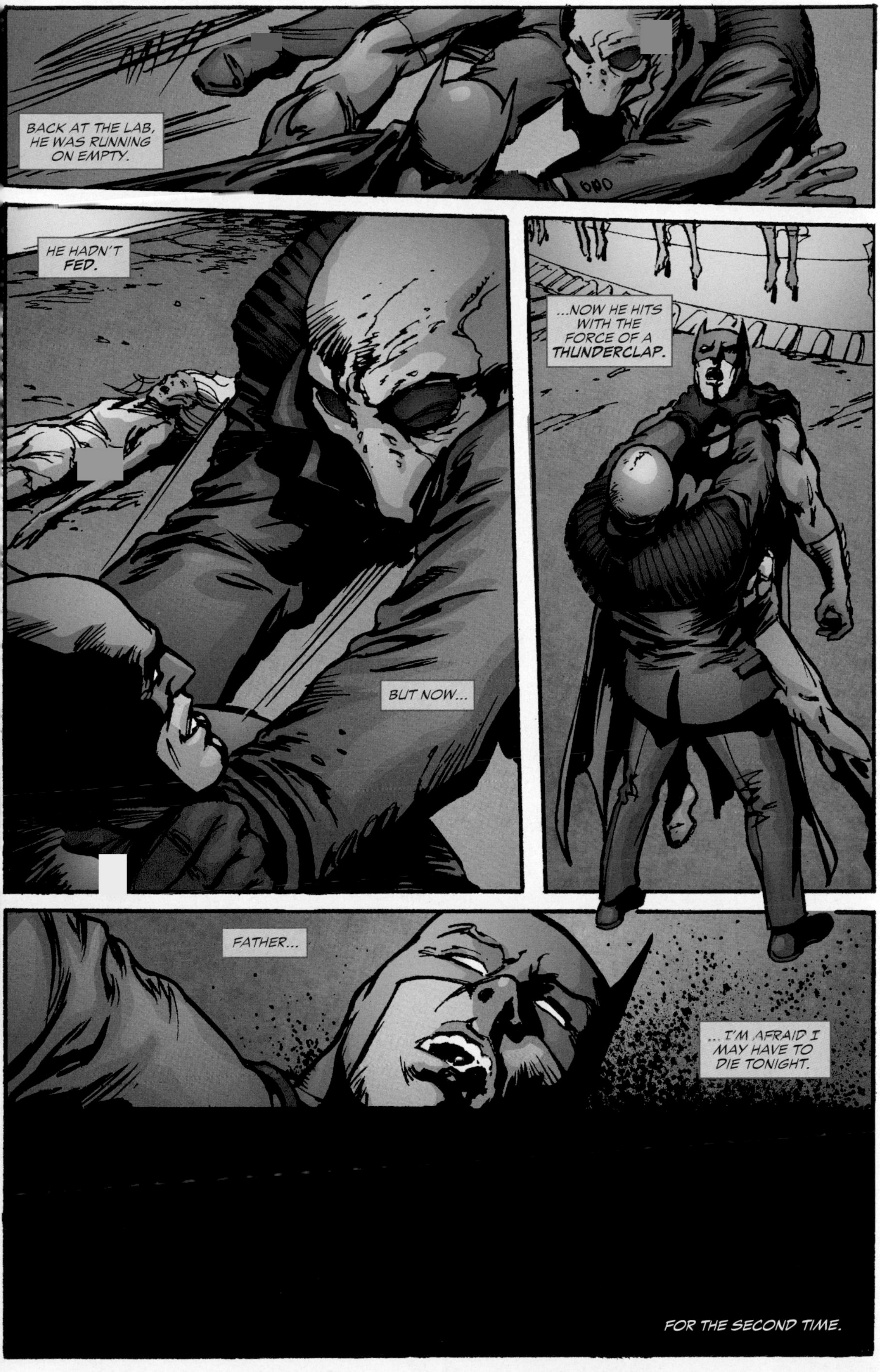
BACK AT THE LAB, HE WAS RUNNING ON EMPTY.
HE HADN'T FED.
BUT NOW...
...NOW HE HITS WITH THE FORCE OF A THUNDERCLAP.
FATHER...
...I'M AFRAID I MAY HAVE TO DIE TONIGHT.
FOR THE SECOND TIME.

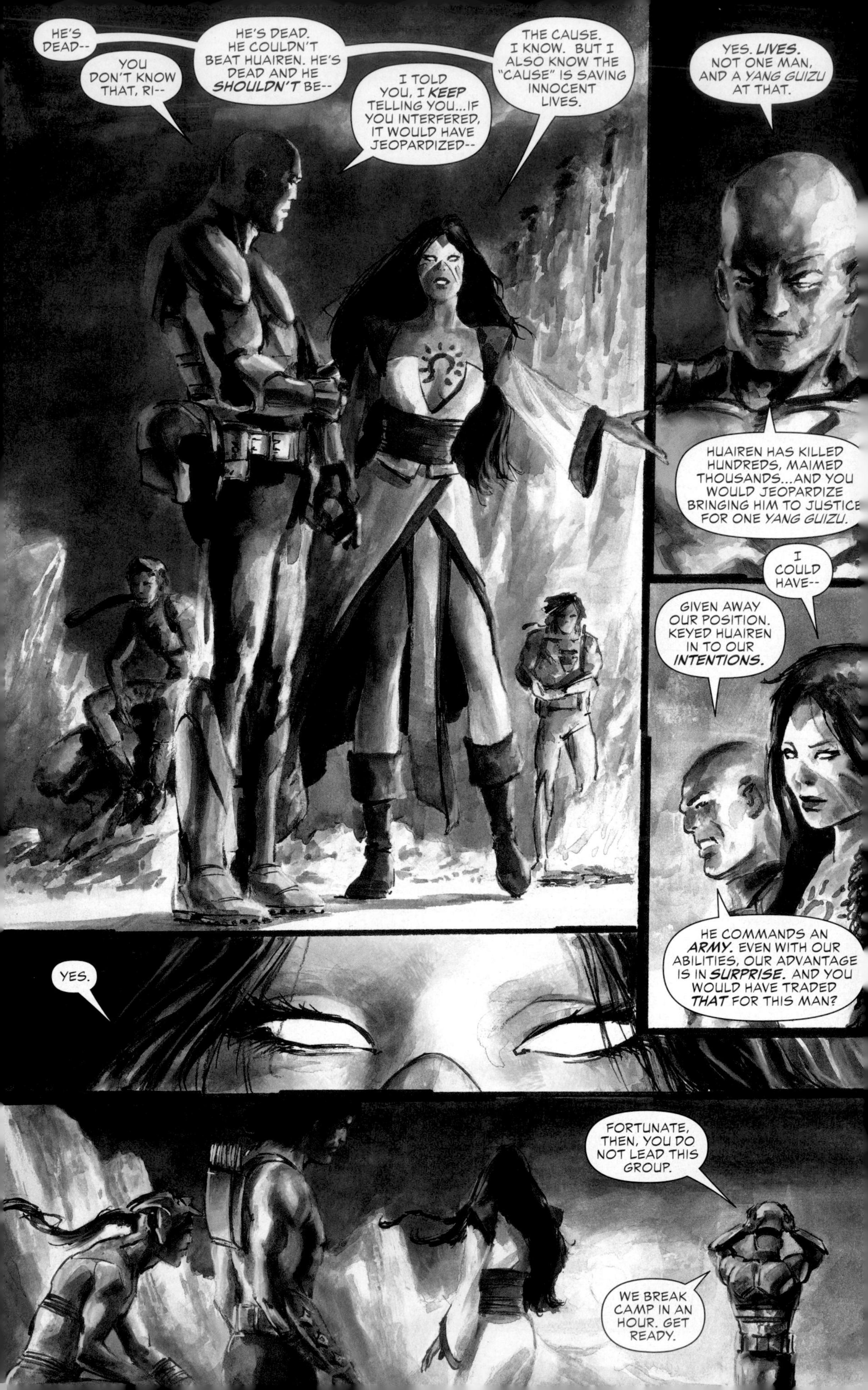
HE'S DEAD--
YOU DON'T KNOW THAT, RI--
HE'S DEAD. HE COULDN'T BEAT HUAIREN. HE'S DEAD AND HE ***SHOULDN'T*** BE--
I TOLD YOU, I ***KEEP*** TELLING YOU...IF YOU INTERFERED, IT WOULD HAVE JEOPARDIZED--
THE CAUSE. I KNOW. BUT I ALSO KNOW THE "CAUSE" IS SAVING INNOCENT LIVES.
YES. ***LIVES.*** NOT ONE MAN, AND A *YANG GUIZU* AT THAT.
HUAIREN HAS KILLED HUNDREDS, MAIMED THOUSANDS...AND YOU WOULD JEOPARDIZE BRINGING HIM TO JUSTICE FOR ONE *YANG GUIZU.*
I COULD HAVE--
GIVEN AWAY OUR POSITION. KEYED HUAIREN IN TO OUR ***INTENTIONS.***
HE COMMANDS AN ***ARMY.*** EVEN WITH OUR ABILITIES, OUR ADVANTAGE IS IN ***SURPRISE.*** AND YOU WOULD HAVE TRADED ***THAT*** FOR THIS MAN?
YES.
FORTUNATE, THEN, YOU DO NOT LEAD THIS GROUP.
WE BREAK CAMP IN AN HOUR. GET READY.

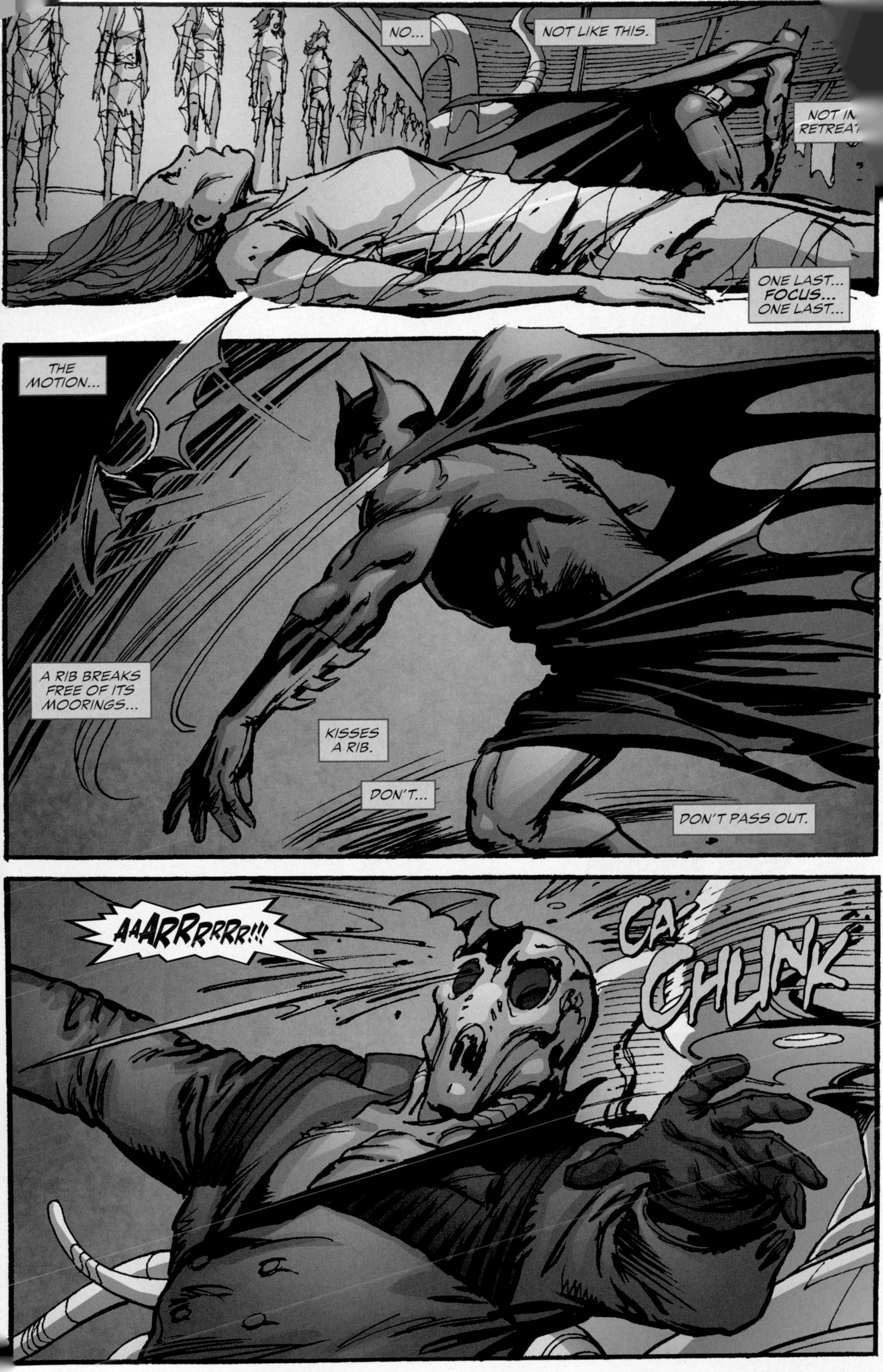
NO...
NOT LIKE THIS.
NOT IN RETREAT
ONE LAST... FOCUS... ONE LAST...
THE MOTION...
A RIB BREAKS FREE OF ITS MOORINGS...
KISSES A RIB.
DON'T...
DON'T PASS OUT.
AAARRRRRR!!!
CA-CHUNK

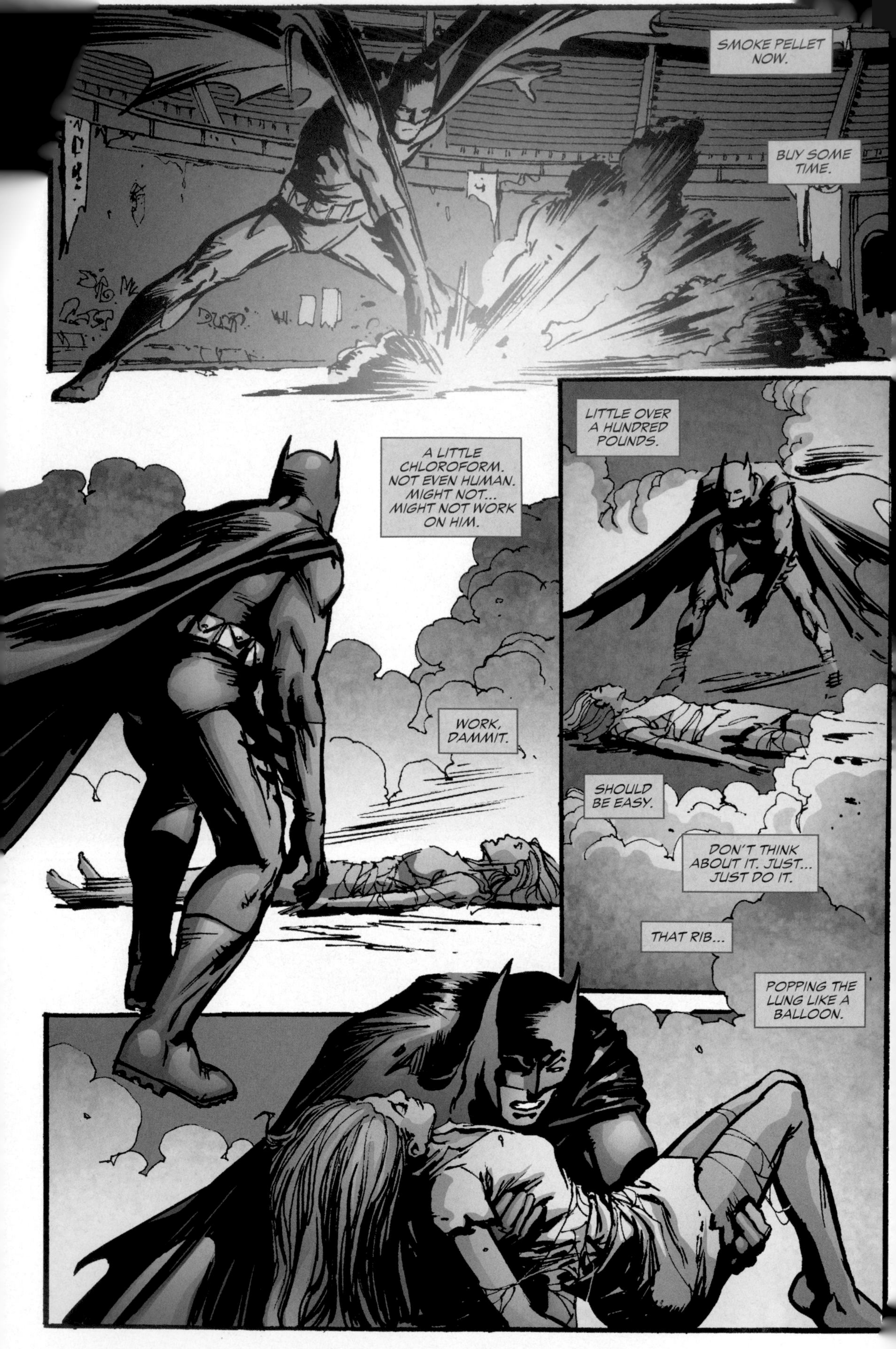
SMOKE PELLET NOW.
BUY SOME TIME.
A LITTLE CHLOROFORM. NOT EVEN HUMAN. MIGHT NOT... MIGHT NOT WORK ON HIM.
WORK, DAMMIT.
LITTLE OVER A HUNDRED POUNDS.
SHOULD BE EASY.
DON'T THINK ABOUT IT. JUST... JUST DO IT.
THAT RIB...
POPPING THE LUNG LIKE A BALLOON.

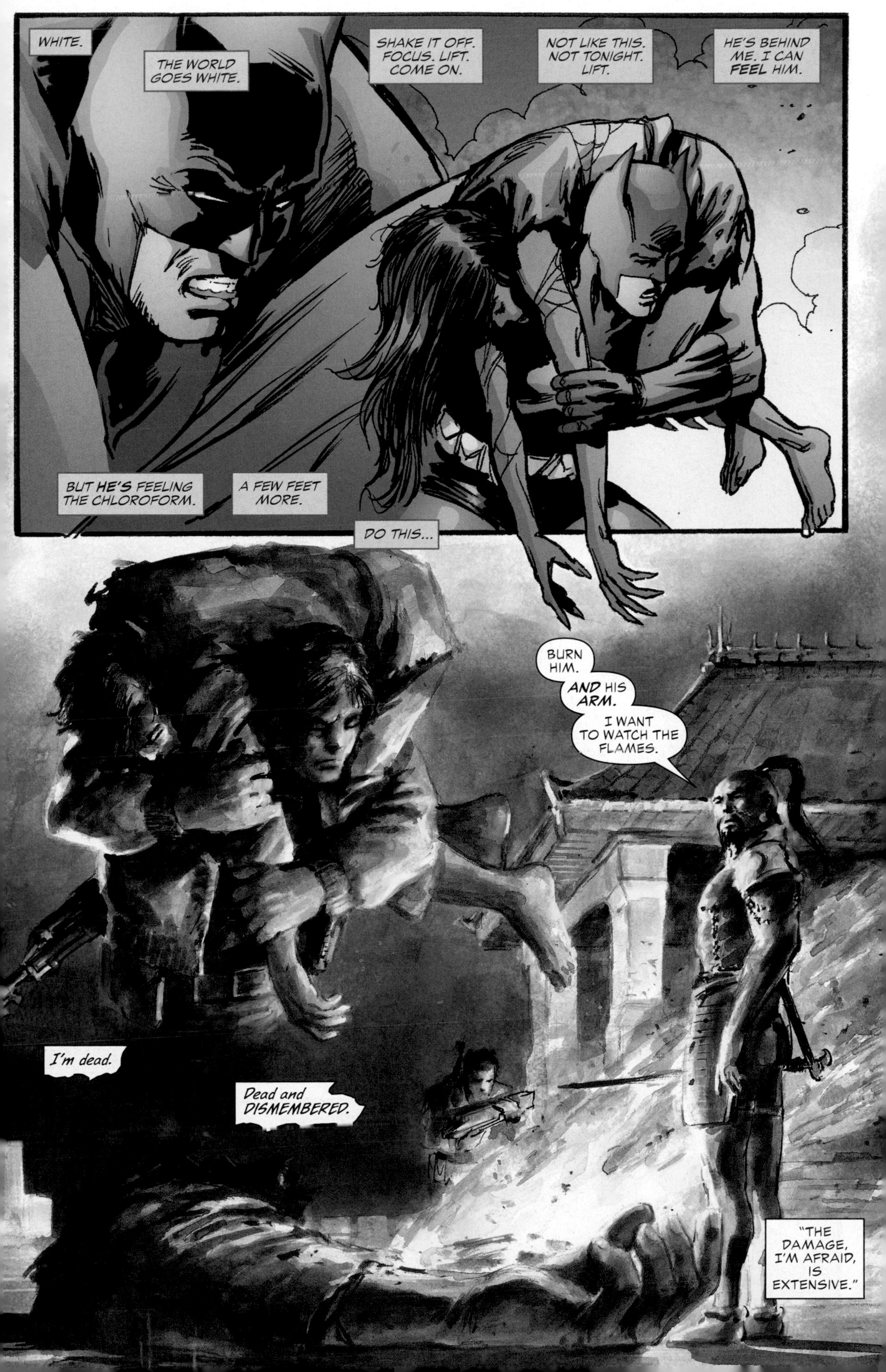
WHITE.
THE WORLD GOES WHITE.
SHAKE IT OFF. FOCUS. LIFT. COME ON.
NOT LIKE THIS. NOT TONIGHT. LIFT.
HE'S BEHIND ME. I CAN FEEL HIM.
BUT HE'S FEELING THE CHLOROFORM.
A FEW FEET MORE.
DO THIS...
BURN HIM. AND HIS ARM.
I WANT TO WATCH THE FLAMES.
I'm dead.
Dead and DISMEMBERED.
"THE DAMAGE, I'M AFRAID, IS EXTENSIVE."

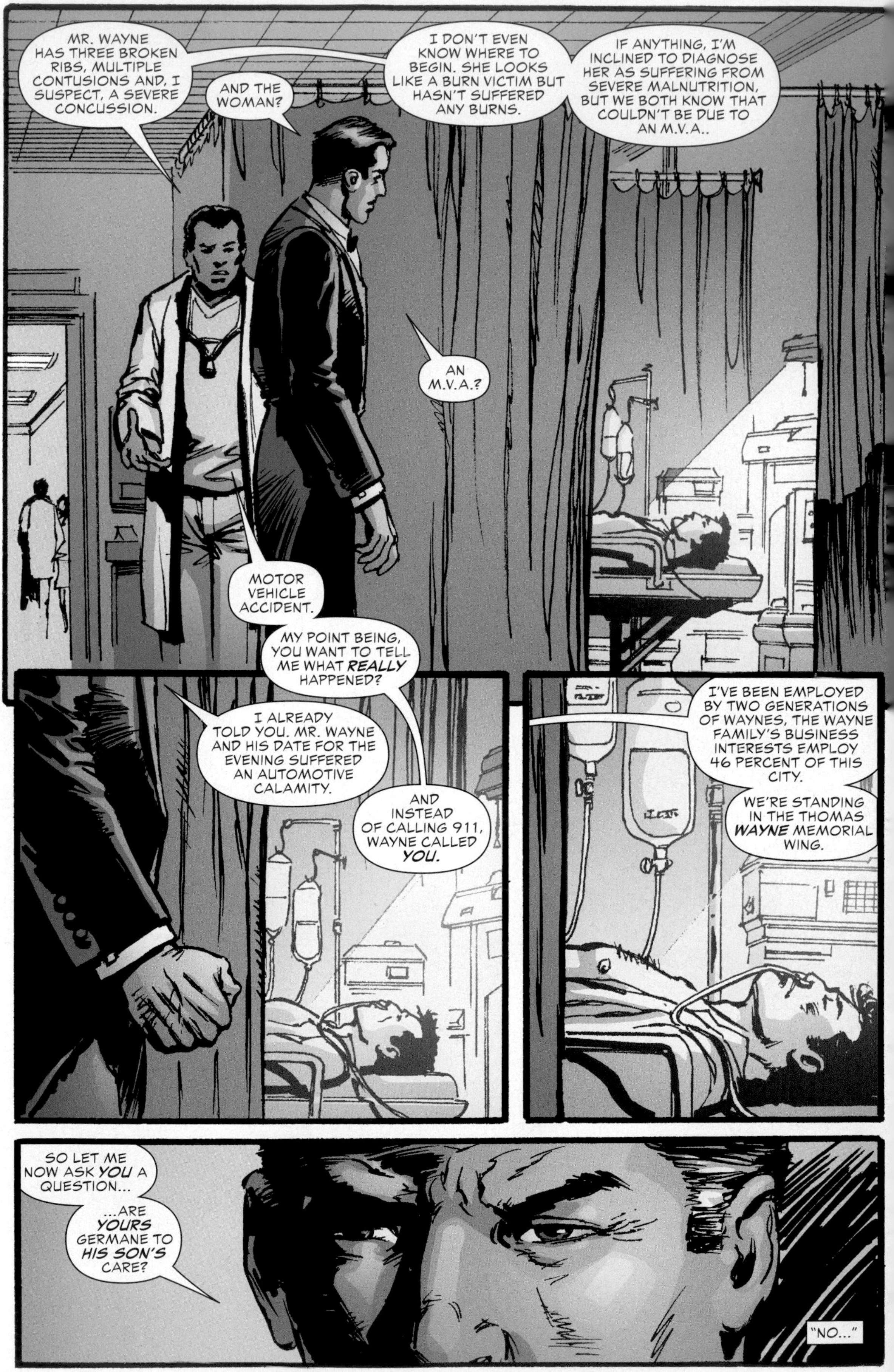
MR. WAYNE HAS THREE BROKEN RIBS, MULTIPLE CONTUSIONS AND, I SUSPECT, A SEVERE CONCUSSION.
AND THE WOMAN?
I DON'T EVEN KNOW WHERE TO BEGIN. SHE LOOKS LIKE A BURN VICTIM BUT HASN'T SUFFERED ANY BURNS.
IF ANYTHING, I'M INCLINED TO DIAGNOSE HER AS SUFFERING FROM SEVERE MALNUTRITION, BUT WE BOTH KNOW THAT COULDN'T BE DUE TO AN M.V.A..
AN M.V.A.?
MOTOR VEHICLE ACCIDENT.
MY POINT BEING, YOU WANT TO TELL ME WHAT REALLY HAPPENED?
I ALREADY TOLD YOU. MR. WAYNE AND HIS DATE FOR THE EVENING SUFFERED AN AUTOMOTIVE CALAMITY.
AND INSTEAD OF CALLING 911, WAYNE CALLED YOU.
I'VE BEEN EMPLOYED BY TWO GENERATIONS OF WAYNES, THE WAYNE FAMILY'S BUSINESS INTERESTS EMPLOY 46 PERCENT OF THIS CITY.
WE'RE STANDING IN THE THOMAS WAYNE MEMORIAL WING.
SO LET ME NOW ASK YOU A QUESTION...
...ARE YOURS GERMANE TO HIS SON'S CARE?
"NO..."

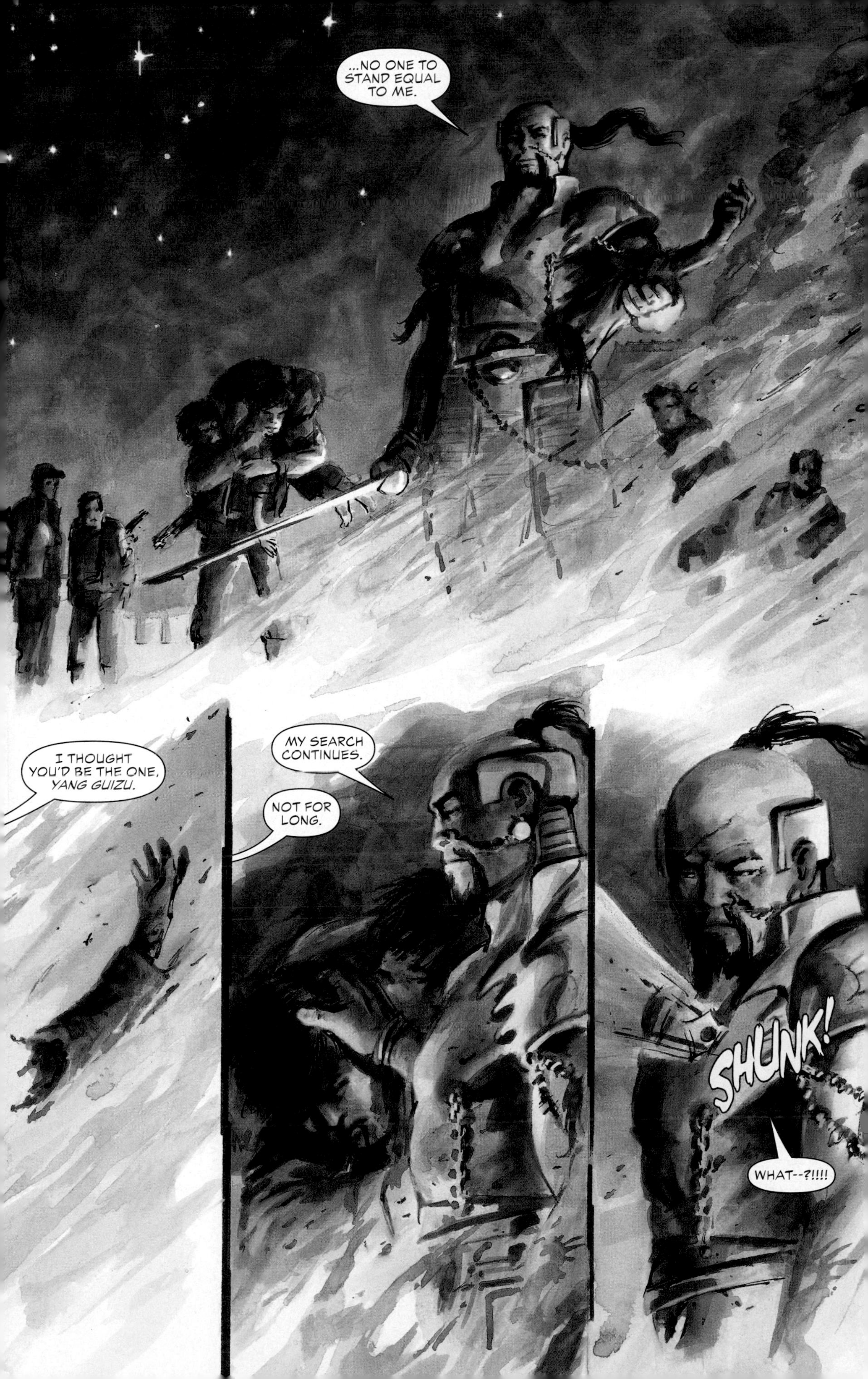
...NO ONE TO STAND EQUAL TO ME.
I THOUGHT YOU'D BE THE ONE, *YANG GUIZU*.
MY SEARCH CONTINUES.
NOT FOR LONG.
SHUNK!
WHAT--?!!!!

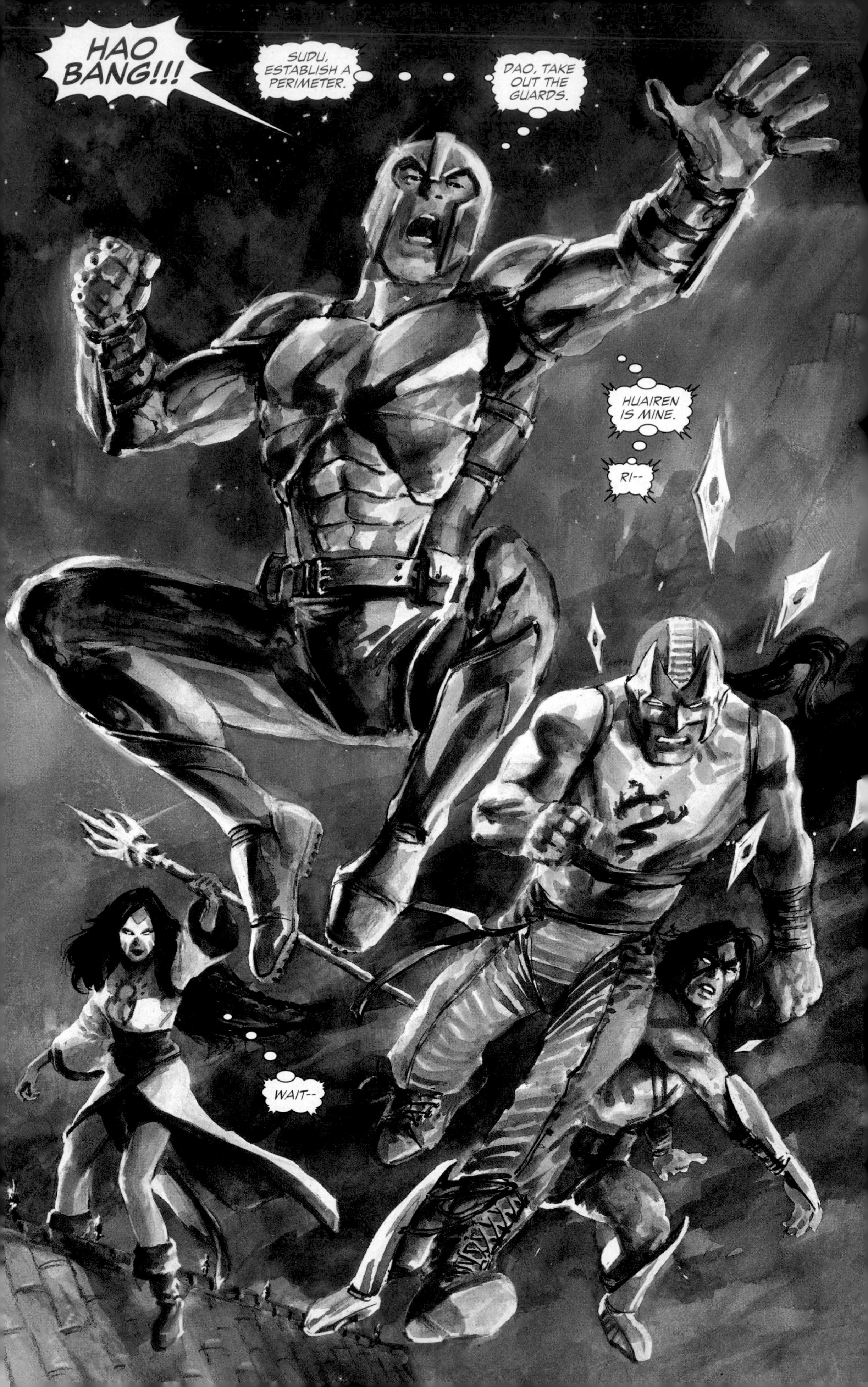
HAO BANG!!!
SUDU, ESTABLISH A PERIMETER.
DAO, TAKE OUT THE GUARDS.
HUAIREN IS MINE.
RI--
WAIT--

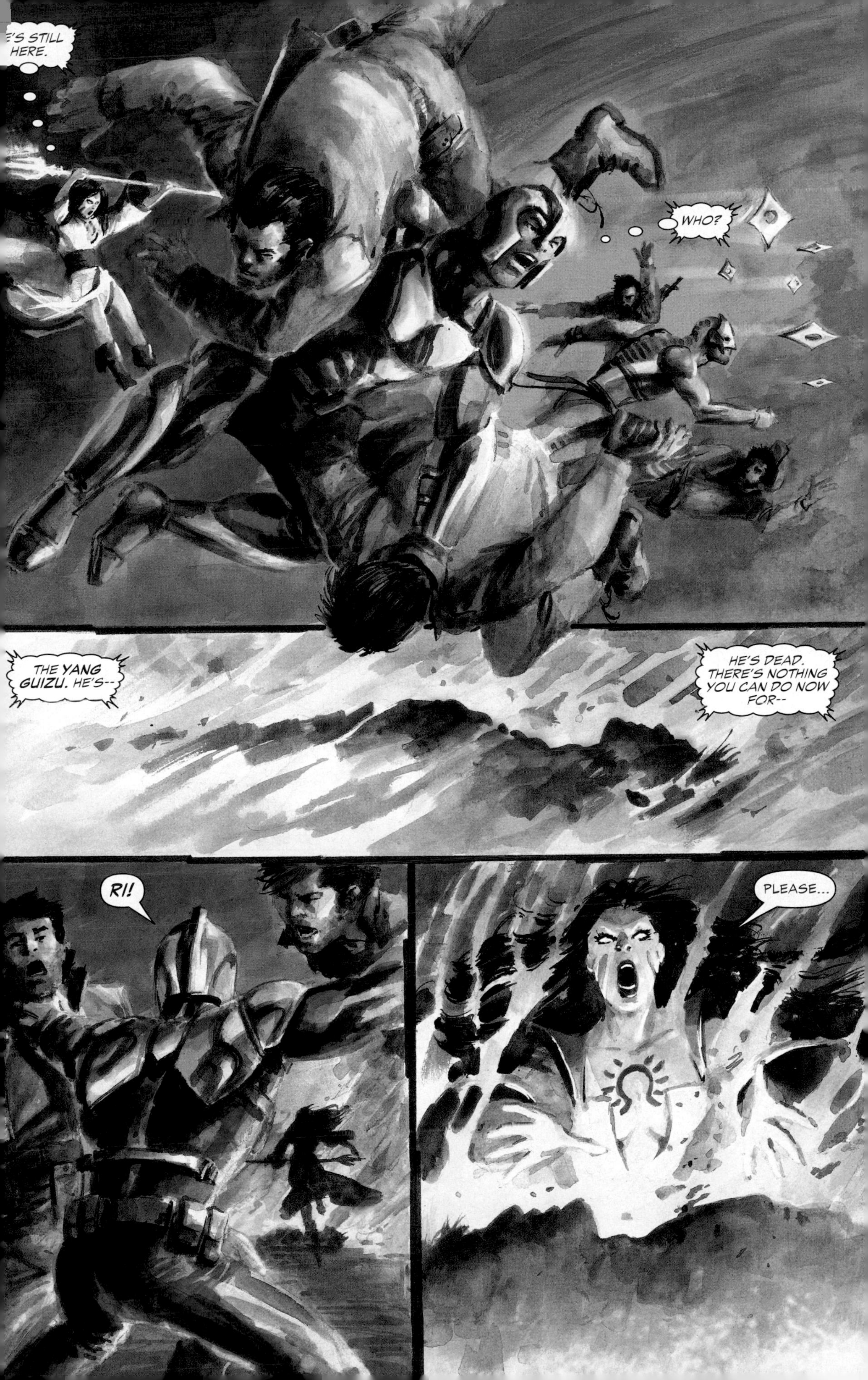
'S STILL HERE.
WHO?
THE YANG GUIZU. HE'S--
HE'S DEAD. THERE'S NOTHING YOU CAN DO NOW FOR--
RI!
PLEASE...

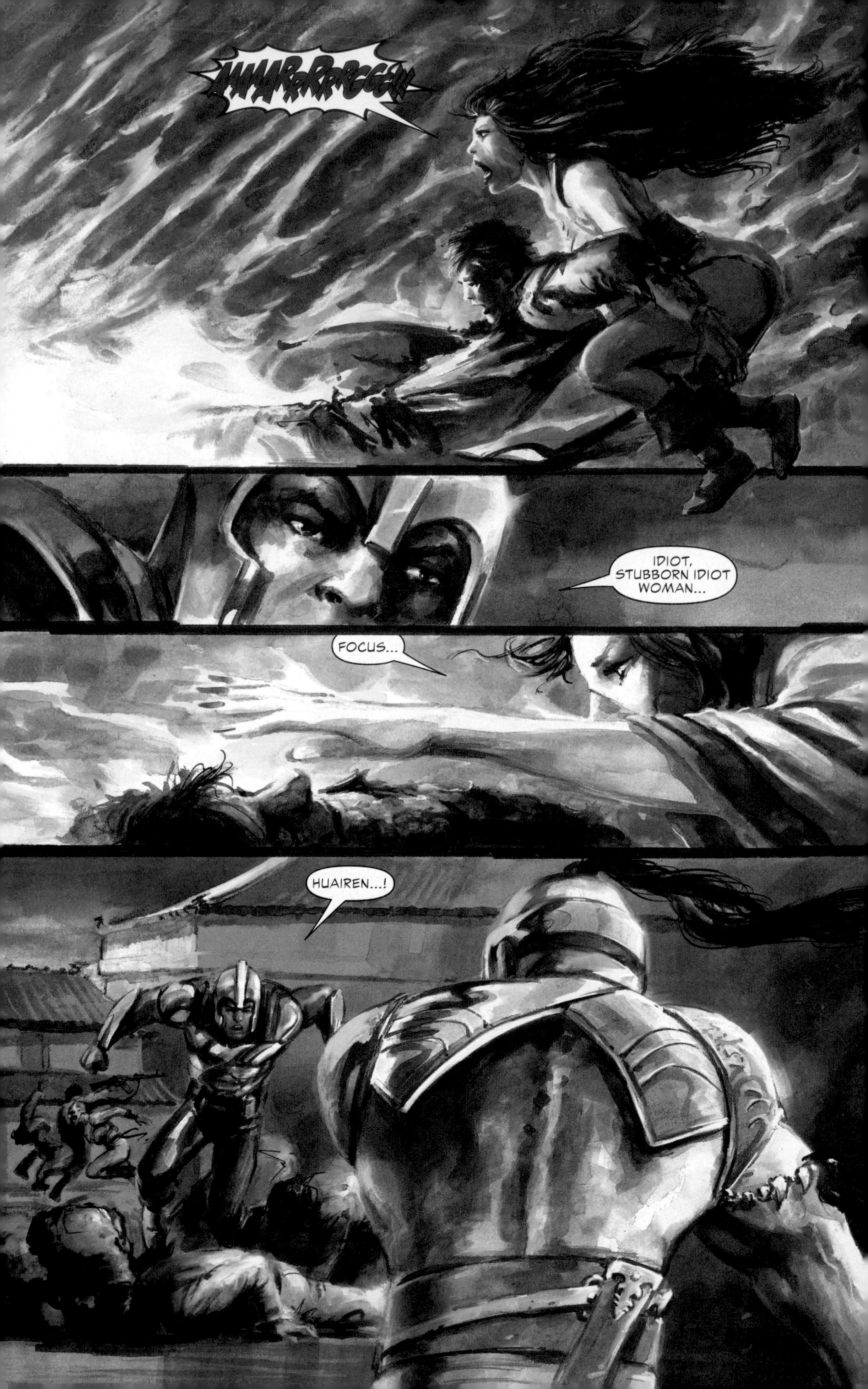
AAAARRRRRGGGH!!
IDIOT, STUBBORN IDIOT WOMAN...
FOCUS...
HUAIREN...!

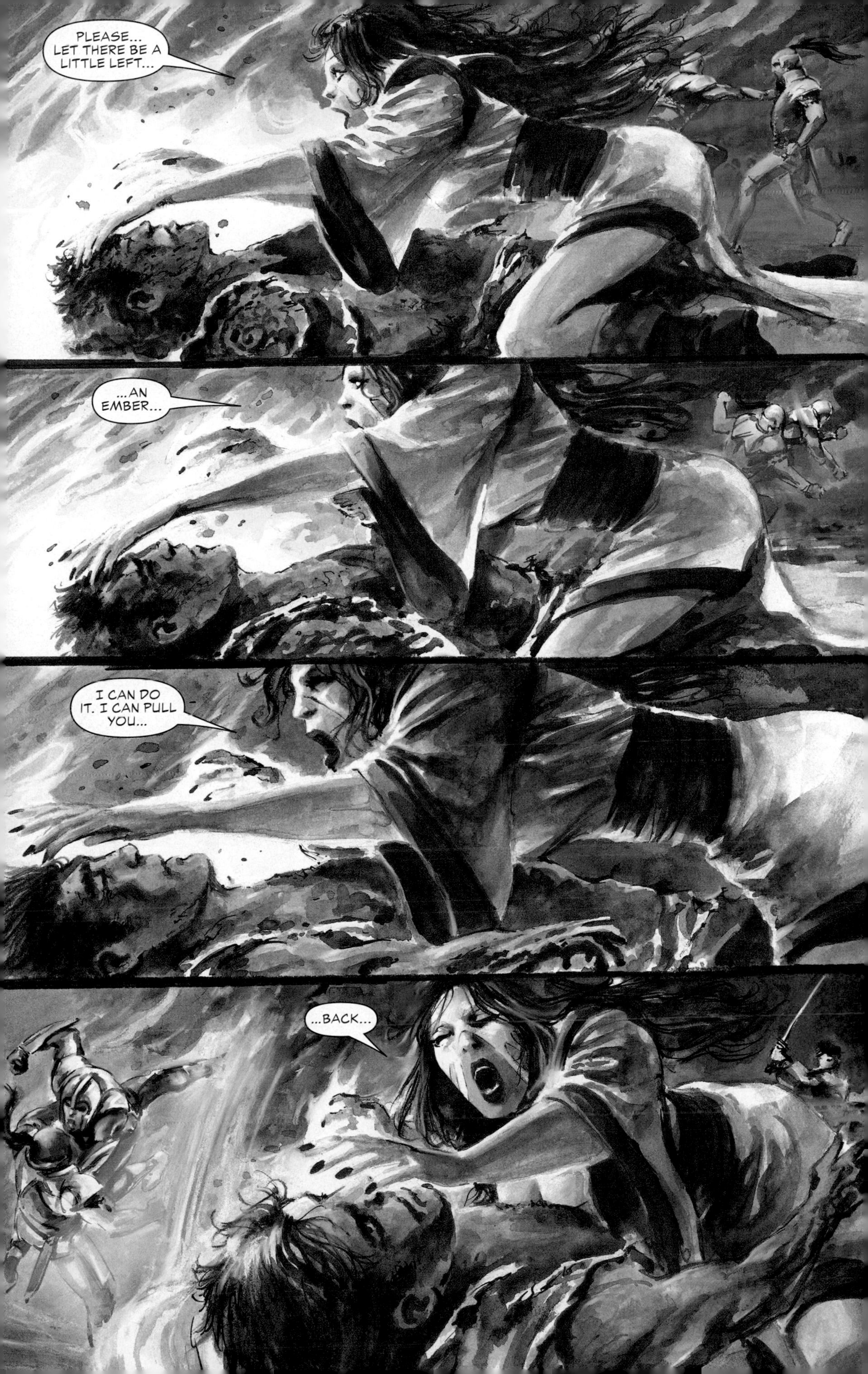
PLEASE... LET THERE BE A LITTLE LEFT...
...AN EMBER...
I CAN DO IT. I CAN PULL YOU...
...BACK...

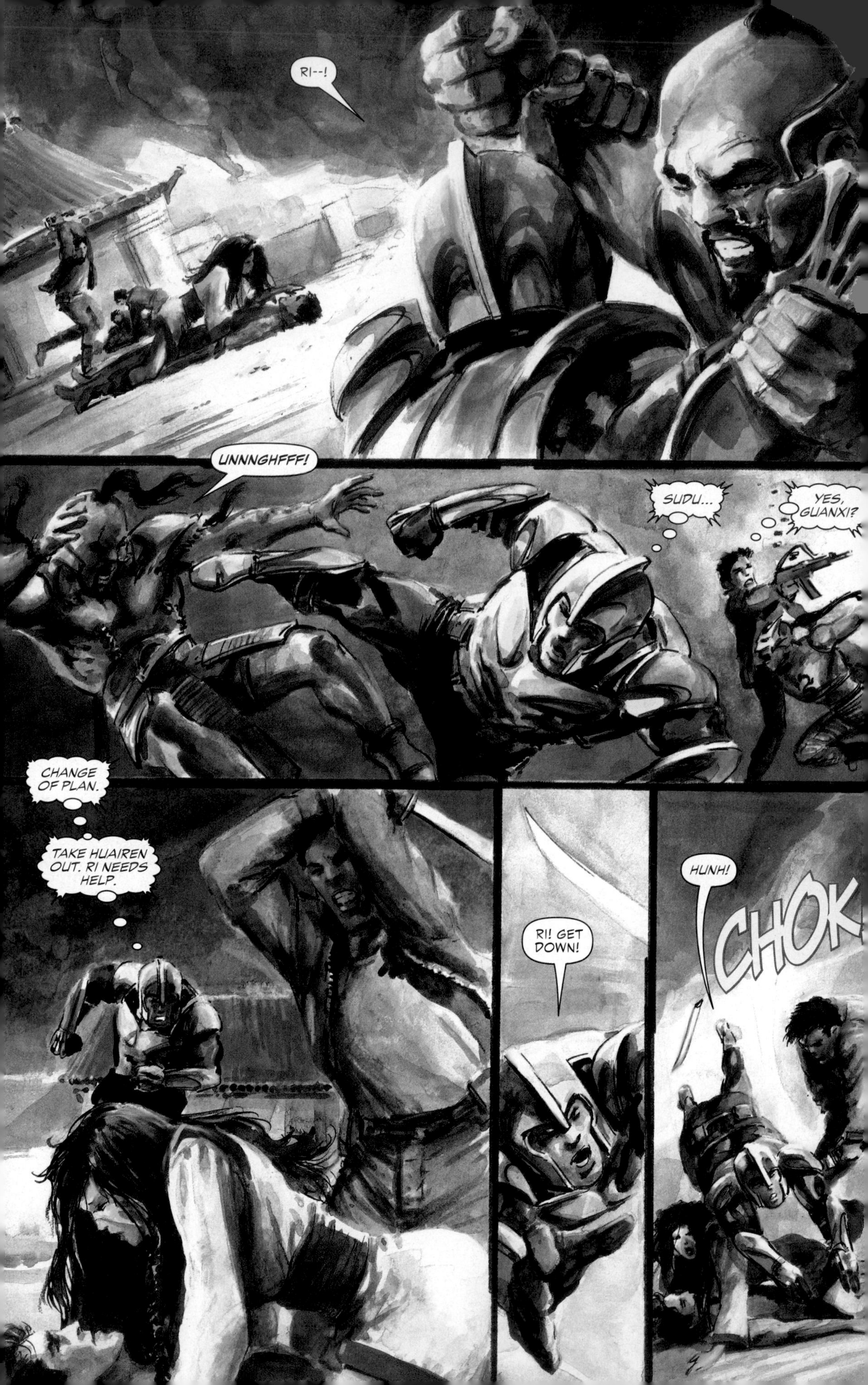
RI--!
UNNNGHFFF!
SUDU...
YES, GUANXI?
CHANGE OF PLAN.
TAKE HUAIREN OUT. RI NEEDS HELP.
RI! GET DOWN!
HUNH!
CHOK

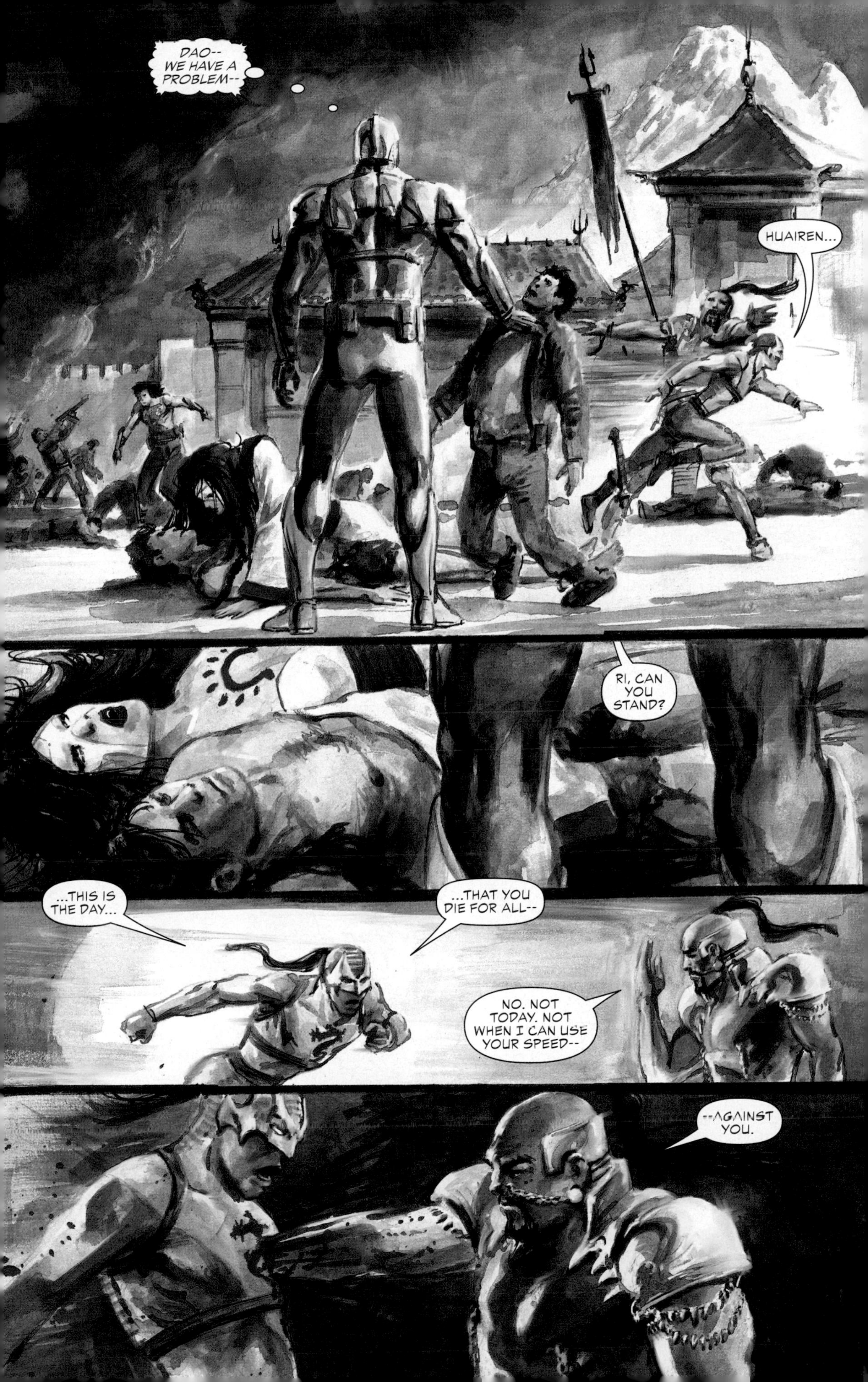
DAO--
WE HAVE A
PROBLEM--
HUAIREN...
RI, CAN
YOU
STAND?
...THIS IS
THE DAY...
...THAT YOU
DIE FOR ALL--
NO. NOT
TODAY. NOT
WHEN I CAN USE
YOUR SPEED--
--AGAINST
YOU.

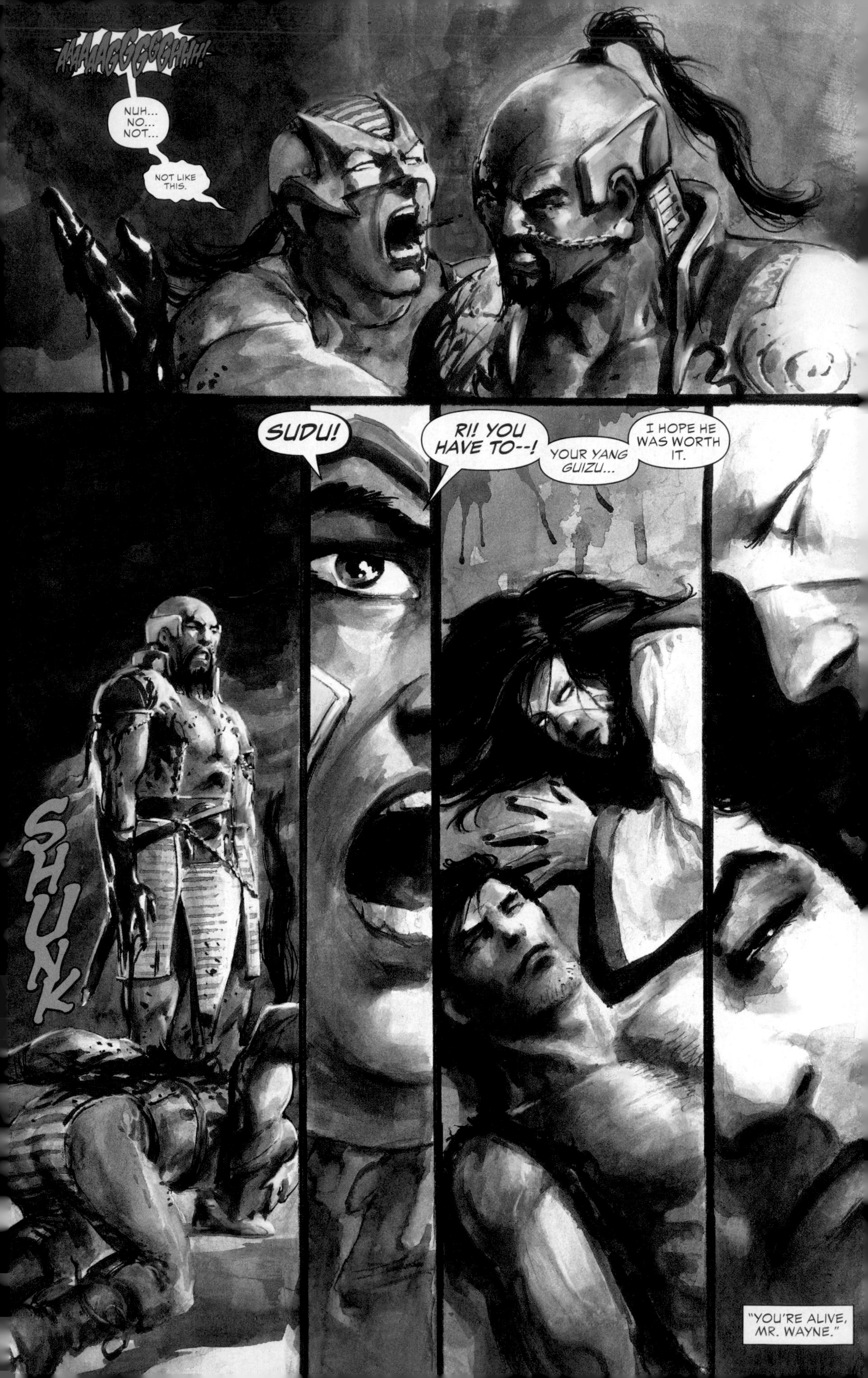
AAAAAAGGGGGHHH!
NUH... NO... NOT...
NOT LIKE THIS.
SUDU!
RI! YOU HAVE TO--!
YOUR YANG GUIZU...
I HOPE HE WAS WORTH IT.
SHUNK
"YOU'RE ALIVE, MR. WAYNE."

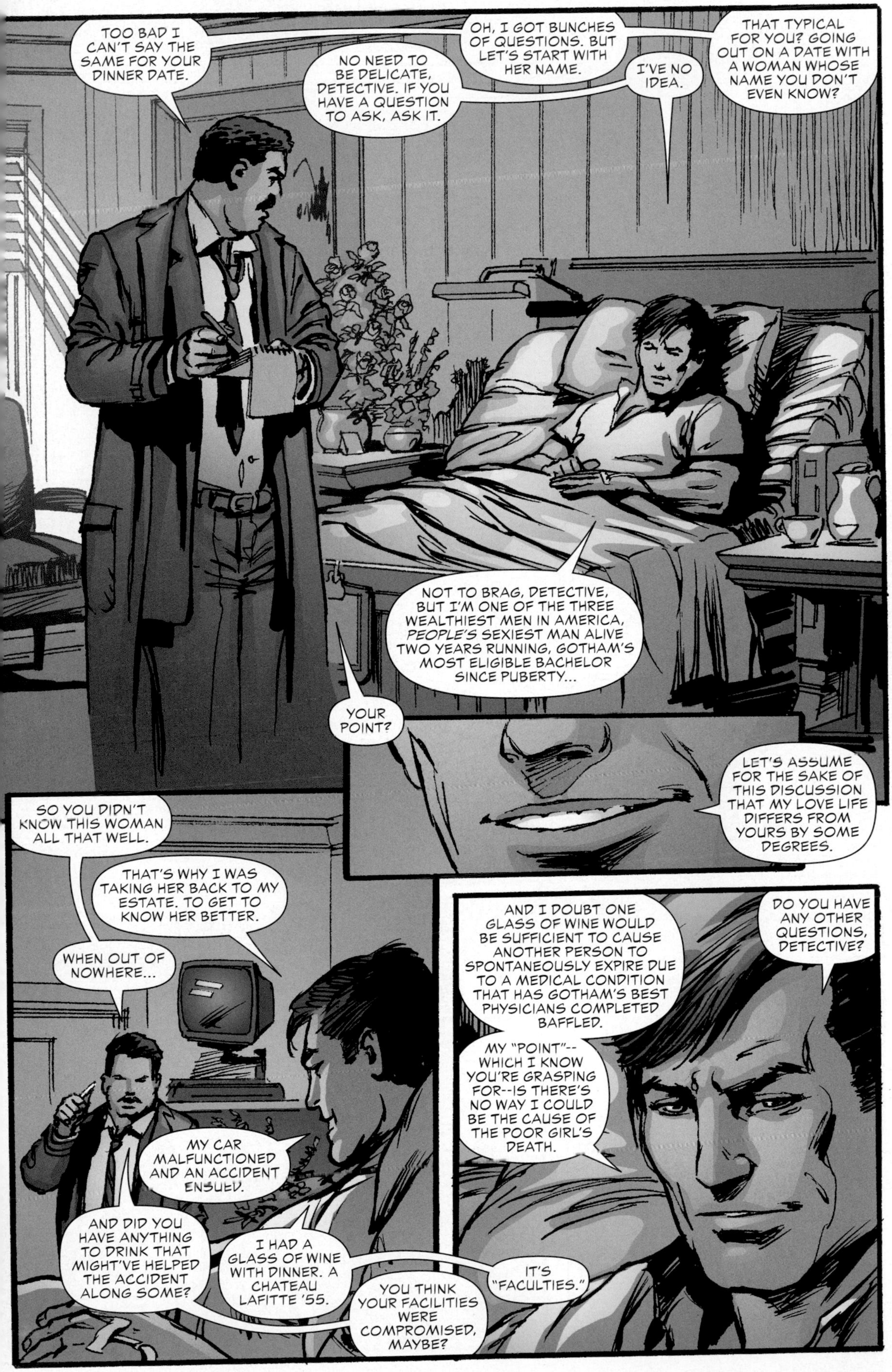
TOO BAD I CAN'T SAY THE SAME FOR YOUR DINNER DATE.
NO NEED TO BE DELICATE, DETECTIVE. IF YOU HAVE A QUESTION TO ASK, ASK IT.
OH, I GOT BUNCHES OF QUESTIONS. BUT LET'S START WITH HER NAME.
I'VE NO IDEA.
THAT TYPICAL FOR YOU? GOING OUT ON A DATE WITH A WOMAN WHOSE NAME YOU DON'T EVEN KNOW?
NOT TO BRAG, DETECTIVE, BUT I'M ONE OF THE THREE WEALTHIEST MEN IN AMERICA, *PEOPLE'S* SEXIEST MAN ALIVE TWO YEARS RUNNING, GOTHAM'S MOST ELIGIBLE BACHELOR SINCE PUBERTY...
YOUR POINT?
LET'S ASSUME FOR THE SAKE OF THIS DISCUSSION THAT MY LOVE LIFE DIFFERS FROM YOURS BY SOME DEGREES.
SO YOU DIDN'T KNOW THIS WOMAN ALL THAT WELL.
THAT'S WHY I WAS TAKING HER BACK TO MY ESTATE. TO GET TO KNOW HER BETTER.
WHEN OUT OF NOWHERE...
MY CAR MALFUNCTIONED AND AN ACCIDENT ENSUED.
AND DID YOU HAVE ANYTHING TO DRINK THAT MIGHT'VE HELPED THE ACCIDENT ALONG SOME?
I HAD A GLASS OF WINE WITH DINNER. A CHATEAU LAFITTE '55.
YOU THINK YOUR FACILITIES WERE COMPROMISED, MAYBE?
IT'S "FACULTIES."
AND I DOUBT ONE GLASS OF WINE WOULD BE SUFFICIENT TO CAUSE ANOTHER PERSON TO SPONTANEOUSLY EXPIRE DUE TO A MEDICAL CONDITION THAT HAS GOTHAM'S BEST PHYSICIANS COMPLETED BAFFLED.
MY "POINT"-- WHICH I KNOW YOU'RE GRASPING FOR--IS THERE'S NO WAY I COULD BE THE CAUSE OF THE POOR GIRL'S DEATH.
DO YOU HAVE ANY OTHER QUESTIONS, DETECTIVE?

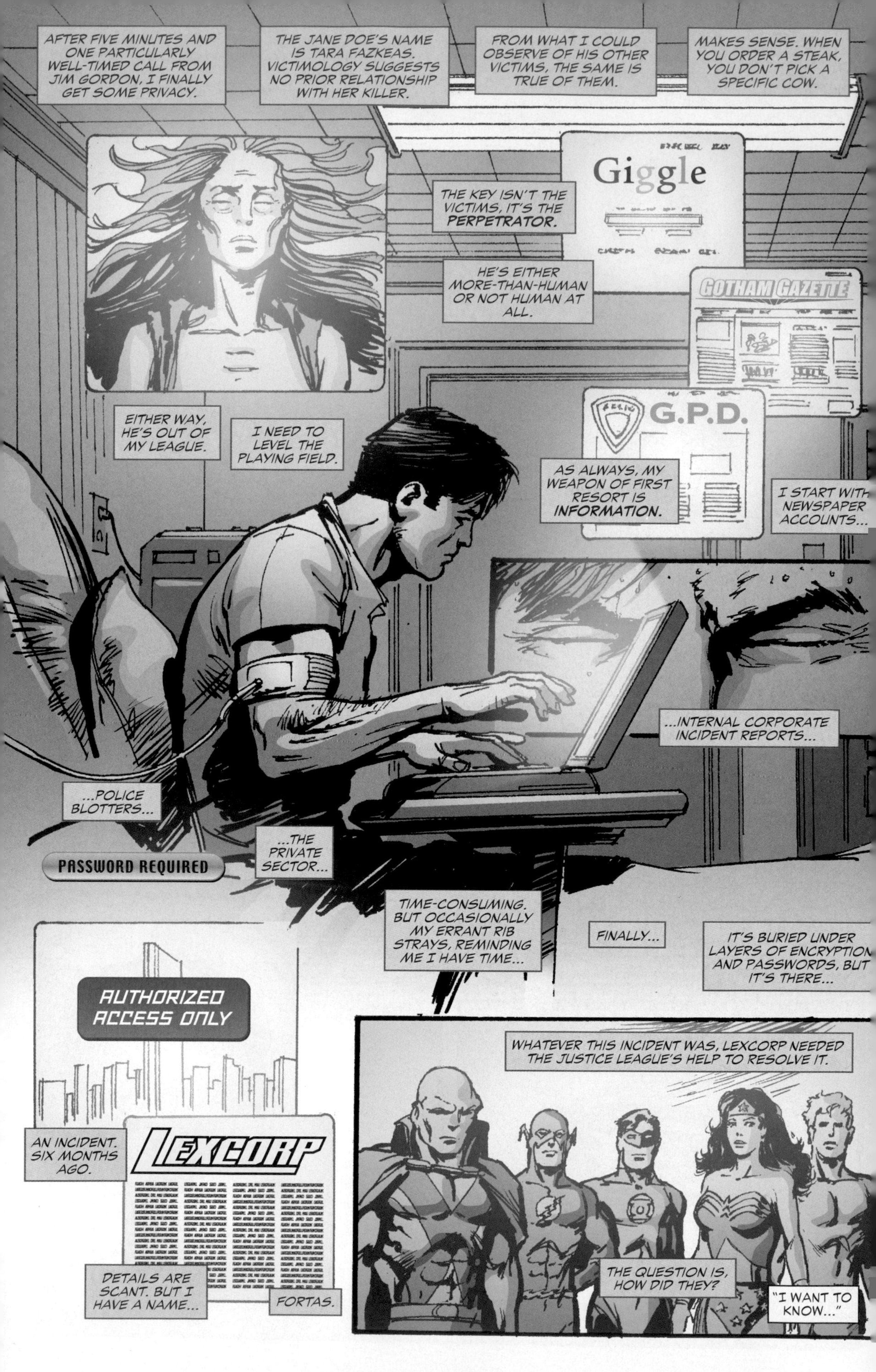
AFTER FIVE MINUTES AND ONE PARTICULARLY WELL-TIMED CALL FROM JIM GORDON, I FINALLY GET SOME PRIVACY.
THE JANE DOE'S NAME IS TARA FAZKEAS. VICTIMOLOGY SUGGESTS NO PRIOR RELATIONSHIP WITH HER KILLER.
FROM WHAT I COULD OBSERVE OF HIS OTHER VICTIMS, THE SAME IS TRUE OF THEM.
MAKES SENSE. WHEN YOU ORDER A STEAK, YOU DON'T PICK A SPECIFIC COW.
Giggle
THE KEY ISN'T THE VICTIMS, IT'S THE PERPETRATOR.
HE'S EITHER MORE-THAN-HUMAN OR NOT HUMAN AT ALL.
GOTHAM GAZETTE
EITHER WAY, HE'S OUT OF MY LEAGUE.
I NEED TO LEVEL THE PLAYING FIELD.
G.P.D.
AS ALWAYS, MY WEAPON OF FIRST RESORT IS INFORMATION.
I START WITH NEWSPAPER ACCOUNTS...
...INTERNAL CORPORATE INCIDENT REPORTS...
...POLICE BLOTTERS...
PASSWORD REQUIRED
...THE PRIVATE SECTOR...
TIME-CONSUMING. BUT OCCASIONALLY MY ERRANT RIB STRAYS, REMINDING ME I HAVE TIME...
FINALLY...
IT'S BURIED UNDER LAYERS OF ENCRYPTION AND PASSWORDS, BUT IT'S THERE...
AUTHORIZED ACCESS ONLY
AN INCIDENT. SIX MONTHS AGO.
LEXCORP
DETAILS ARE SCANT. BUT I HAVE A NAME...
FORTAS.
WHATEVER THIS INCIDENT WAS, LEXCORP NEEDED THE JUSTICE LEAGUE'S HELP TO RESOLVE IT.
THE QUESTION IS, HOW DID THEY?
"I WANT TO KNOW..."

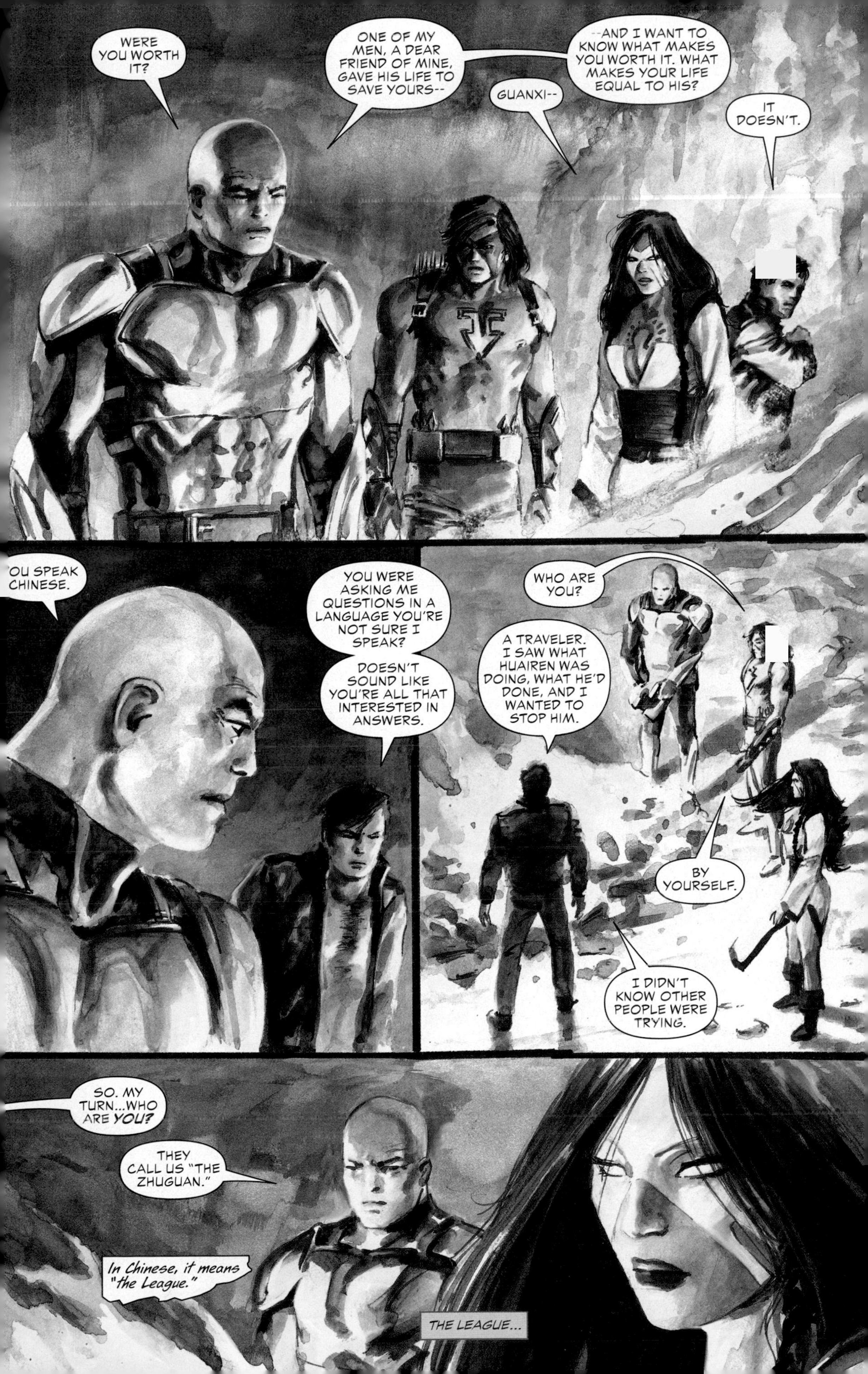
WERE YOU WORTH IT?
ONE OF MY MEN, A DEAR FRIEND OF MINE, GAVE HIS LIFE TO SAVE YOURS--
--AND I WANT TO KNOW WHAT MAKES YOU WORTH IT. WHAT MAKES YOUR LIFE EQUAL TO HIS?
GUANXI--
IT DOESN'T.
OU SPEAK CHINESE.
YOU WERE ASKING ME QUESTIONS IN A LANGUAGE YOU'RE NOT SURE I SPEAK?
DOESN'T SOUND LIKE YOU'RE ALL THAT INTERESTED IN ANSWERS.
WHO ARE YOU?
A TRAVELER. I SAW WHAT HUAIREN WAS DOING, WHAT HE'D DONE, AND I WANTED TO STOP HIM.
BY YOURSELF.
I DIDN'T KNOW OTHER PEOPLE WERE TRYING.
SO. MY TURN...WHO ARE *YOU?*
THEY CALL US "THE ZHUGUAN."
In Chinese, it means "the League."
THE LEAGUE...

...MAINTAINS WHAT THEY CALL THEIR "SECRET SANCTUARY" IN RHODE ISLAND.

BUT "SECRET" IS A RELATIVE TERM.

AND A "SANCTUARY" IS ONLY AS SECURE AS ITS DEFENSES.

WHETHER THOSE DEFENSES BE MOTION SENSORS...

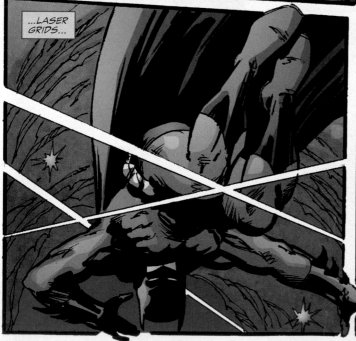

...LASER GRIDS...

...OR SUPPOSEDLY PICKPROOF LOCKS.

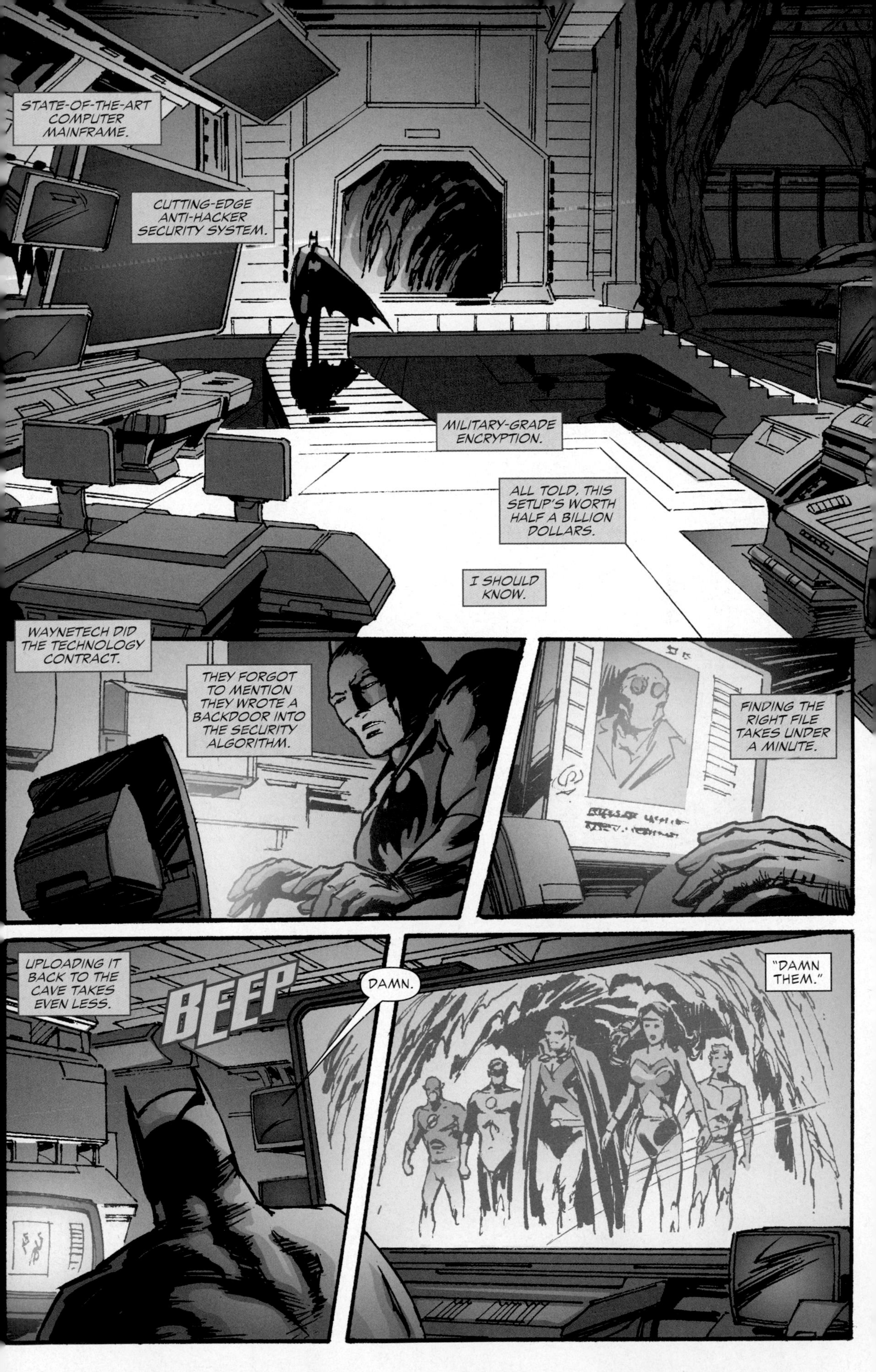
STATE-OF-THE-ART COMPUTER MAINFRAME.
CUTTING-EDGE ANTI-HACKER SECURITY SYSTEM.
MILITARY-GRADE ENCRYPTION.
ALL TOLD, THIS SETUP'S WORTH HALF A BILLION DOLLARS.
I SHOULD KNOW.
WAYNETECH DID THE TECHNOLOGY CONTRACT.
THEY FORGOT TO MENTION THEY WROTE A BACKDOOR INTO THE SECURITY ALGORITHM.
FINDING THE RIGHT FILE TAKES UNDER A MINUTE.
UPLOADING IT BACK TO THE CAVE TAKES EVEN LESS.
BEEP
DAMN.
"DAMN THEM."

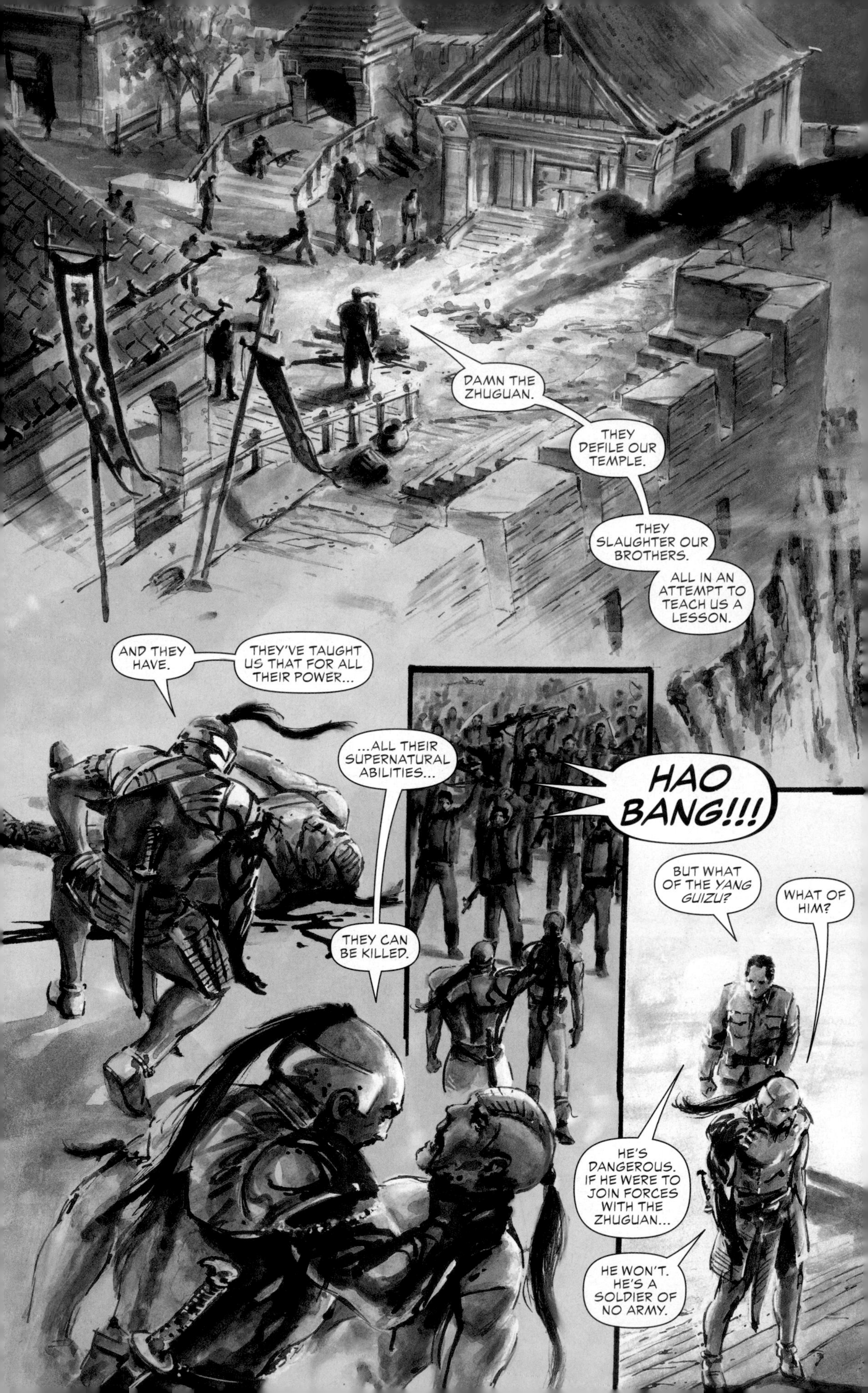
DAMN THE ZHUGUAN.
THEY DEFILE OUR TEMPLE.
THEY SLAUGHTER OUR BROTHERS.
ALL IN AN ATTEMPT TO TEACH US A LESSON.
AND THEY HAVE.
THEY'VE TAUGHT US THAT FOR ALL THEIR POWER...
...ALL THEIR SUPERNATURAL ABILITIES...
THEY CAN BE KILLED.
HAO BANG!!!
BUT WHAT OF THE YANG GUIZU?
WHAT OF HIM?
HE'S DANGEROUS. IF HE WERE TO JOIN FORCES WITH THE ZHUGUAN...
HE WON'T. HE'S A SOLDIER OF NO ARMY.

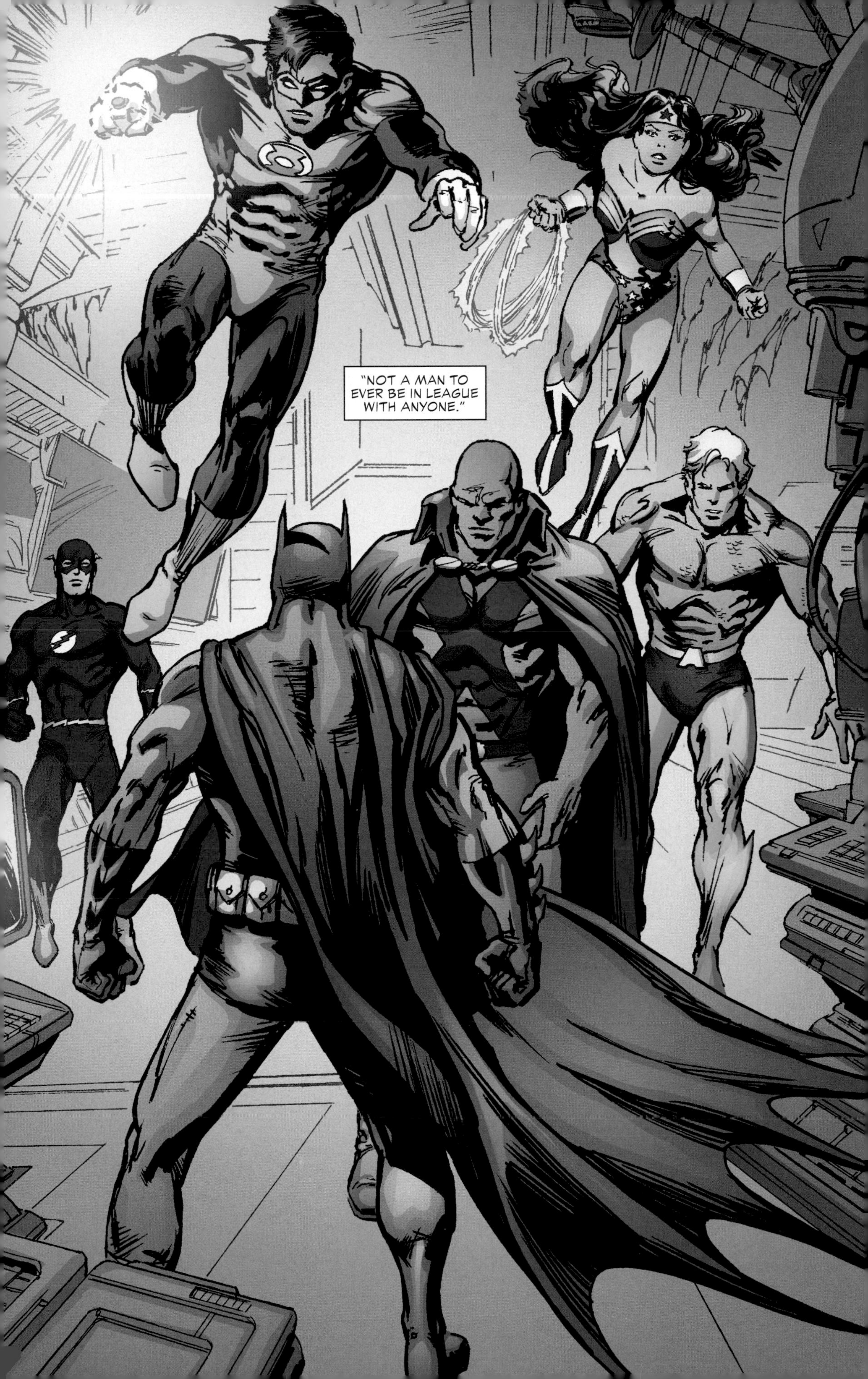
"NOT A MAN TO EVER BE IN LEAGUE WITH ANYONE."

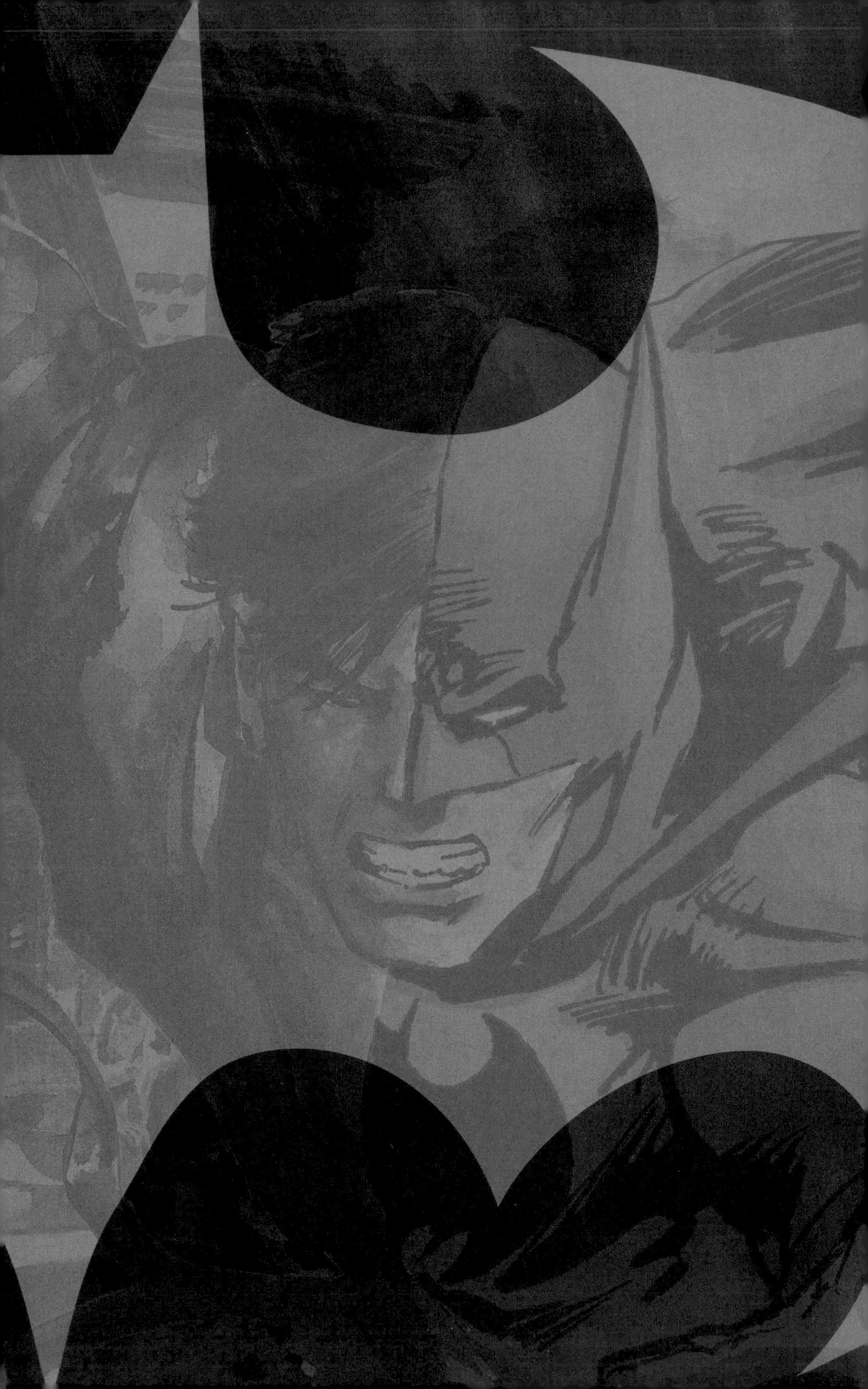

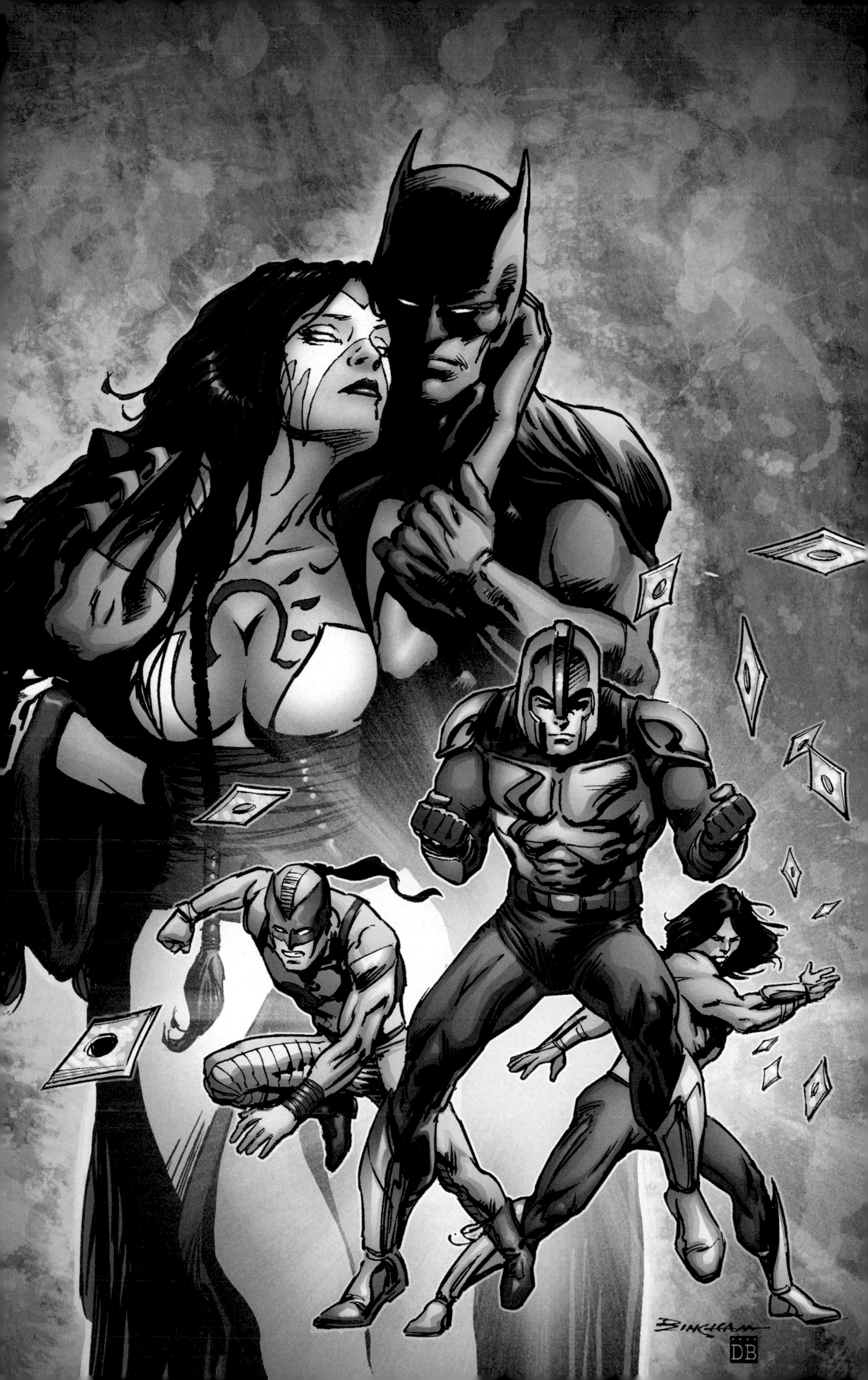
DB

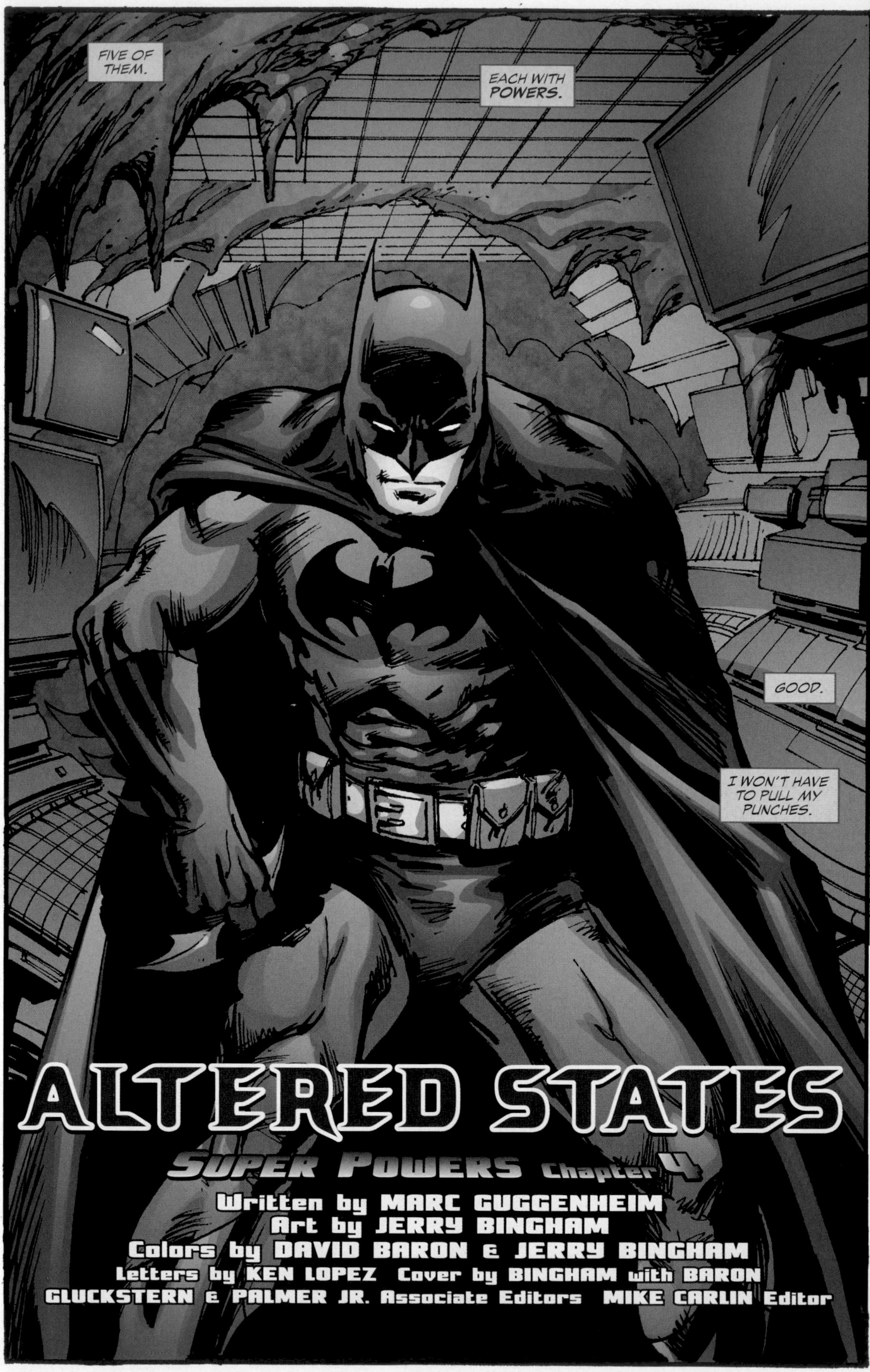

FIVE OF THEM.
EACH WITH POWERS.
GOOD.
I WON'T HAVE TO PULL MY PUNCHES.
ALTERED STATES
SUPER POWERS Chapter 4
Written by MARC GUGGENHEIM
Art by JERRY BINGHAM
Colors by DAVID BARON & JERRY BINGHAM
Letters by KEN LOPEZ Cover by BINGHAM with BARON
GLUCKSTERN & PALMER JR. Associate Editors MIKE CARLIN Editor

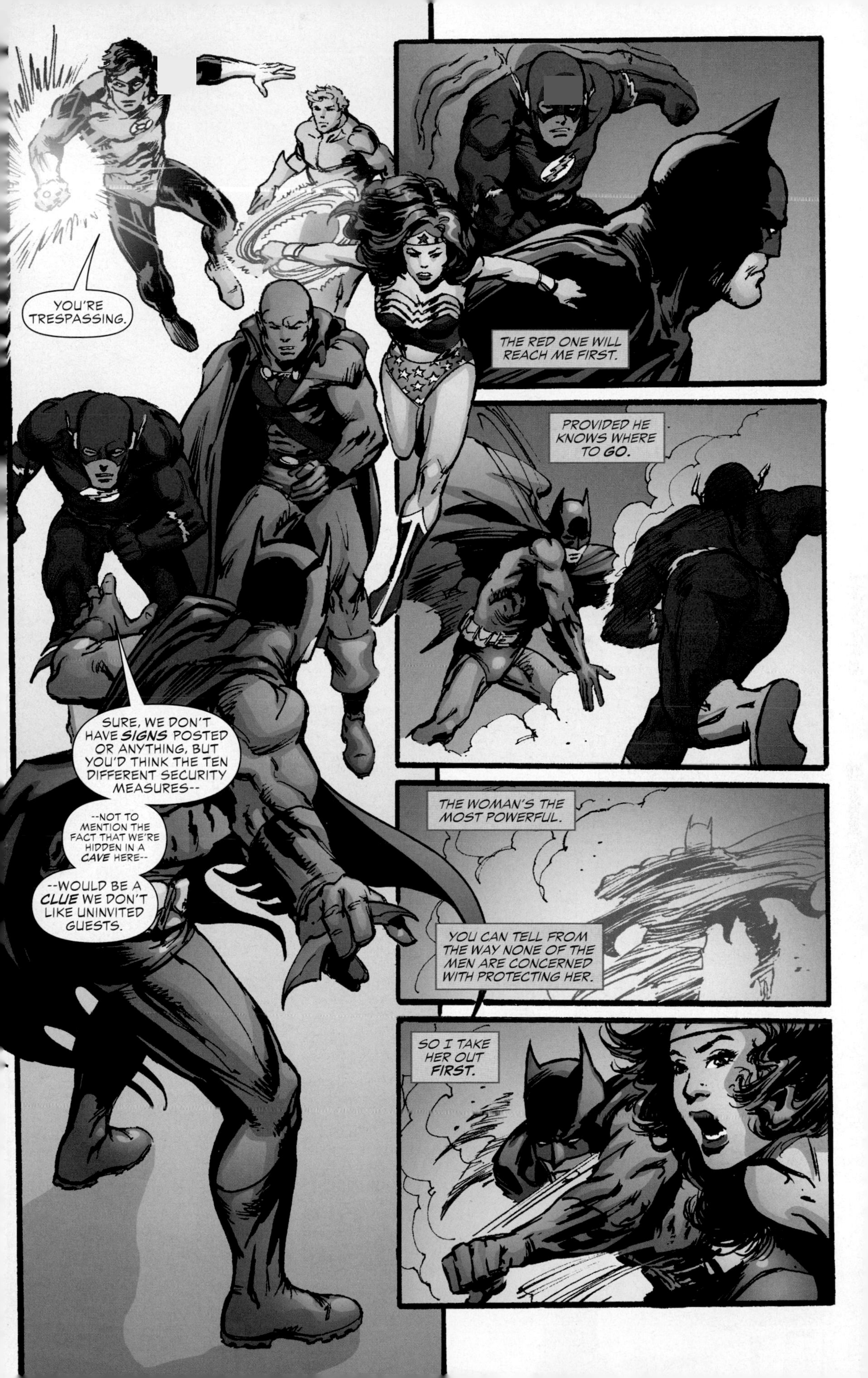

YOU'RE TRESPASSING.
SURE, WE DON'T HAVE SIGNS POSTED OR ANYTHING, BUT YOU'D THINK THE TEN DIFFERENT SECURITY MEASURES--
--NOT TO MENTION THE FACT THAT WE'RE HIDDEN IN A CAVE HERE--
--WOULD BE A CLUE WE DON'T LIKE UNINVITED GUESTS.
THE RED ONE WILL REACH ME FIRST.
PROVIDED HE KNOWS WHERE TO GO.
THE WOMAN'S THE MOST POWERFUL.
YOU CAN TELL FROM THE WAY NONE OF THE MEN ARE CONCERNED WITH PROTECTING HER.
SO I TAKE HER OUT FIRST.

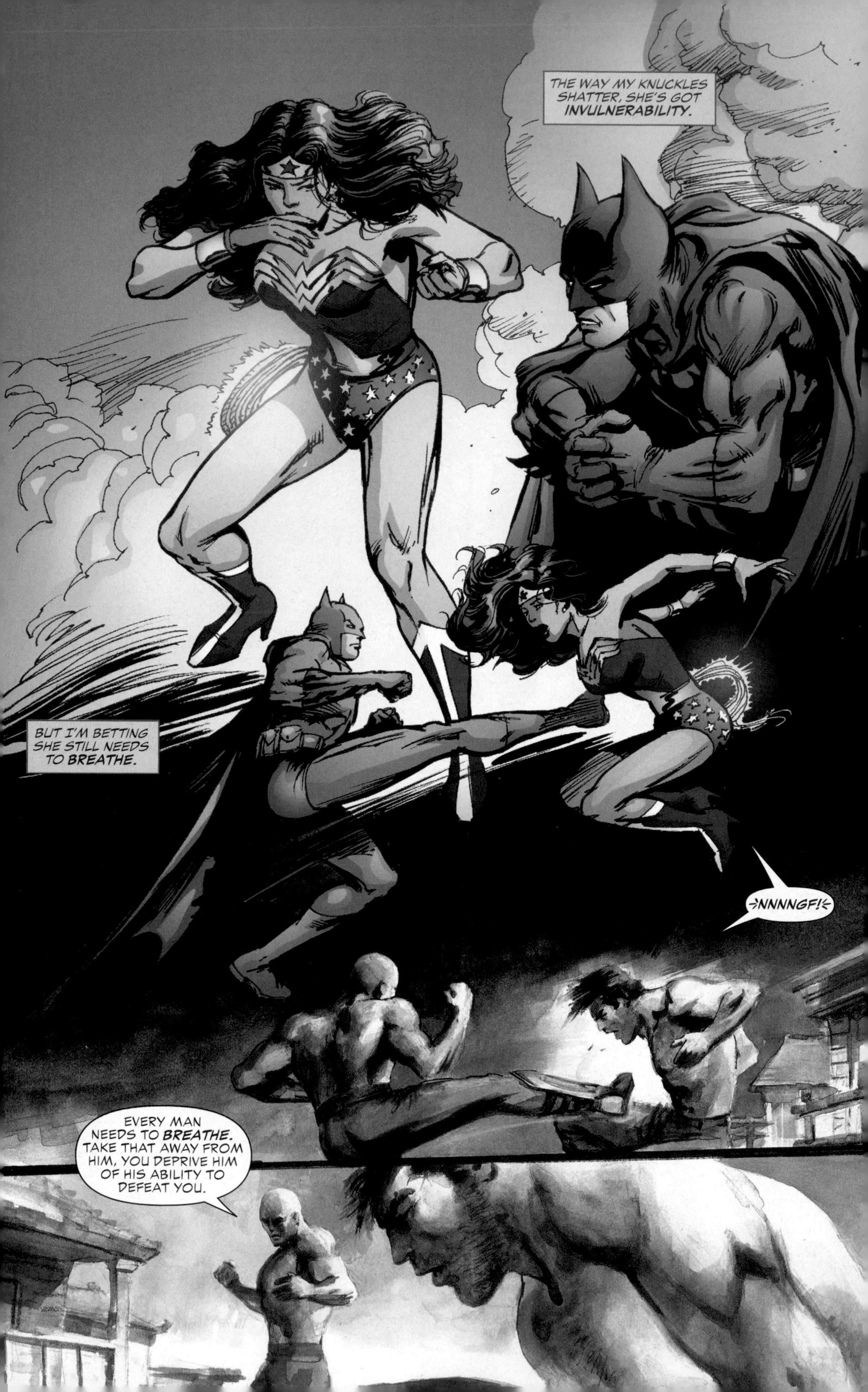
THE WAY MY KNUCKLES SHATTER, SHE'S GOT INVULNERABILITY.
BUT I'M BETTING SHE STILL NEEDS TO BREATHE.
NNNNGF!
EVERY MAN NEEDS TO BREATHE. TAKE THAT AWAY FROM HIM, YOU DEPRIVE HIM OF HIS ABILITY TO DEFEAT YOU.

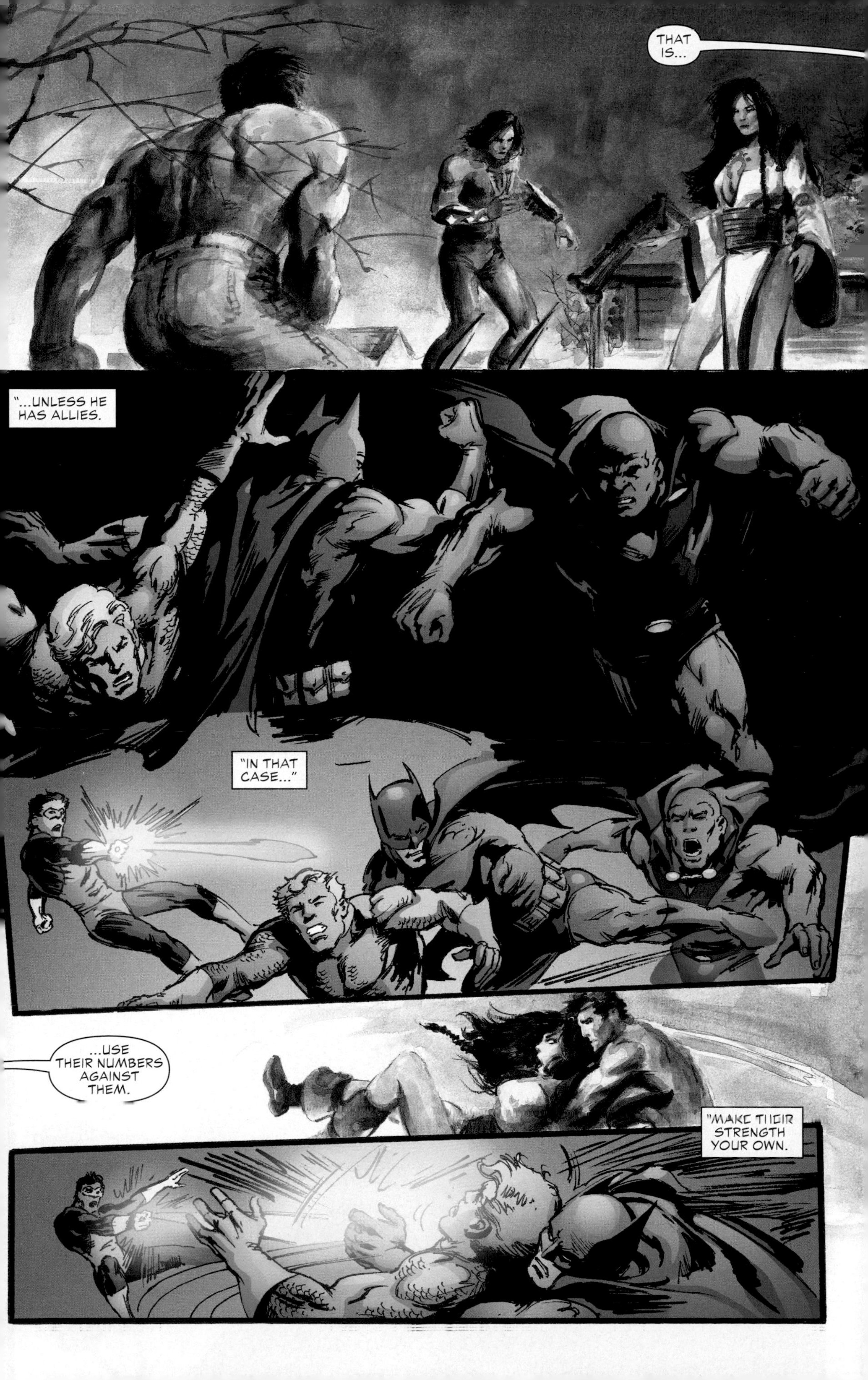
THAT IS...
"...UNLESS HE HAS ALLIES.
"IN THAT CASE..."
...USE THEIR NUMBERS AGAINST THEM.
"MAKE THEIR STRENGTH YOUR OWN.

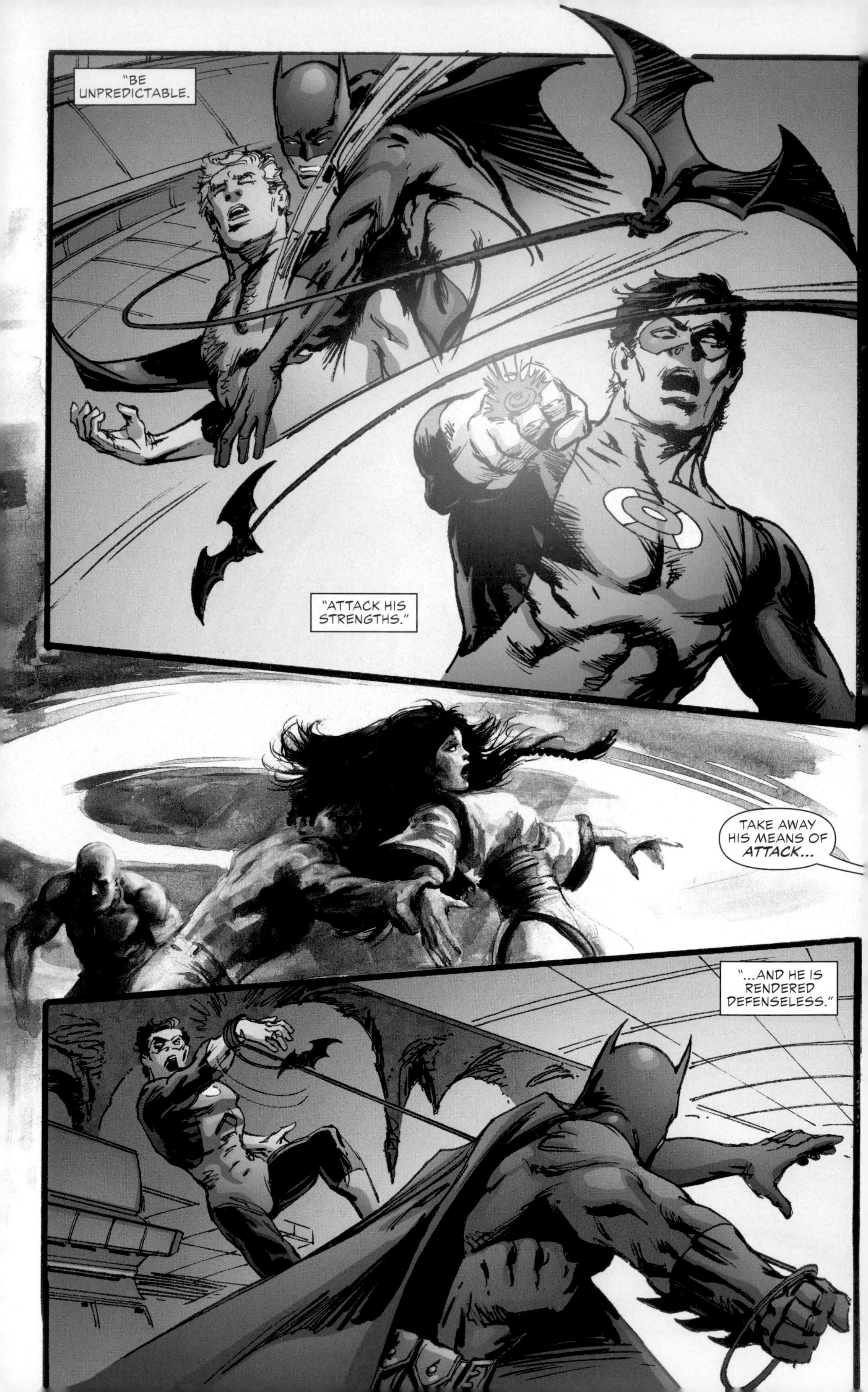
"BE UNPREDICTABLE.
"ATTACK HIS STRENGTHS."
TAKE AWAY HIS MEANS OF *ATTACK*...
"...AND HE IS RENDERED DEFENSELESS."

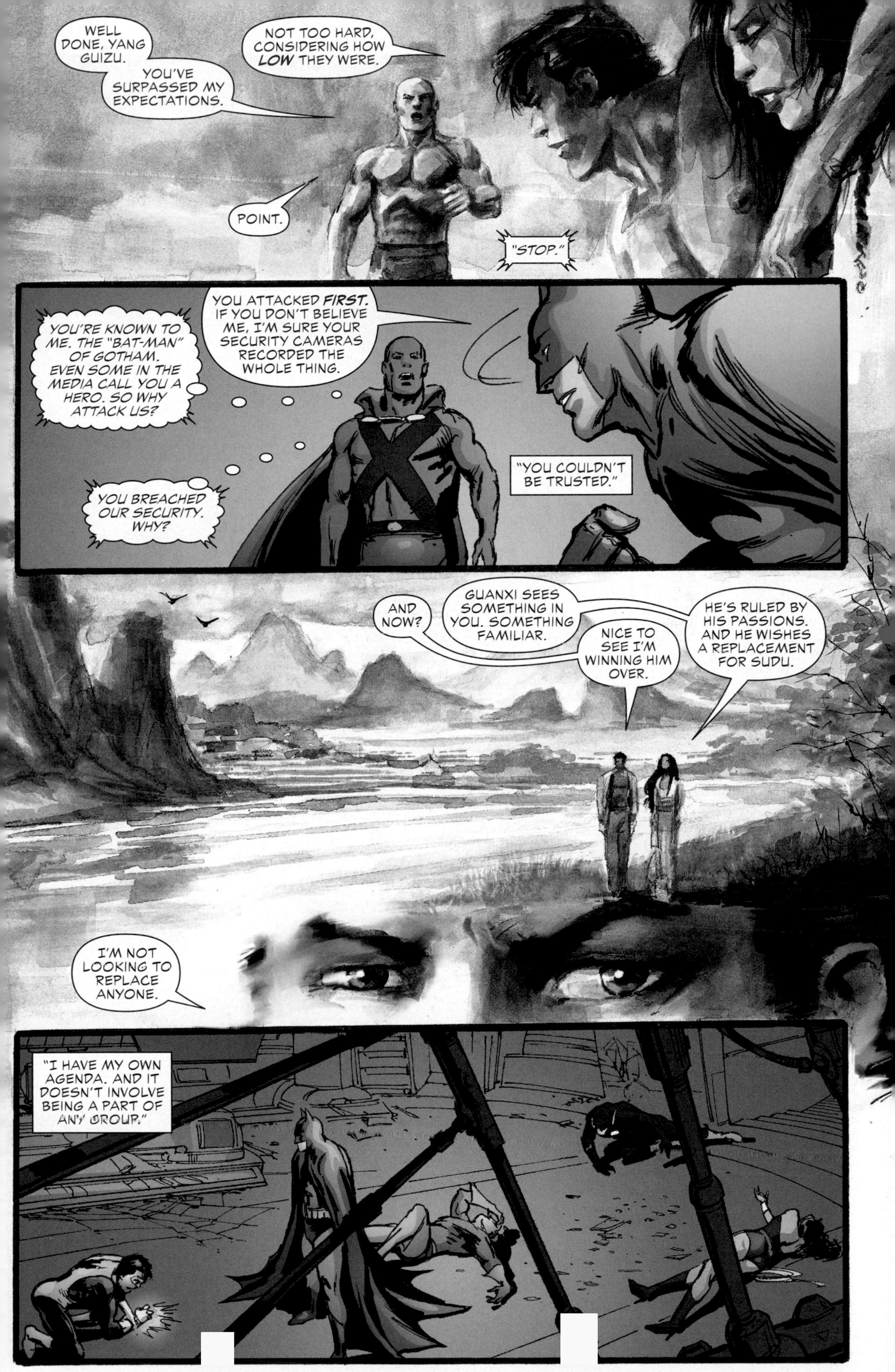
WELL DONE, YANG GUIZU.
YOU'VE SURPASSED MY EXPECTATIONS.
NOT TOO HARD, CONSIDERING HOW LOW THEY WERE.
POINT.
"STOP."
YOU'RE KNOWN TO ME. THE "BAT-MAN" OF GOTHAM. EVEN SOME IN THE MEDIA CALL YOU A HERO. SO WHY ATTACK US?
YOU ATTACKED FIRST. IF YOU DON'T BELIEVE ME, I'M SURE YOUR SECURITY CAMERAS RECORDED THE WHOLE THING.
YOU BREACHED OUR SECURITY. WHY?
"YOU COULDN'T BE TRUSTED."
AND NOW?
GUANXI SEES SOMETHING IN YOU. SOMETHING FAMILIAR.
NICE TO SEE I'M WINNING HIM OVER.
HE'S RULED BY HIS PASSIONS. AND HE WISHES A REPLACEMENT FOR SUDU.
I'M NOT LOOKING TO REPLACE ANYONE.
"I HAVE MY OWN AGENDA. AND IT DOESN'T INVOLVE BEING A PART OF ANY GROUP."

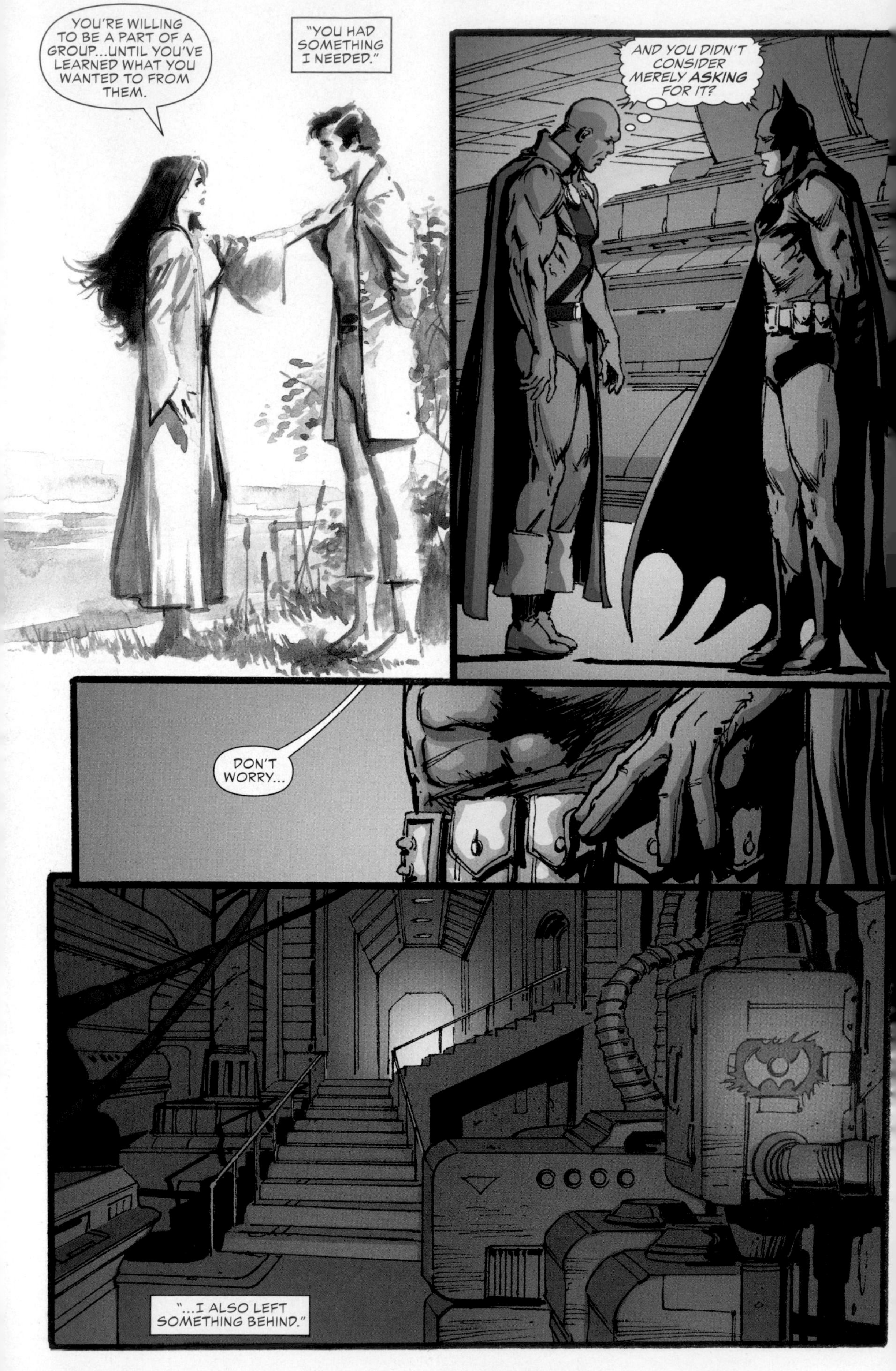
YOU'RE WILLING TO BE A PART OF A GROUP...UNTIL YOU'VE LEARNED WHAT YOU WANTED TO FROM THEM.
"YOU HAD SOMETHING I NEEDED."
AND YOU DIDN'T CONSIDER MERELY ASKING FOR IT?
DON'T WORRY...
"...I ALSO LEFT SOMETHING BEHIND."

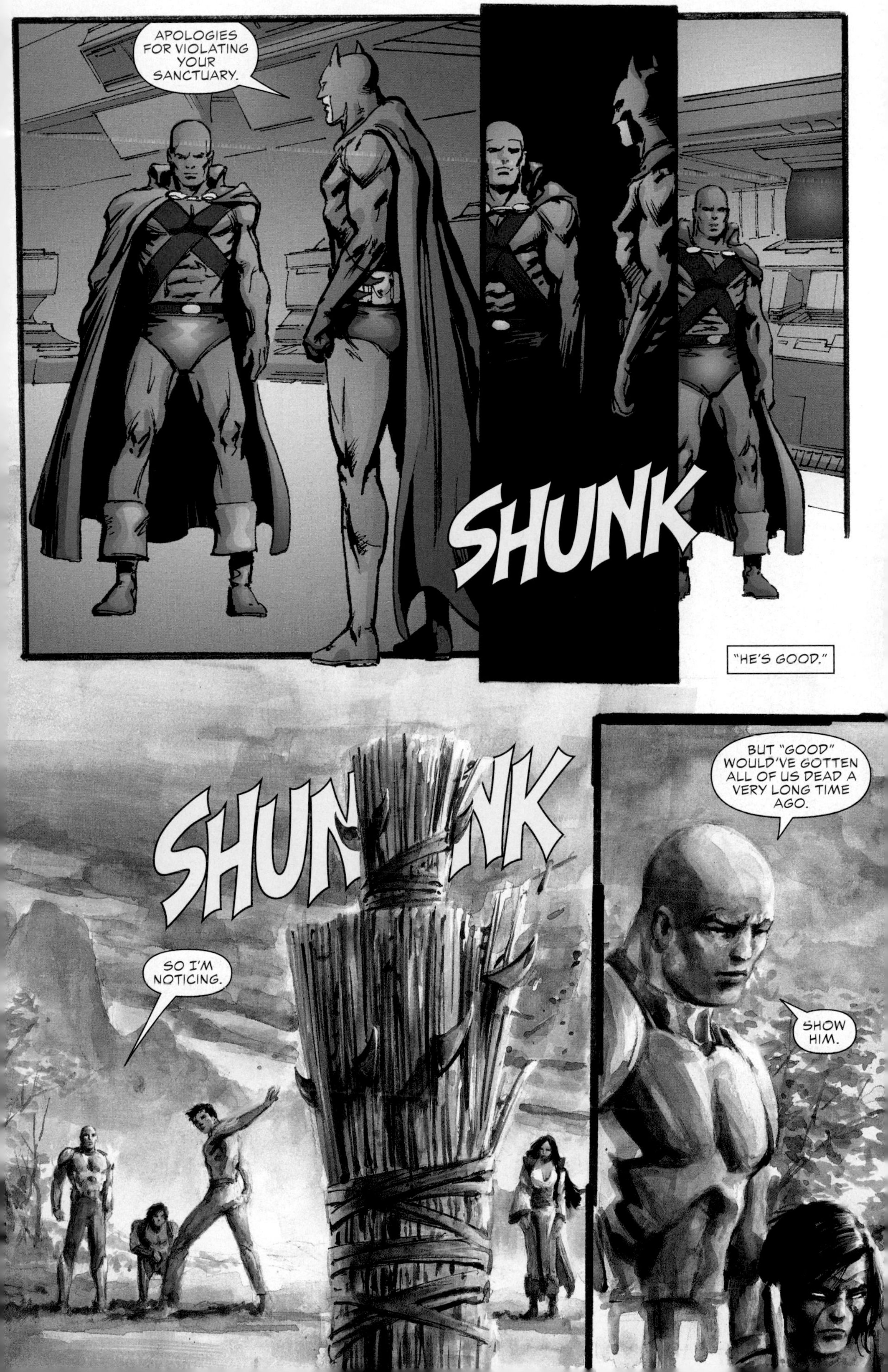
APOLOGIES FOR VIOLATING YOUR SANCTUARY.
SHUNK
"HE'S GOOD."
SHUNK
BUT "GOOD" WOULD'VE GOTTEN ALL OF US DEAD A VERY LONG TIME AGO.
SO I'M NOTICING.
SHOW HIM.

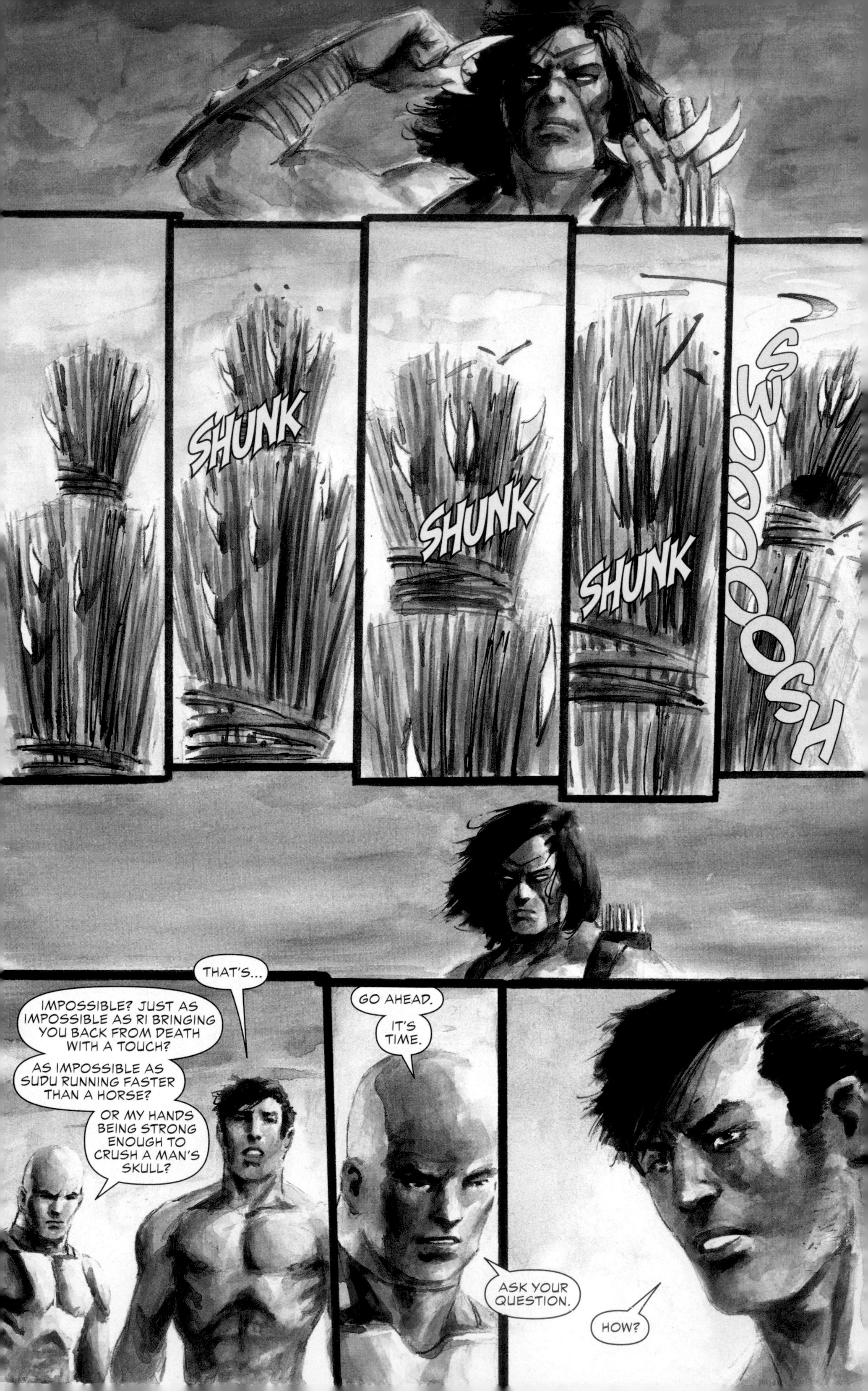
SHUNK
SHUNK
SHUNK
SWOOOOOOSH
THAT'S...
IMPOSSIBLE? JUST AS IMPOSSIBLE AS RI BRINGING YOU BACK FROM DEATH WITH A TOUCH?
AS IMPOSSIBLE AS SUDU RUNNING FASTER THAN A HORSE?
OR MY HANDS BEING STRONG ENOUGH TO CRUSH A MAN'S SKULL?
GO AHEAD.
IT'S TIME.
ASK YOUR QUESTION.
HOW?

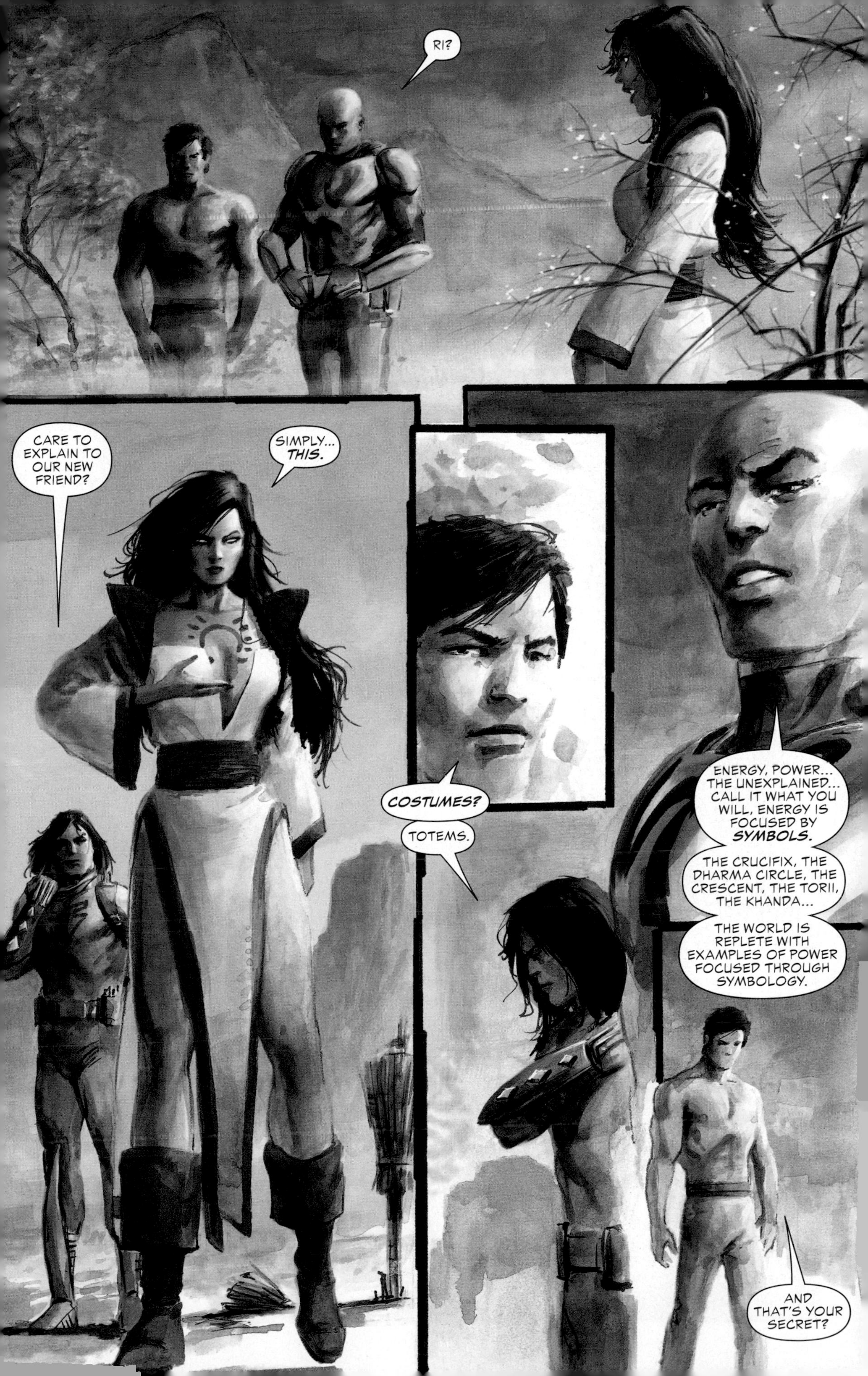
RI?
CARE TO EXPLAIN TO OUR NEW FRIEND?
SIMPLY... THIS.
COSTUMES?
TOTEMS.
ENERGY, POWER... THE UNEXPLAINED... CALL IT WHAT YOU WILL, ENERGY IS FOCUSED BY SYMBOLS.
THE CRUCIFIX, THE DHARMA CIRCLE, THE CRESCENT, THE TORII, THE KHANDA...
THE WORLD IS REPLETE WITH EXAMPLES OF POWER FOCUSED THROUGH SYMBOLOGY.
AND THAT'S YOUR SECRET?

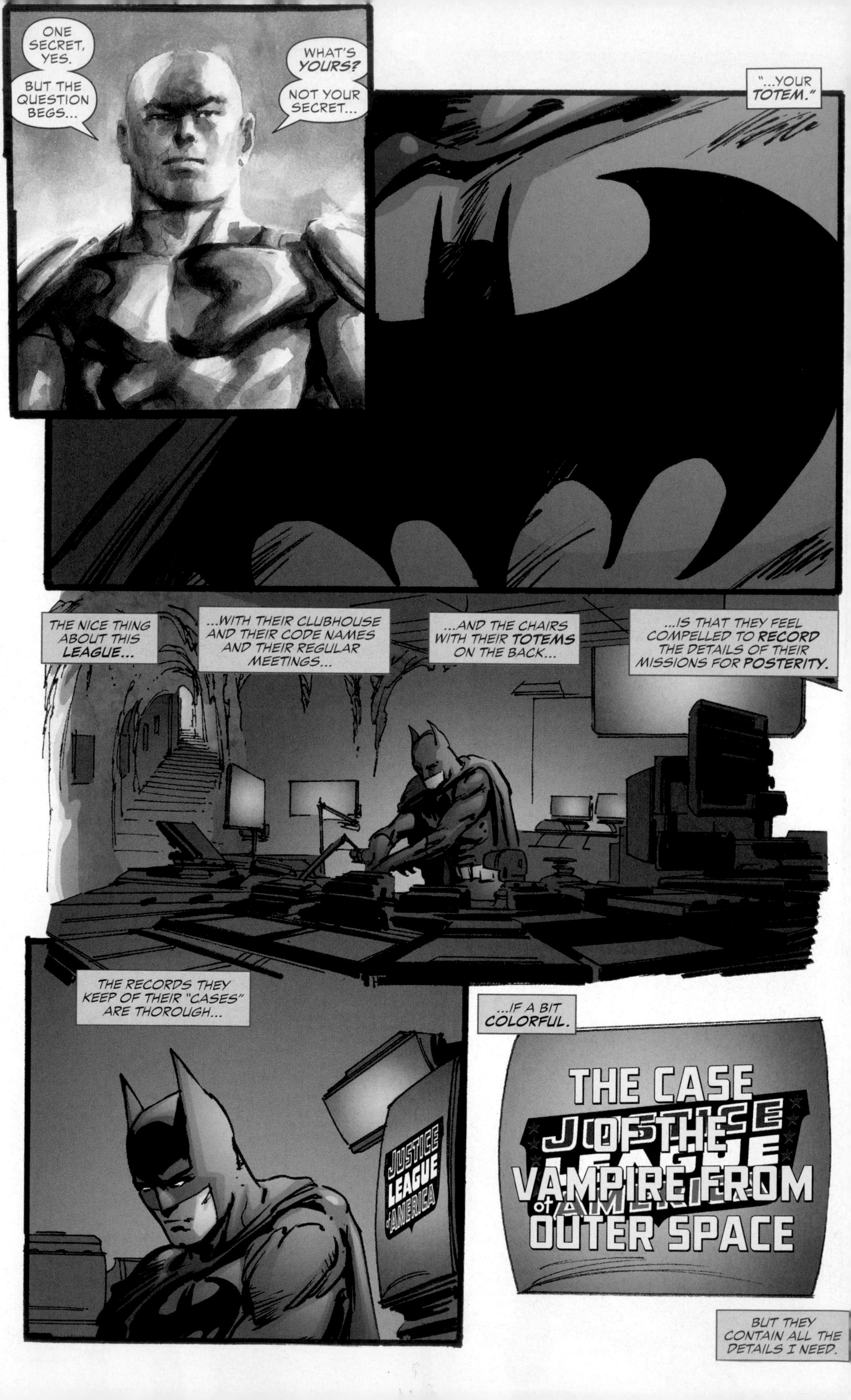
ONE SECRET, YES.
BUT THE QUESTION BEGS...
WHAT'S YOURS?
NOT YOUR SECRET...
"...YOUR TOTEM."
THE NICE THING ABOUT THIS LEAGUE...
...WITH THEIR CLUBHOUSE AND THEIR CODE NAMES AND THEIR REGULAR MEETINGS...
...AND THE CHAIRS WITH THEIR TOTEMS ON THE BACK...
...IS THAT THEY FEEL COMPELLED TO RECORD THE DETAILS OF THEIR MISSIONS FOR POSTERITY.
THE RECORDS THEY KEEP OF THEIR "CASES" ARE THOROUGH...
JUSTICE LEAGUE of AMERICA
...IF A BIT COLORFUL.
THE CASE OF THE VAMPIRE FROM OUTER SPACE
BUT THEY CONTAIN ALL THE DETAILS I NEED.

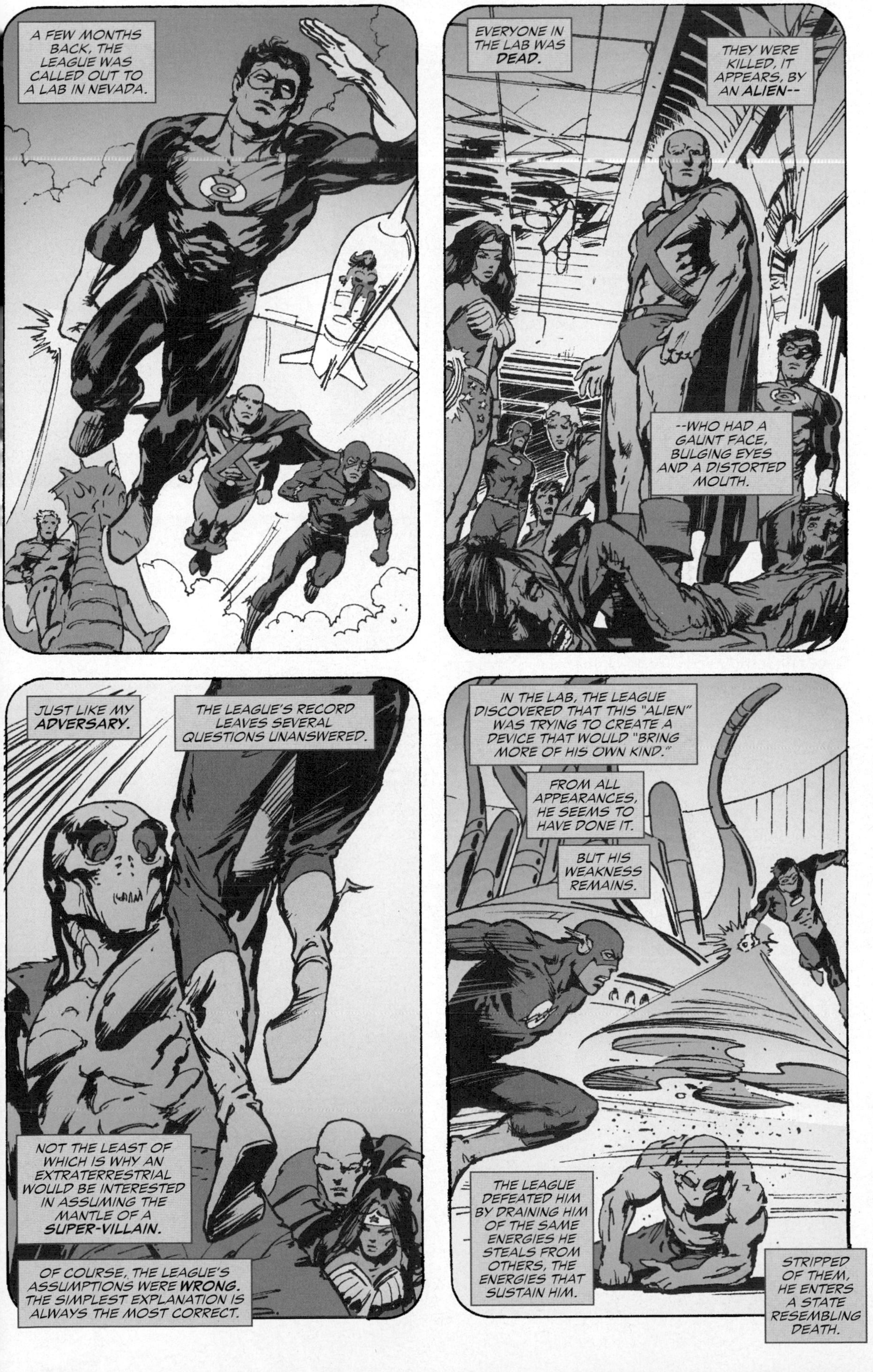
A FEW MONTHS BACK, THE LEAGUE WAS CALLED OUT TO A LAB IN NEVADA.
EVERYONE IN THE LAB WAS DEAD.
THEY WERE KILLED, IT APPEARS, BY AN ALIEN--
--WHO HAD A GAUNT FACE, BULGING EYES AND A DISTORTED MOUTH.
JUST LIKE MY ADVERSARY.
THE LEAGUE'S RECORD LEAVES SEVERAL QUESTIONS UNANSWERED.
NOT THE LEAST OF WHICH IS WHY AN EXTRATERRESTRIAL WOULD BE INTERESTED IN ASSUMING THE MANTLE OF A SUPER-VILLAIN.
OF COURSE, THE LEAGUE'S ASSUMPTIONS WERE WRONG. THE SIMPLEST EXPLANATION IS ALWAYS THE MOST CORRECT.
IN THE LAB, THE LEAGUE DISCOVERED THAT THIS "ALIEN" WAS TRYING TO CREATE A DEVICE THAT WOULD "BRING MORE OF HIS OWN KIND."
FROM ALL APPEARANCES, HE SEEMS TO HAVE DONE IT.
BUT HIS WEAKNESS REMAINS.
THE LEAGUE DEFEATED HIM BY DRAINING HIM OF THE SAME ENERGIES HE STEALS FROM OTHERS, THE ENERGIES THAT SUSTAIN HIM.
STRIPPED OF THEM, HE ENTERS A STATE RESEMBLING DEATH.

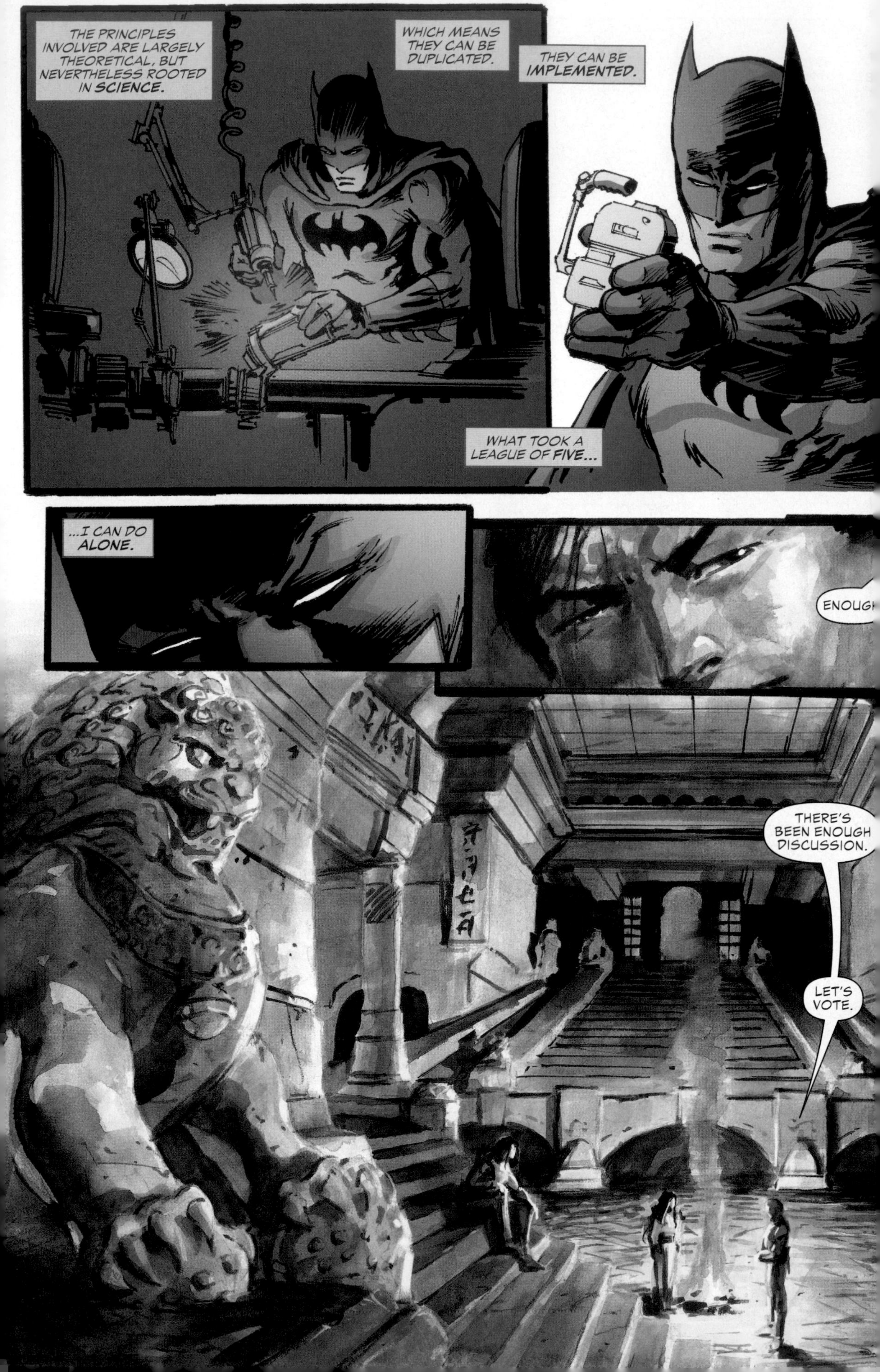
THE PRINCIPLES INVOLVED ARE LARGELY THEORETICAL, BUT NEVERTHELESS ROOTED IN SCIENCE.
WHICH MEANS THEY CAN BE DUPLICATED.
THEY CAN BE IMPLEMENTED.
WHAT TOOK A LEAGUE OF FIVE...
...I CAN DO ALONE.
ENOUG
THERE'S BEEN ENOUGH DISCUSSION.
LET'S VOTE.

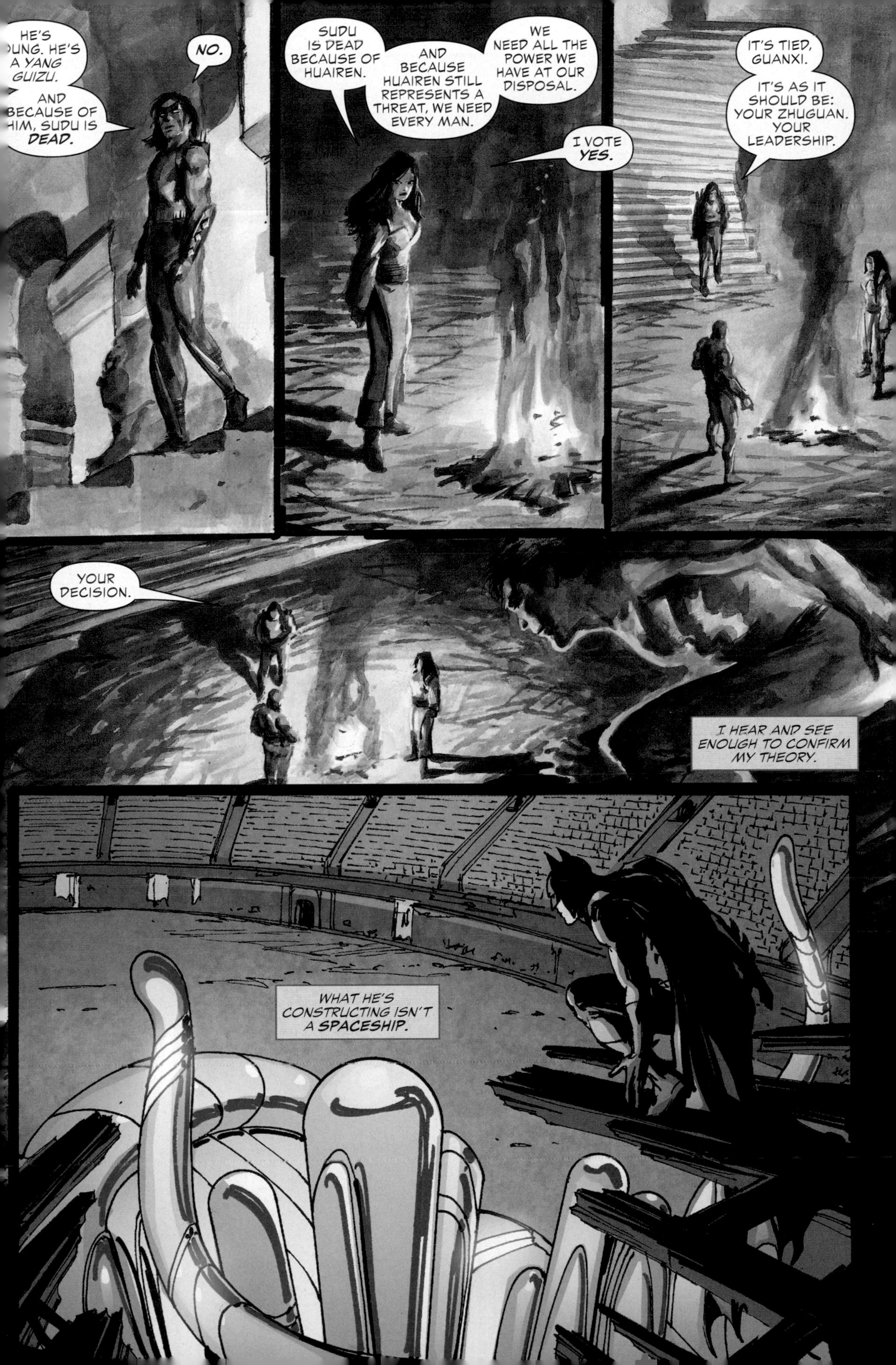

HE'S OUNG. HE'S A YANG GUIZU.
AND BECAUSE OF HIM, SUDU IS DEAD.
NO.
SUDU IS DEAD BECAUSE OF HUAIREN.
AND BECAUSE HUAIREN STILL REPRESENTS A THREAT, WE NEED EVERY MAN.
WE NEED ALL THE POWER WE HAVE AT OUR DISPOSAL.
I VOTE YES.
IT'S TIED, GUANXI.
IT'S AS IT SHOULD BE: YOUR ZHUGUAN. YOUR LEADERSHIP.
YOUR DECISION.
I HEAR AND SEE ENOUGH TO CONFIRM MY THEORY.
WHAT HE'S CONSTRUCTING ISN'T A SPACESHIP.

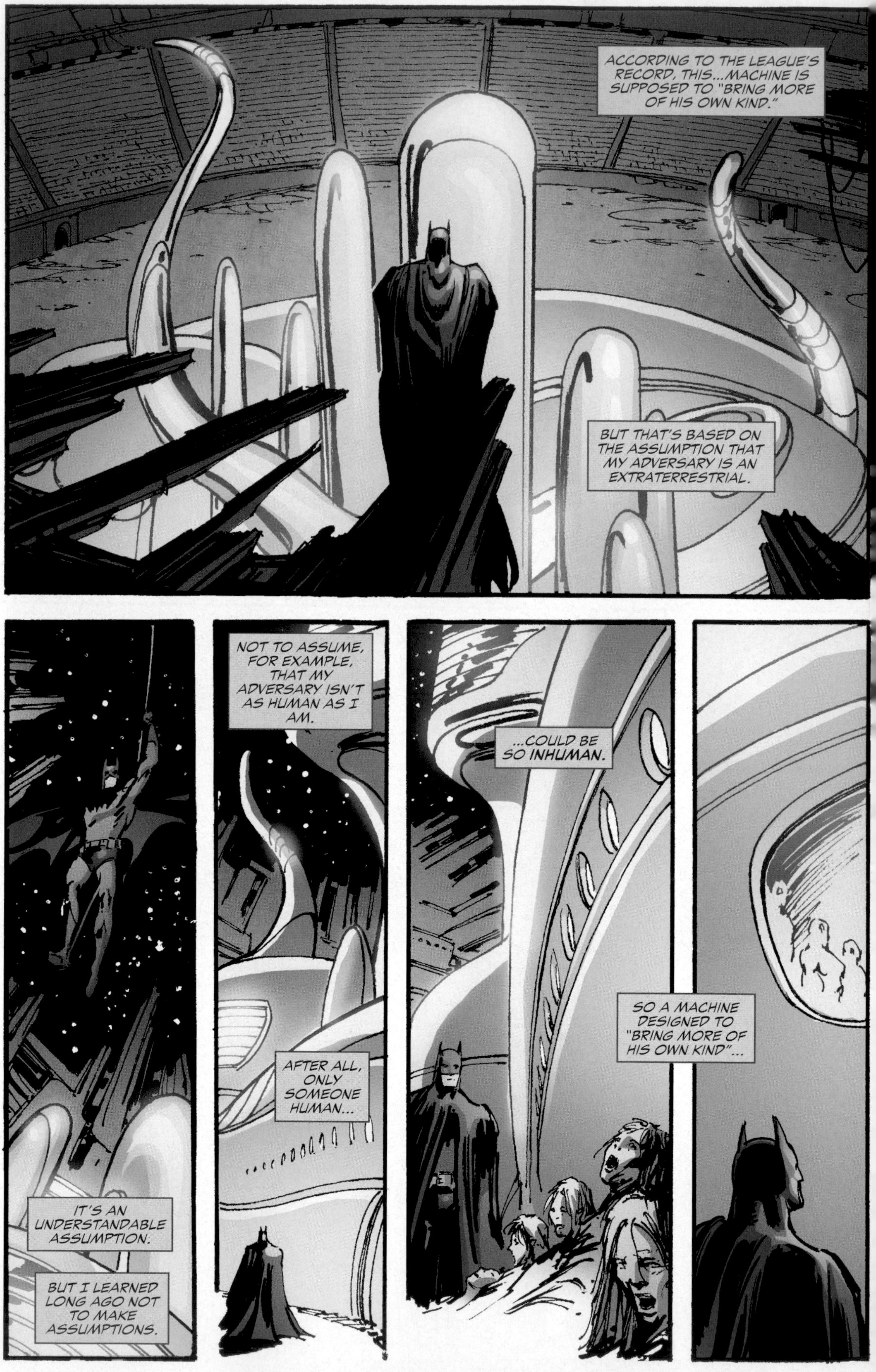
ACCORDING TO THE LEAGUE'S RECORD, THIS...MACHINE IS SUPPOSED TO "BRING MORE OF HIS OWN KIND."
BUT THAT'S BASED ON THE ASSUMPTION THAT MY ADVERSARY IS AN EXTRATERRESTRIAL.
IT'S AN UNDERSTANDABLE ASSUMPTION.
BUT I LEARNED LONG AGO NOT TO MAKE ASSUMPTIONS.
NOT TO ASSUME, FOR EXAMPLE, THAT MY ADVERSARY ISN'T AS HUMAN AS I AM.
AFTER ALL, ONLY SOMEONE HUMAN...
...COULD BE SO INHUMAN.
SO A MACHINE DESIGNED TO "BRING MORE OF HIS OWN KIND"...

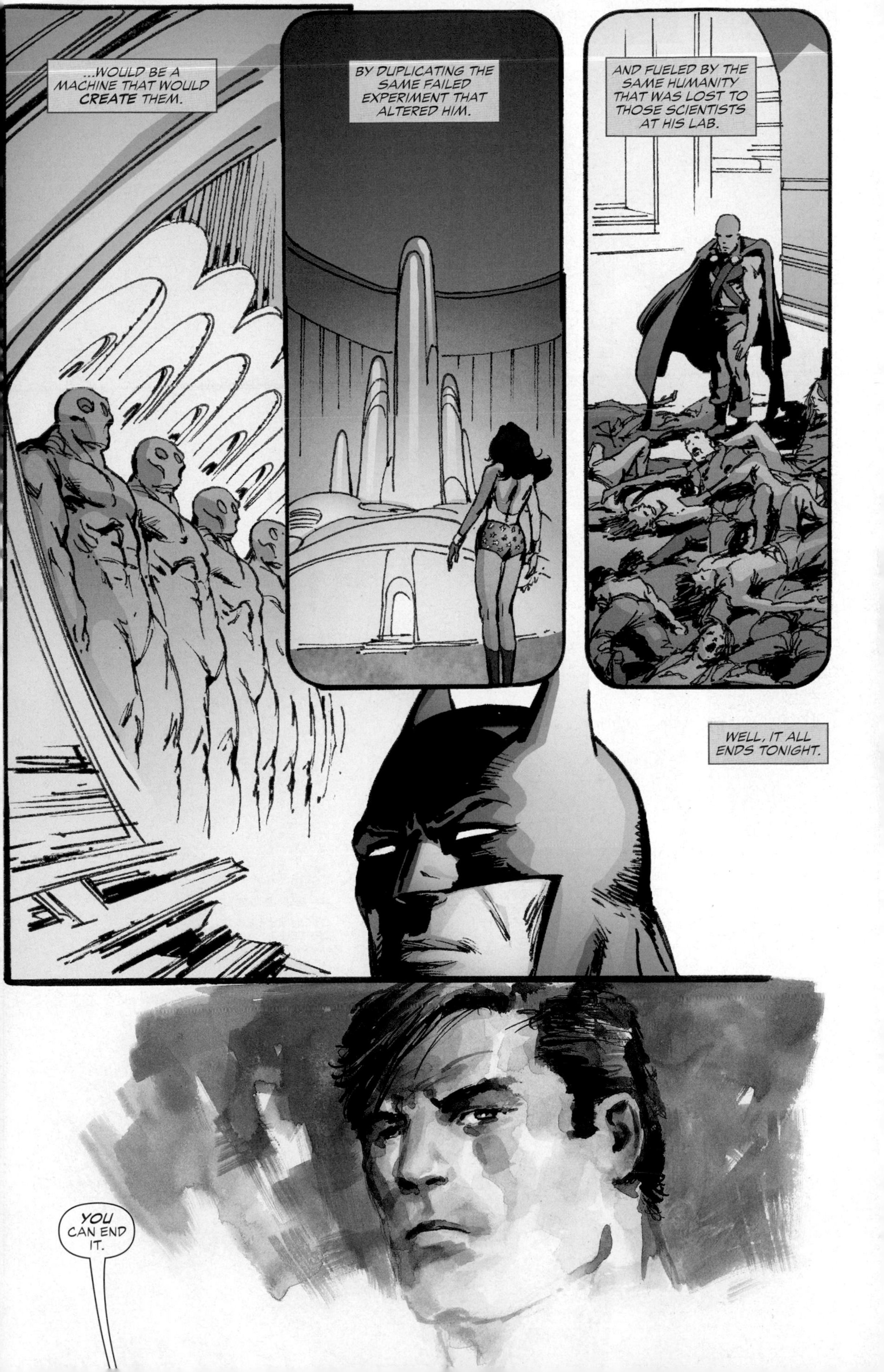
...WOULD BE A MACHINE THAT WOULD CREATE THEM.
BY DUPLICATING THE SAME FAILED EXPERIMENT THAT ALTERED HIM.
AND FUELED BY THE SAME HUMANITY THAT WAS LOST TO THOSE SCIENTISTS AT HIS LAB.
WELL, IT ALL ENDS TONIGHT.
YOU CAN END IT.

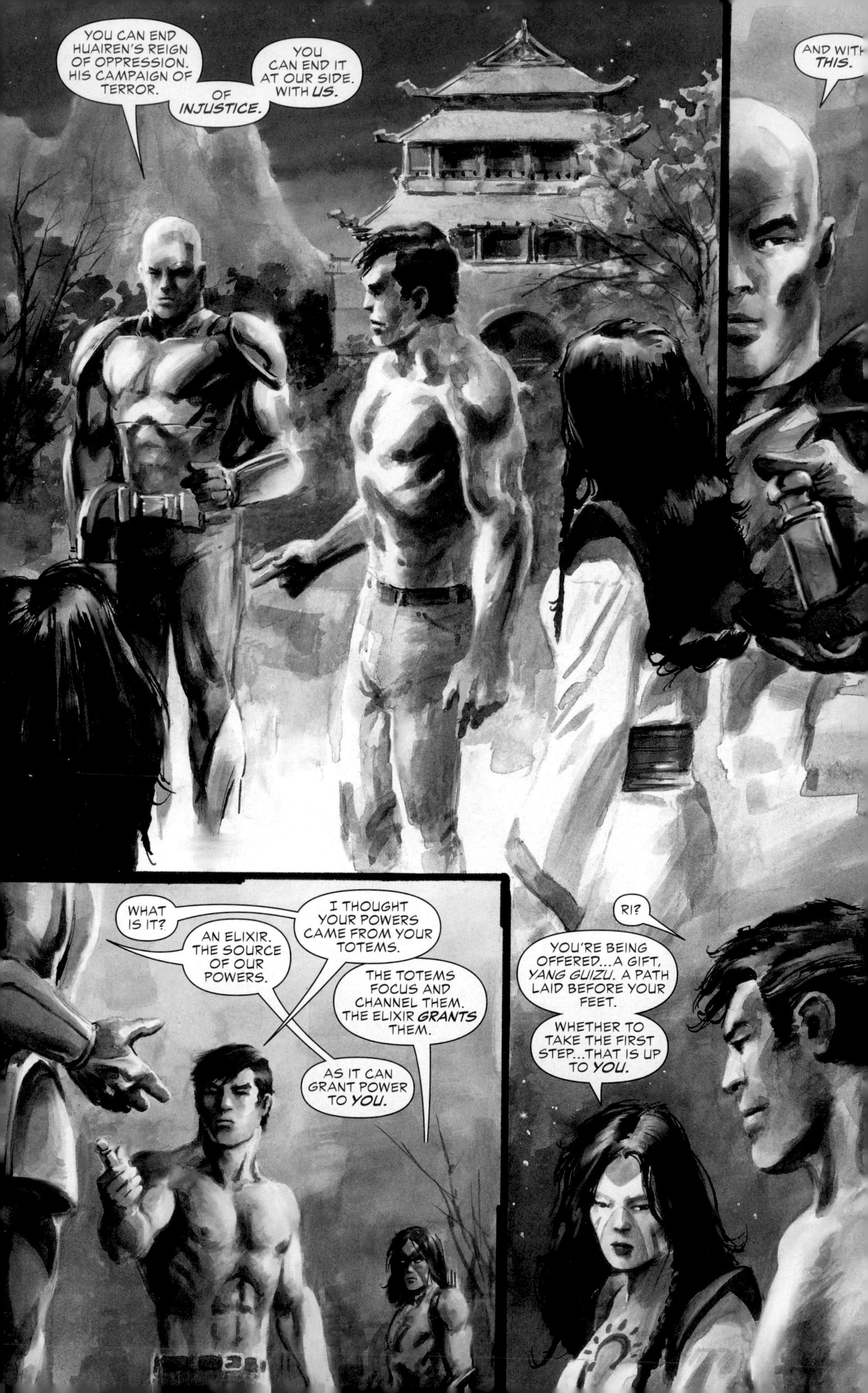

YOU CAN END HUAIREN'S REIGN OF OPPRESSION. HIS CAMPAIGN OF TERROR.
OF INJUSTICE.
YOU CAN END IT AT OUR SIDE. WITH US.
AND WITH THIS.
WHAT IS IT?
AN ELIXIR. THE SOURCE OF OUR POWERS.
I THOUGHT YOUR POWERS CAME FROM YOUR TOTEMS.
THE TOTEMS FOCUS AND CHANNEL THEM. THE ELIXIR GRANTS THEM.
AS IT CAN GRANT POWER TO YOU.
RI?
YOU'RE BEING OFFERED...A GIFT, YANG GUIZU. A PATH LAID BEFORE YOUR FEET.
WHETHER TO TAKE THE FIRST STEP...THAT IS UP TO YOU.

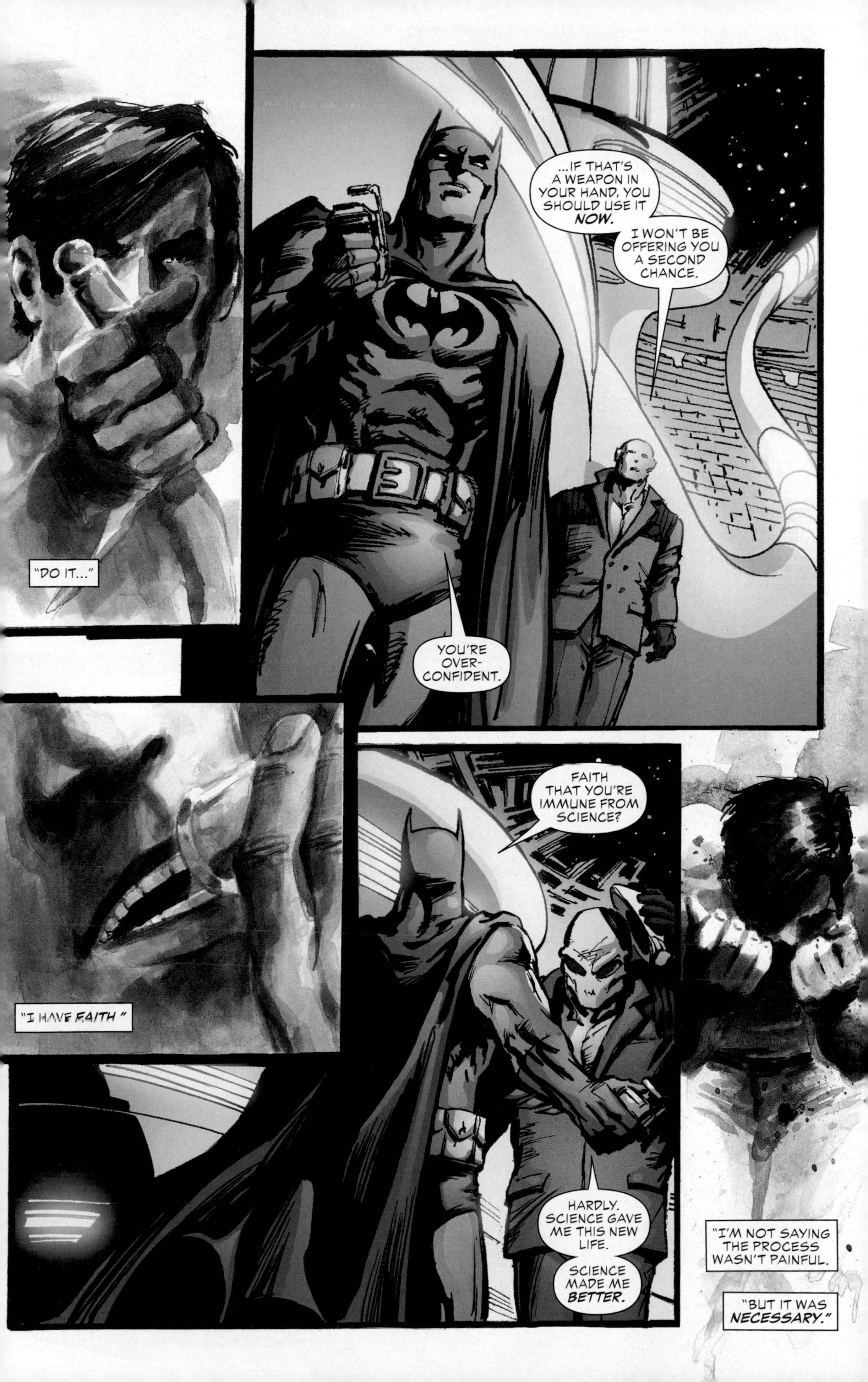
...IF THAT'S A WEAPON IN YOUR HAND, YOU SHOULD USE IT NOW.
I WON'T BE OFFERING YOU A SECOND CHANCE.
"DO IT..."
YOU'RE OVER-CONFIDENT.
"I HAVE FAITH"
FAITH THAT YOU'RE IMMUNE FROM SCIENCE?
HARDLY. SCIENCE GAVE ME THIS NEW LIFE.
SCIENCE MADE ME BETTER.
"I'M NOT SAYING THE PROCESS WASN'T PAINFUL.
"BUT IT WAS NECESSARY."

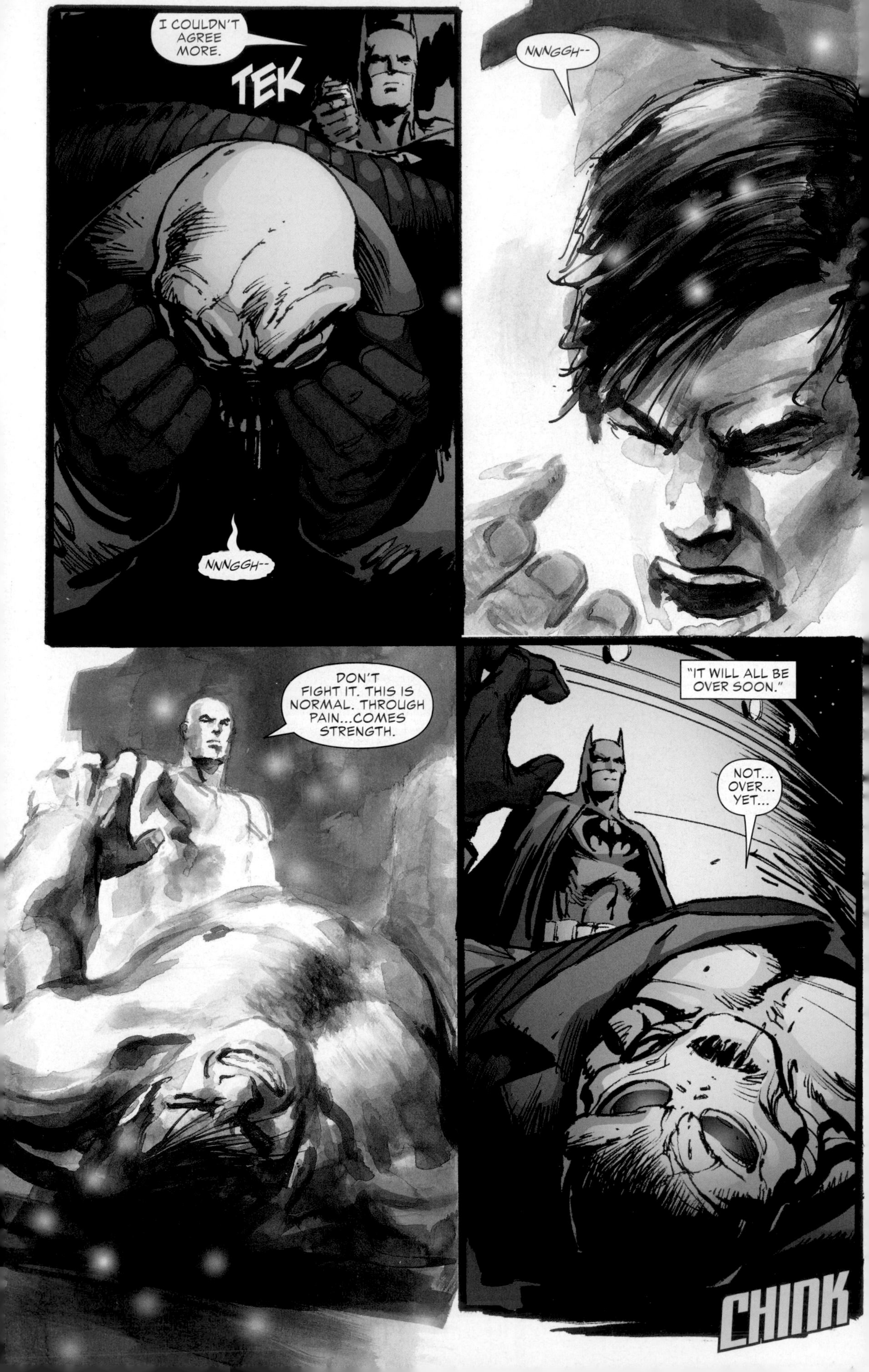
I COULDN'T AGREE MORE.
TEK
NNNGGH--
NNNGGH--
DON'T FIGHT IT. THIS IS NORMAL. THROUGH PAIN...COMES STRENGTH.
"IT WILL ALL BE OVER SOON."
NOT... OVER... YET...
CHINK

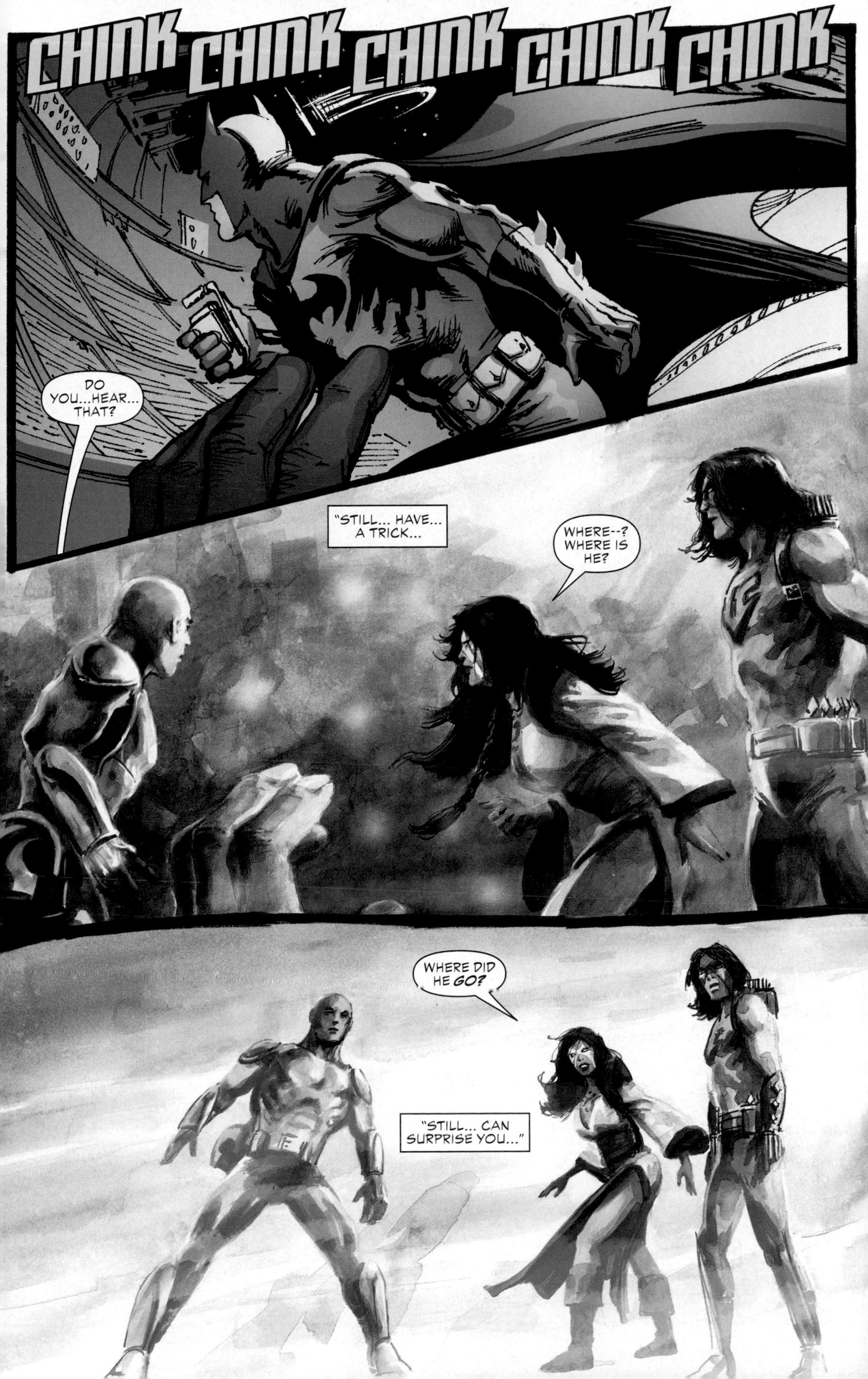
CHINK CHINK CHINK CHINK CHINK
DO YOU...HEAR... THAT?
"STILL... HAVE... A TRICK...
WHERE--? WHERE IS HE?
WHERE DID HE GO?
"STILL... CAN SURPRISE YOU..."

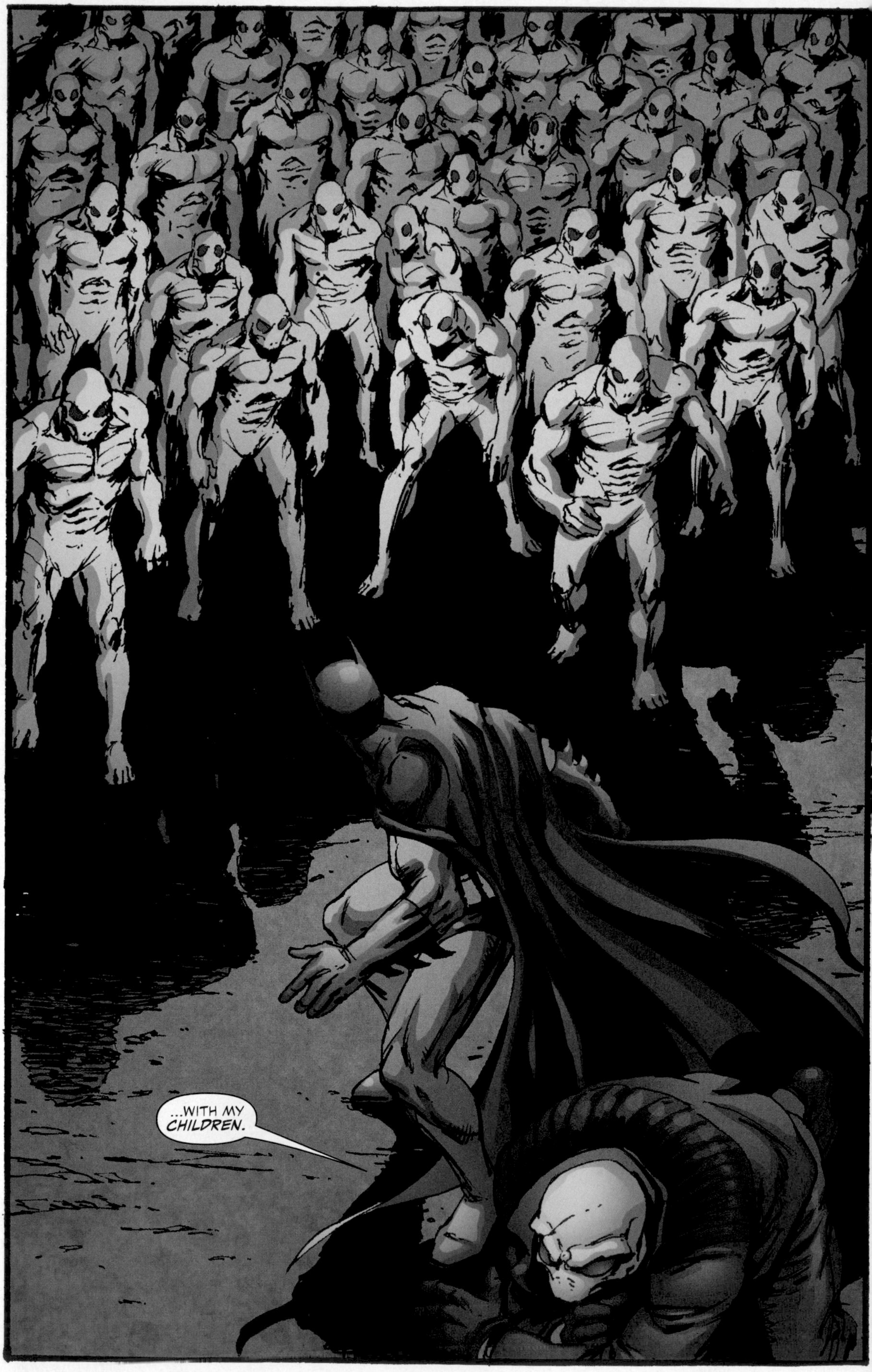
...WITH MY CHILDREN.

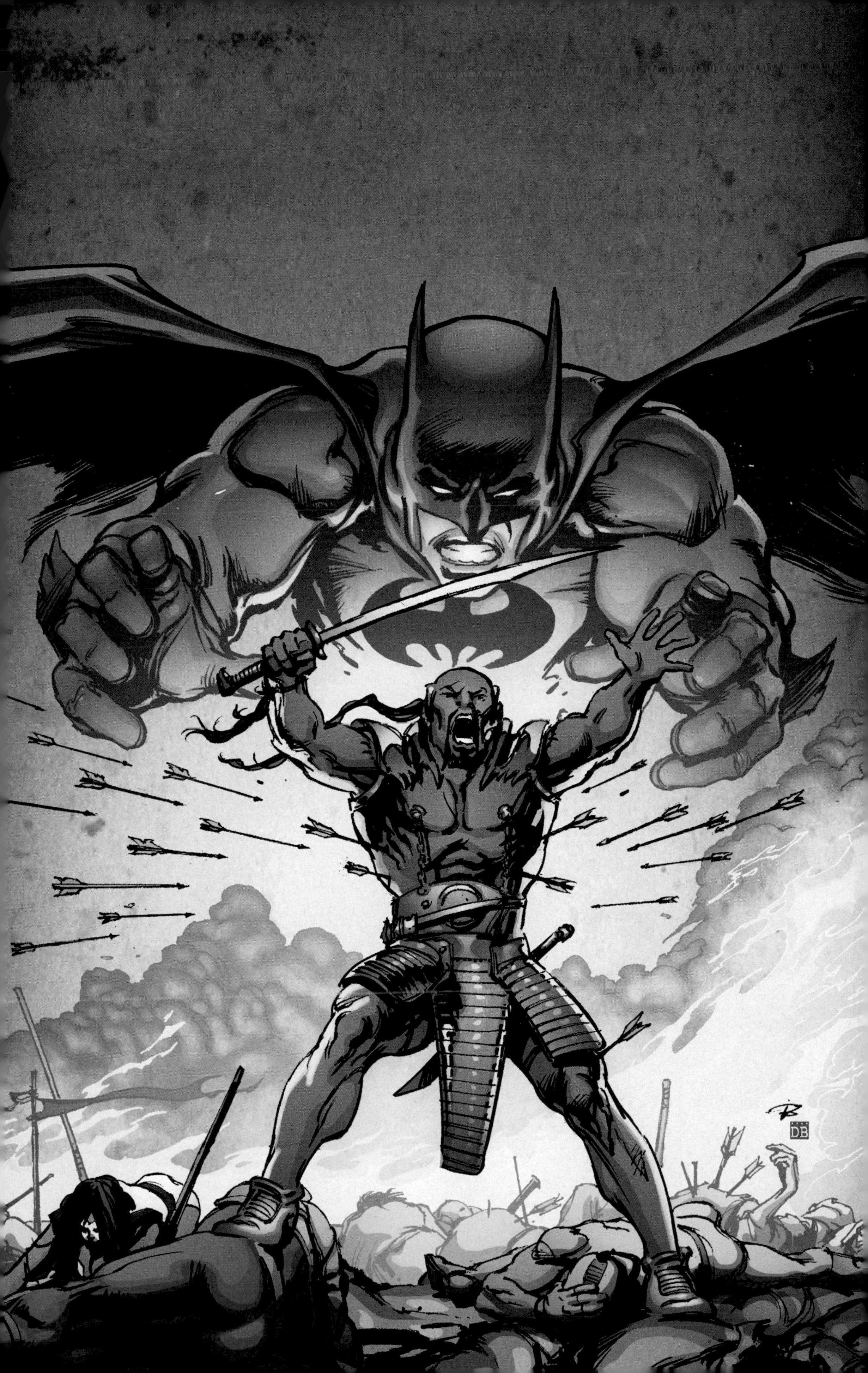

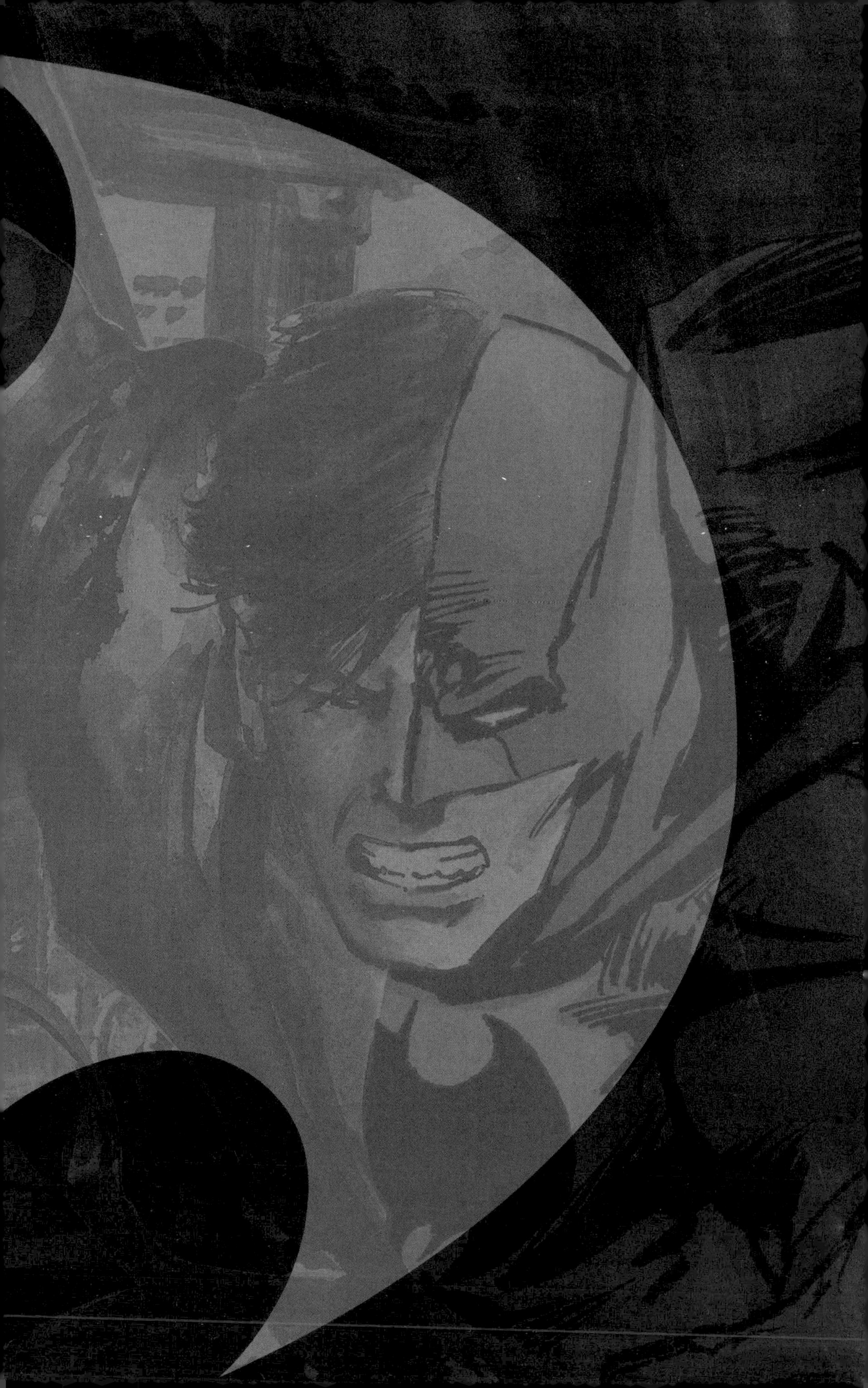

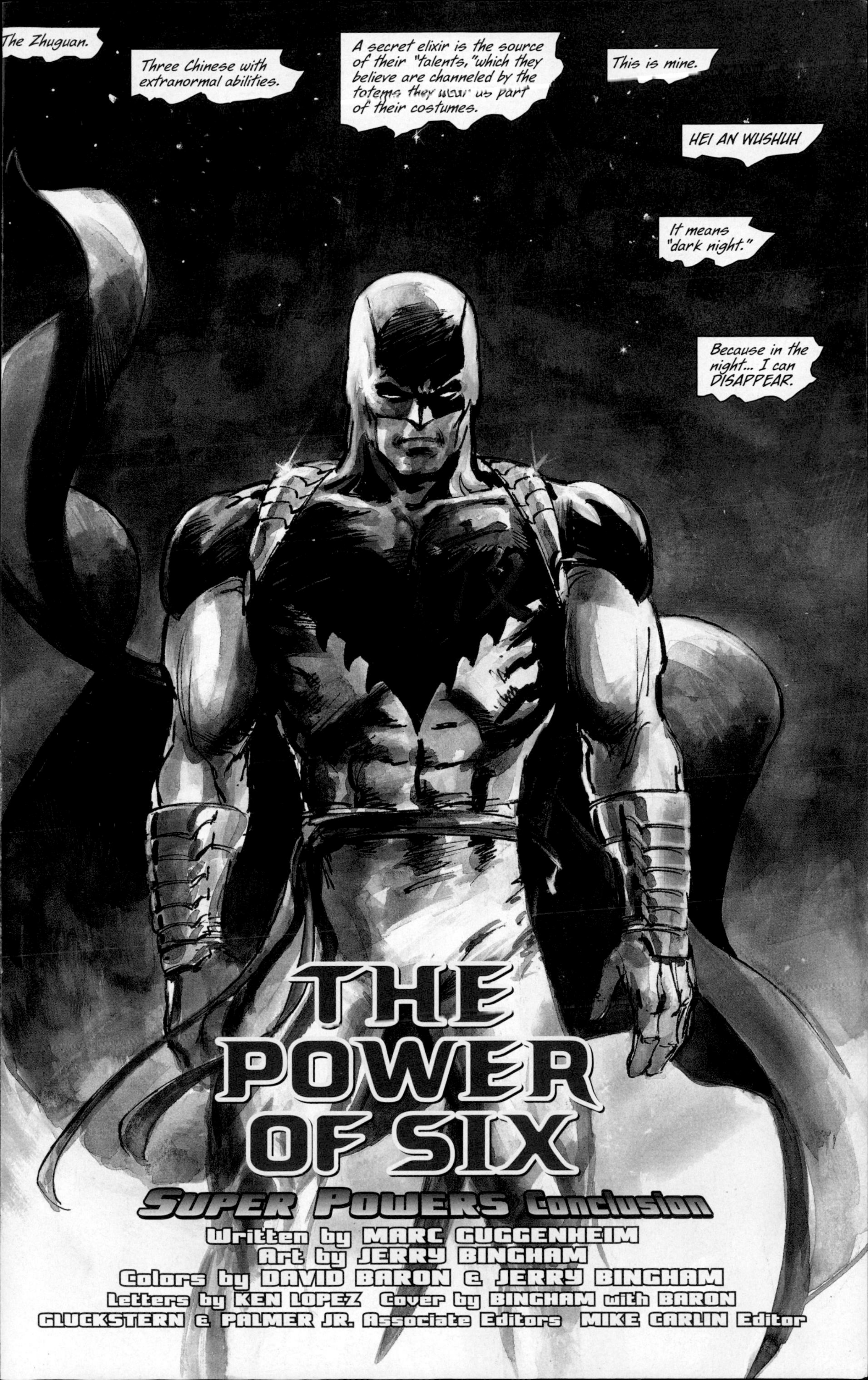
The Zhuguan.
Three Chinese with extranormal abilities.
A secret elixir is the source of their "talents," which they believe are channeled by the totems they wear as part of their costumes.
This is mine.
HEI AN WUSHUH
It means "dark night."
Because in the night... I can DISAPPEAR.
THE POWER OF SIX
SUPER POWERS Conclusion
Written by MARC GUGGENHEIM
Art by JERRY BINGHAM
Colors by DAVID BARON & JERRY BINGHAM
Letters by KEN LOPEZ Cover by BINGHAM with BARON
GLUCKSTERN & PALMER JR. Associate Editors MIKE CARLIN Editor

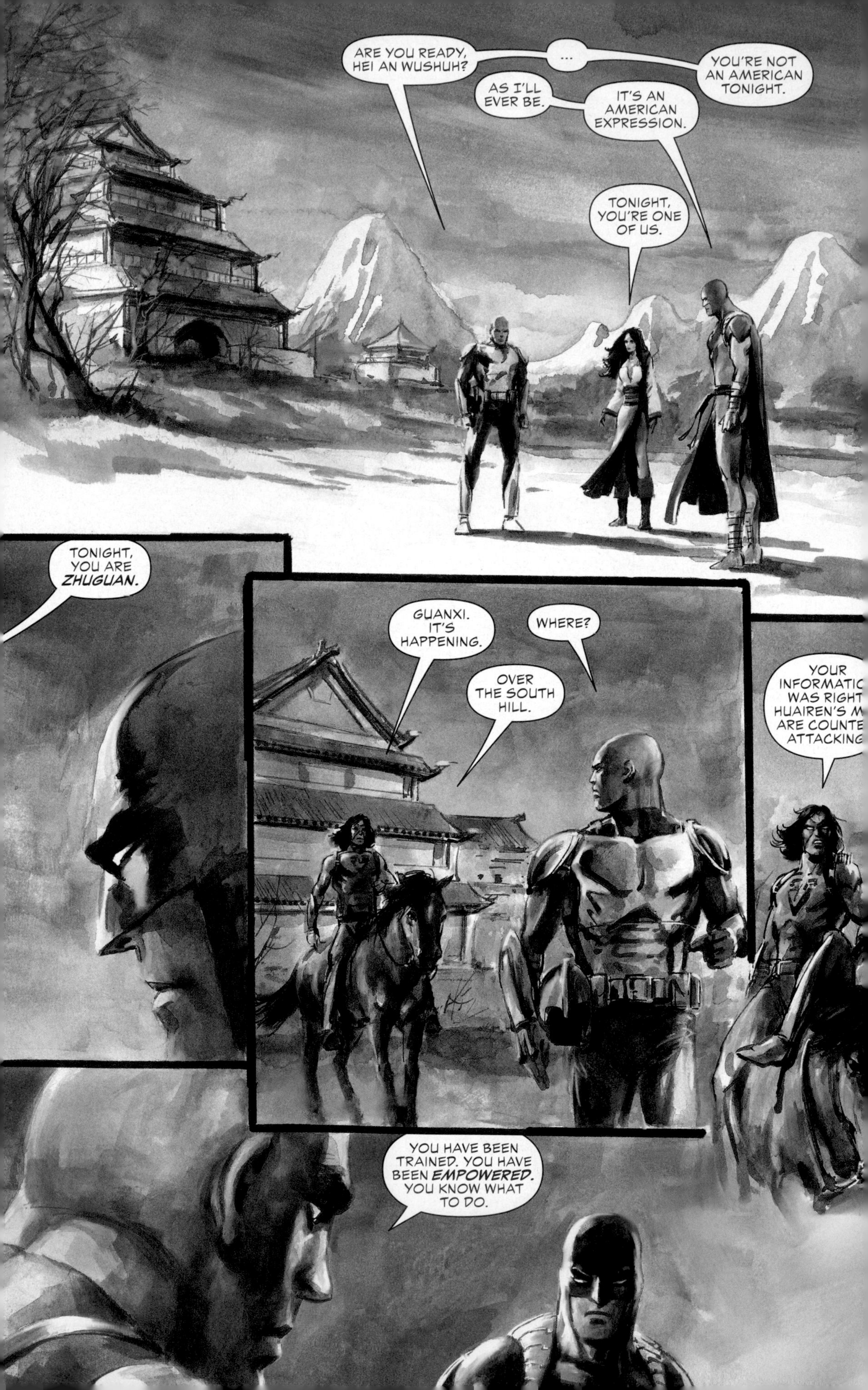
ARE YOU READY, HEI AN WUSHUH?
...
YOU'RE NOT AN AMERICAN TONIGHT.
AS I'LL EVER BE.
IT'S AN AMERICAN EXPRESSION.
TONIGHT, YOU'RE ONE OF US.
TONIGHT, YOU ARE ZHUGUAN.
GUANXI. IT'S HAPPENING.
WHERE?
OVER THE SOUTH HILL.
YOUR INFORMATIC WAS RIGHT HUAIREN'S M ARE COUNTE ATTACKING
YOU HAVE BEEN TRAINED. YOU HAVE BEEN EMPOWERED. YOU KNOW WHAT TO DO.

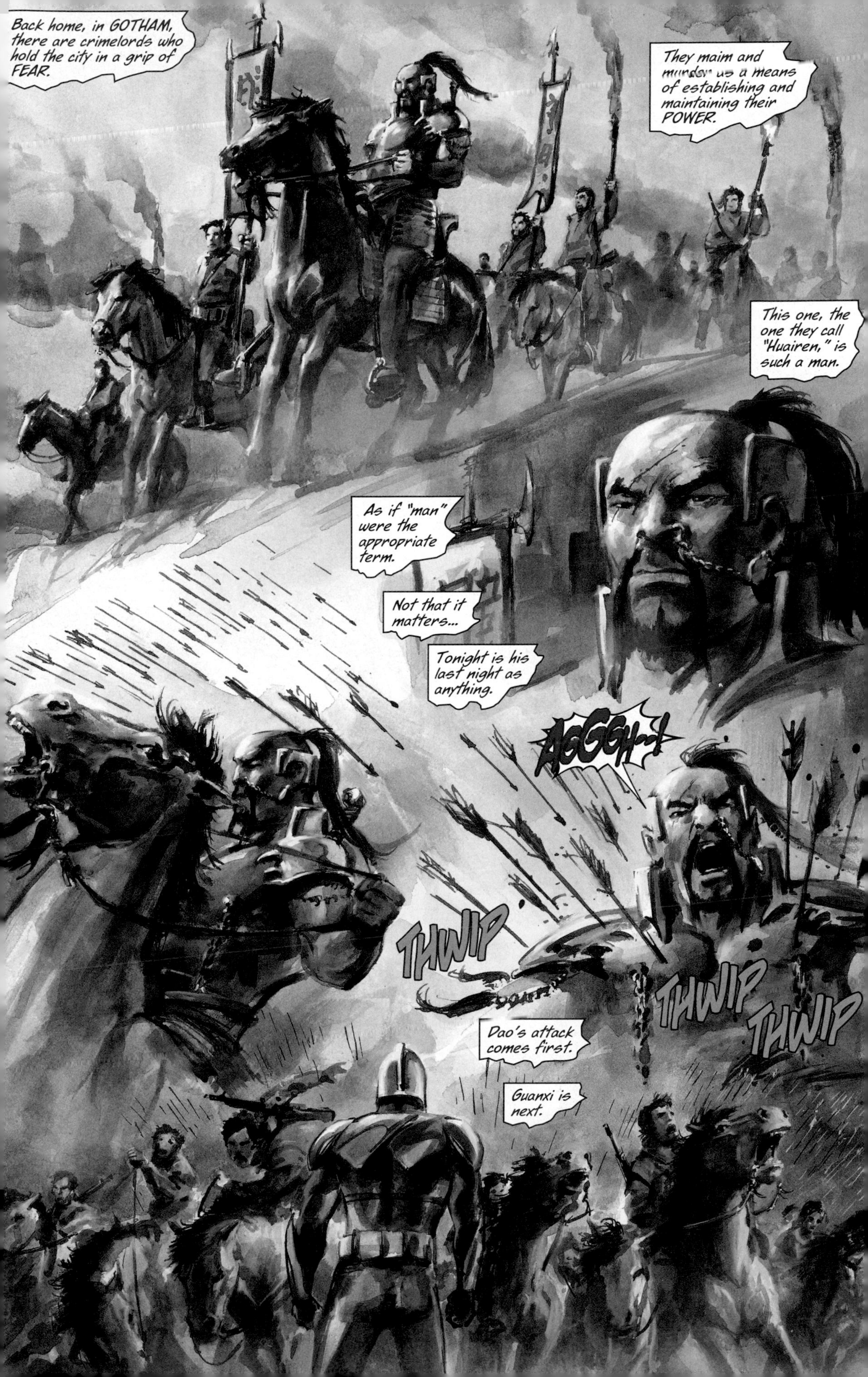
Back home, in GOTHAM, there are crimelords who hold the city in a grip of FEAR.
They maim and murder as a means of establishing and maintaining their POWER.
This one, the one they call "Huairen," is such a man.
As if "man" were the appropriate term.
Not that it matters...
Tonight is his last night as anything.
AGGGH--!
THWIP
THWIP
THWIP
Dao's attack comes first.
Guanxi is next.

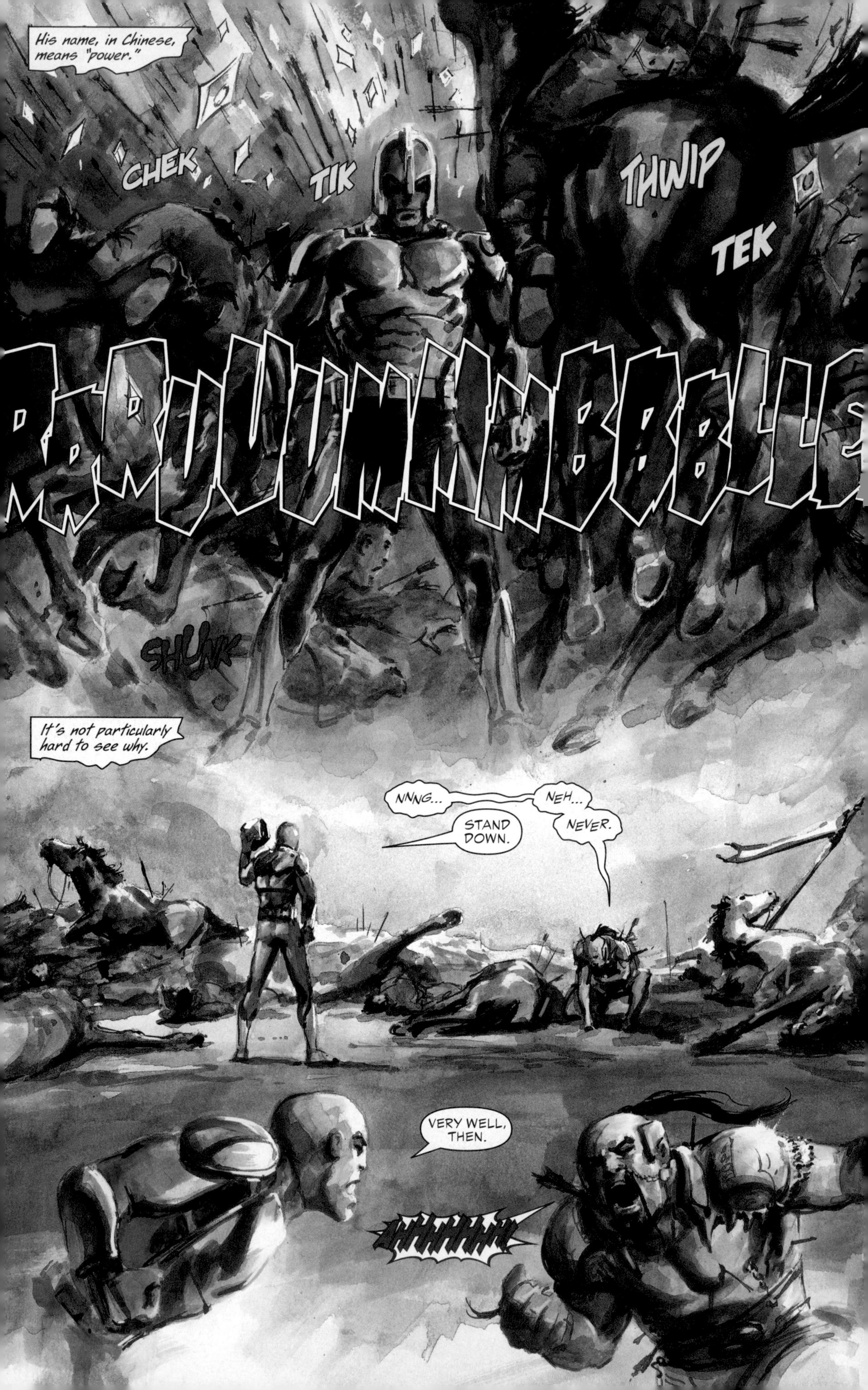
His name, in Chinese, means "power."
CHEK
TIK
THWIP
TEK
It's not particularly hard to see why.
NNNG...
NEH...
STAND DOWN.
NEVER.
VERY WELL, THEN.

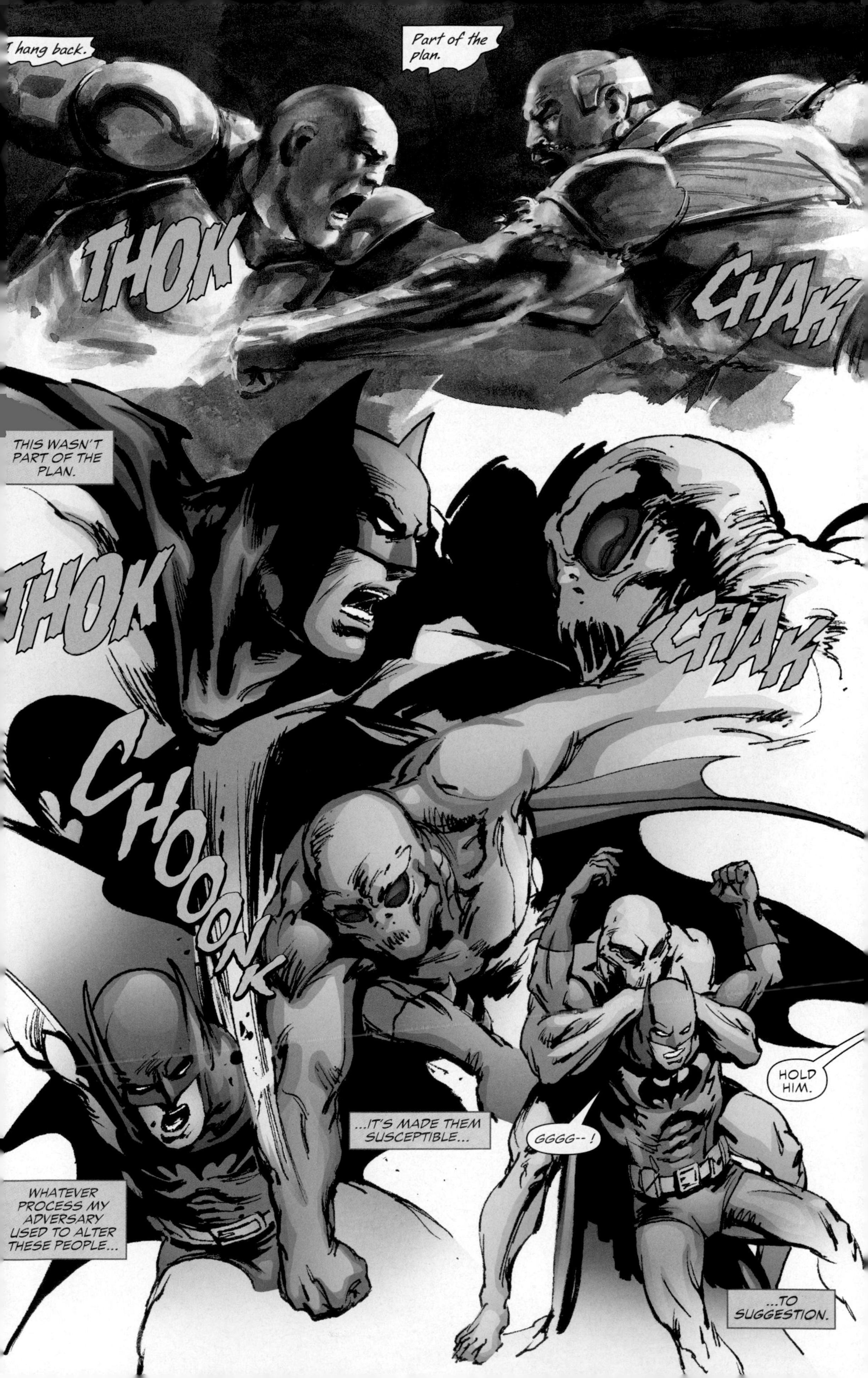
I hang back.
Part of the plan.
THOK
CHAK
THIS WASN'T PART OF THE PLAN.
THOK
CHAK
CHOOOONK
WHATEVER PROCESS MY ADVERSARY USED TO ALTER THESE PEOPLE...
...IT'S MADE THEM SUSCEPTIBLE...
HOLD HIM.
GGGG-- !
...TO SUGGESTION.

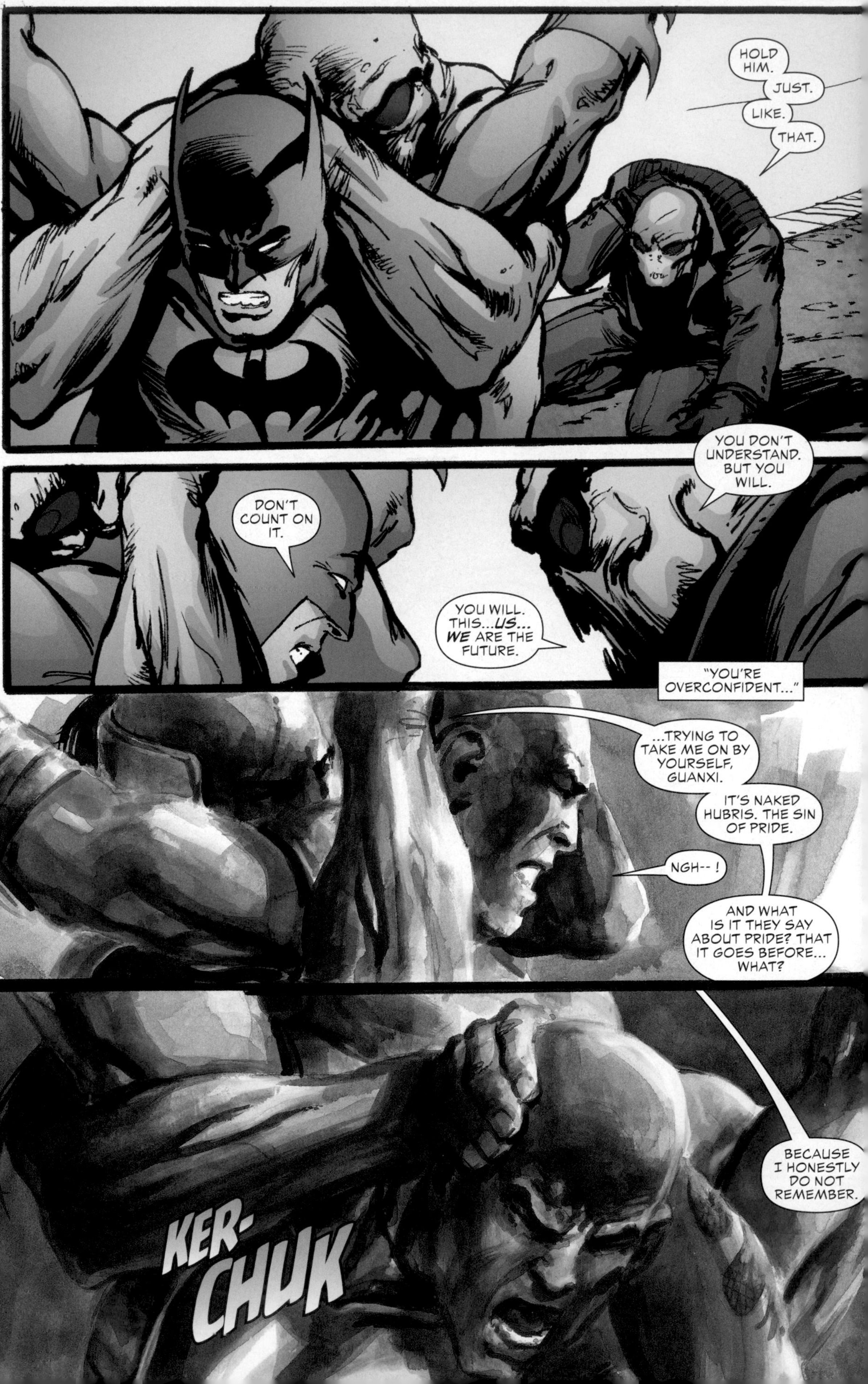
HOLD HIM.
JUST.
LIKE.
THAT.
YOU DON'T UNDERSTAND. BUT YOU WILL.
DON'T COUNT ON IT.
YOU WILL. THIS...US... WE ARE THE FUTURE.
"YOU'RE OVERCONFIDENT..."
...TRYING TO TAKE ME ON BY YOURSELF, GUANXI.
IT'S NAKED HUBRIS. THE SIN OF PRIDE.
NGH-- !
AND WHAT IS IT THEY SAY ABOUT PRIDE? THAT IT GOES BEFORE... WHAT?
BECAUSE I HONESTLY DO NOT REMEMBER.
KER-CHUK

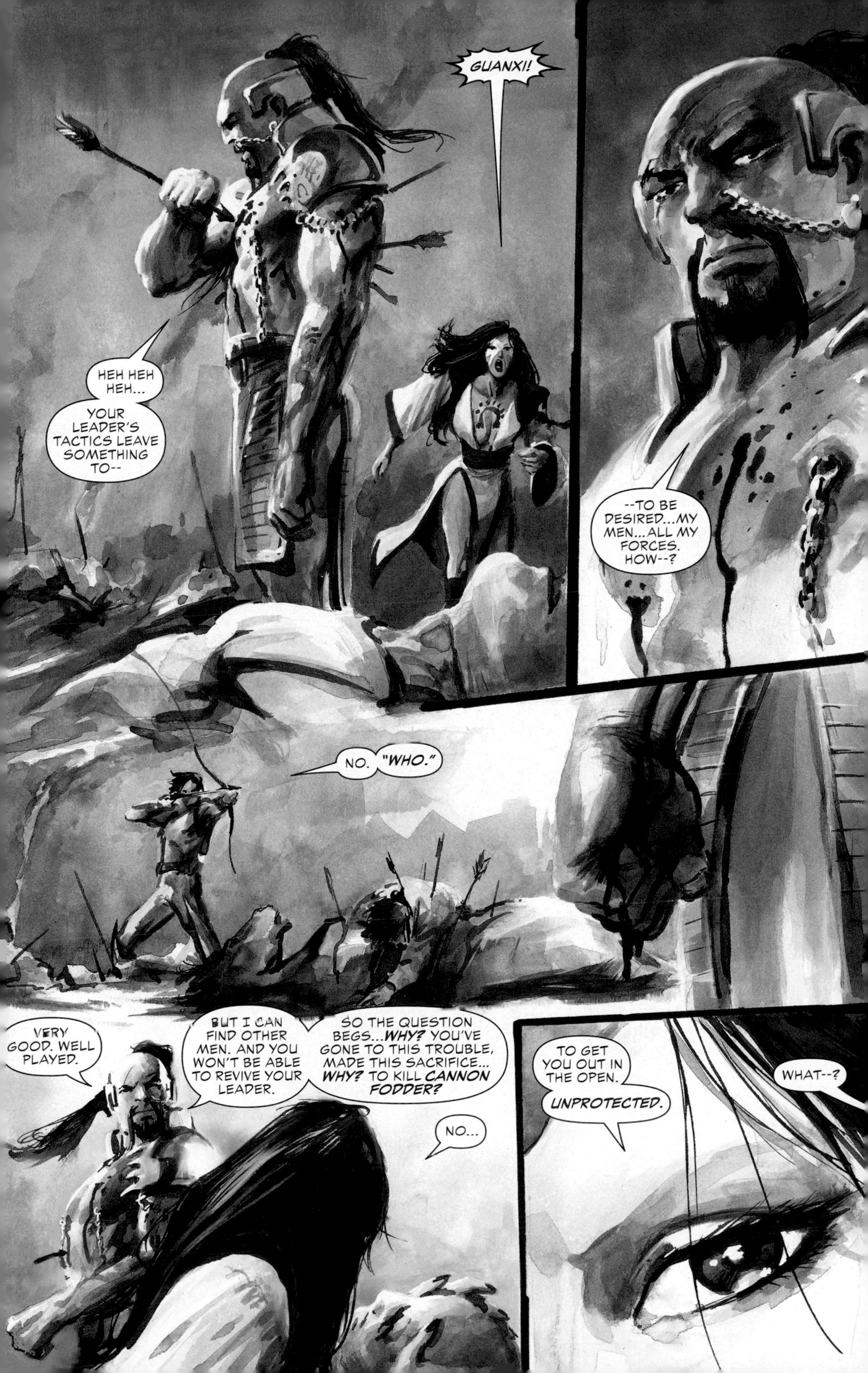
GUANXI!
HEH HEH HEH...
YOUR LEADER'S TACTICS LEAVE SOMETHING TO--
--TO BE DESIRED...MY MEN...ALL MY FORCES. HOW--?
NO. "WHO."
VERY GOOD. WELL PLAYED.
BUT I CAN FIND OTHER MEN. AND YOU WON'T BE ABLE TO REVIVE YOUR LEADER.
SO THE QUESTION BEGS...WHY? YOU'VE GONE TO THIS TROUBLE, MADE THIS SACRIFICE... WHY? TO KILL CANNON FODDER?
NO...
TO GET YOU OUT IN THE OPEN.
UNPROTECTED.
WHAT--?

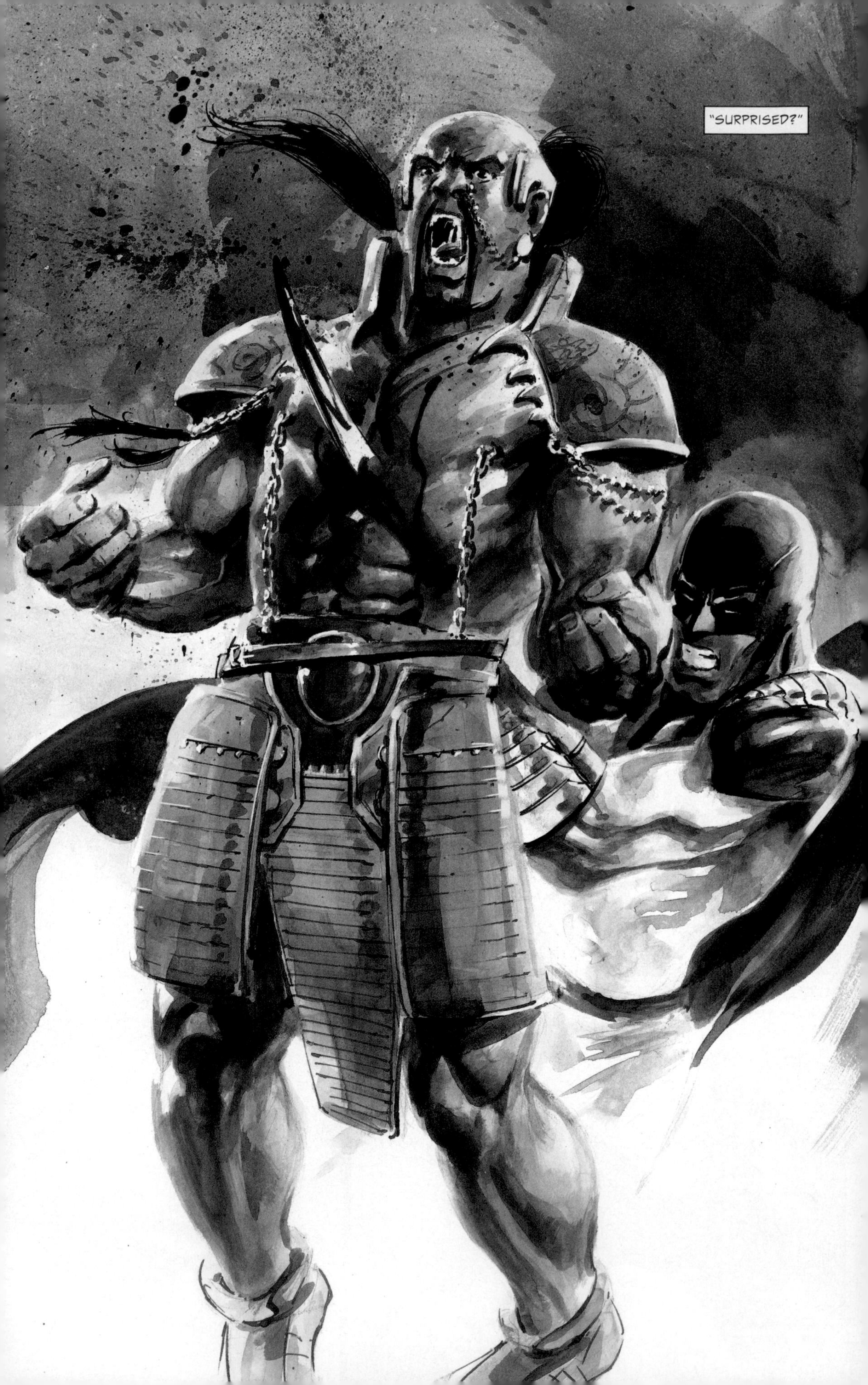
"SURPRISED?"

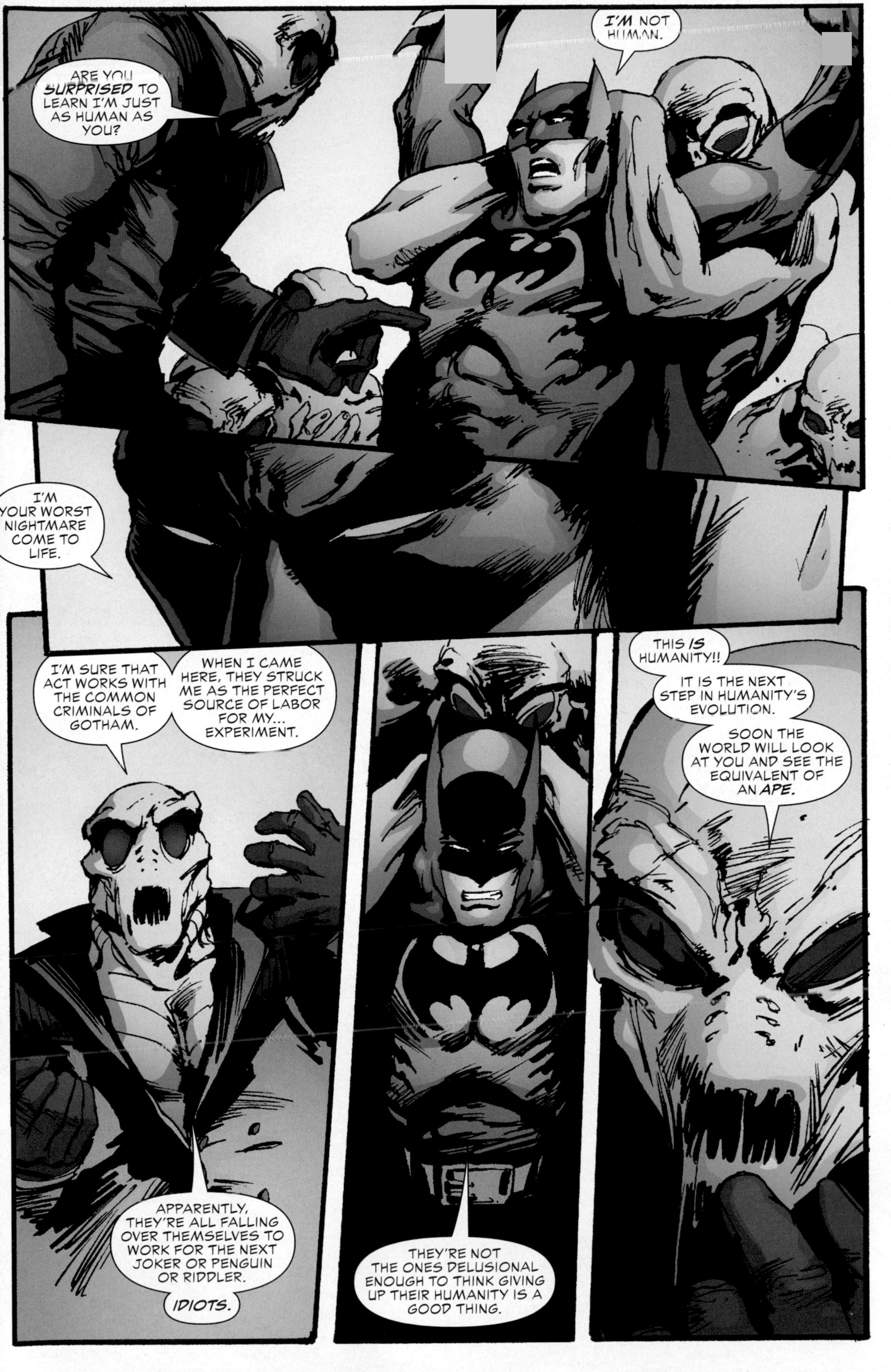

ARE YOU SURPRISED TO LEARN I'M JUST AS HUMAN AS YOU?
I'M NOT HUMAN.
I'M YOUR WORST NIGHTMARE COME TO LIFE.
I'M SURE THAT ACT WORKS WITH THE COMMON CRIMINALS OF GOTHAM.
WHEN I CAME HERE, THEY STRUCK ME AS THE PERFECT SOURCE OF LABOR FOR MY... EXPERIMENT.
APPARENTLY, THEY'RE ALL FALLING OVER THEMSELVES TO WORK FOR THE NEXT JOKER OR PENGUIN OR RIDDLER.
IDIOTS.
THEY'RE NOT THE ONES DELUSIONAL ENOUGH TO THINK GIVING UP THEIR HUMANITY IS A GOOD THING.
THIS IS HUMANITY!!
IT IS THE NEXT STEP IN HUMANITY'S EVOLUTION.
SOON THE WORLD WILL LOOK AT YOU AND SEE THE EQUIVALENT OF AN APE.

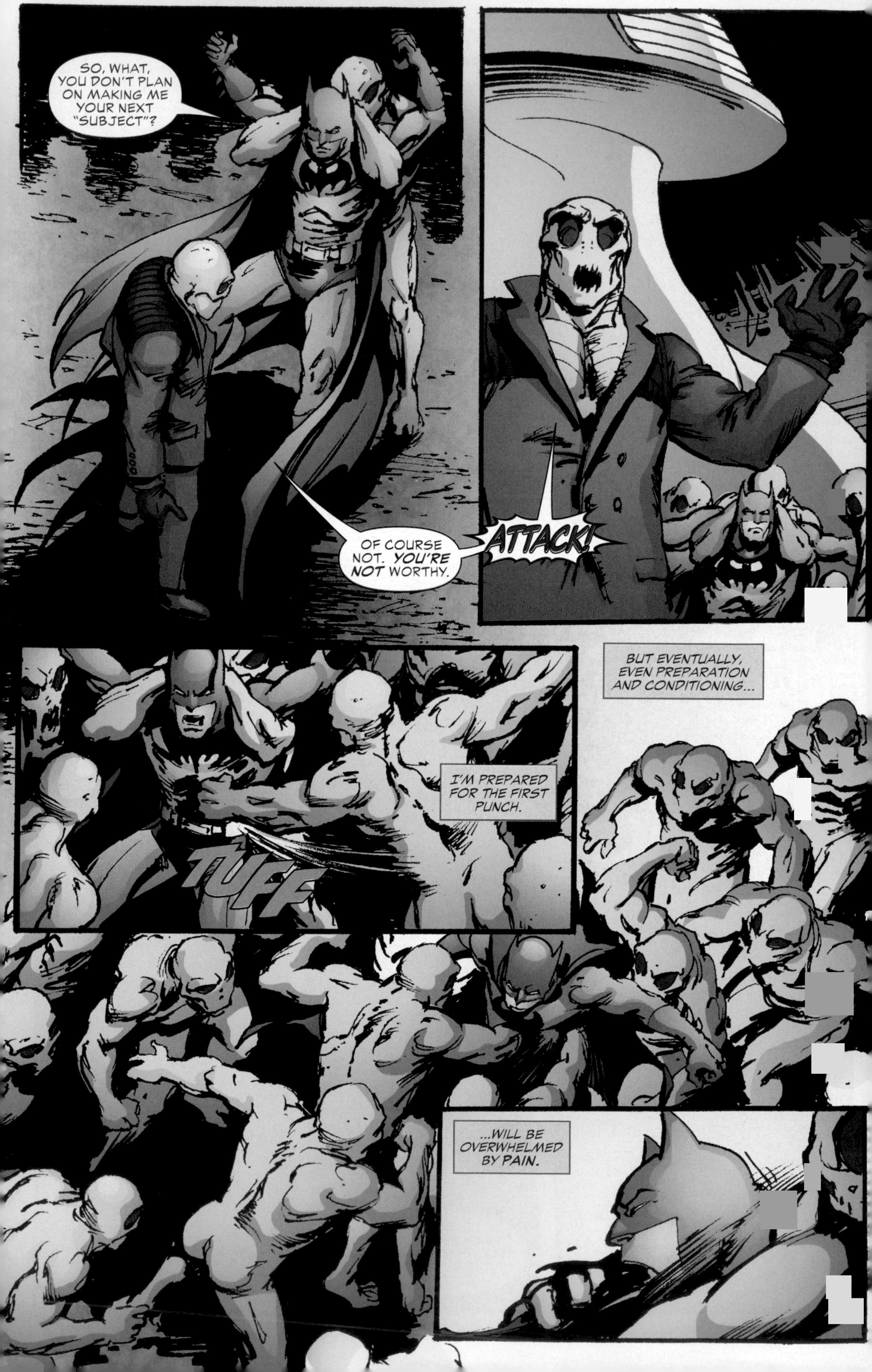
SO, WHAT, YOU DON'T PLAN ON MAKING ME YOUR NEXT "SUBJECT"?
OF COURSE NOT. *YOU'RE NOT* WORTHY.
ATTACK!
I'M PREPARED FOR THE FIRST PUNCH.
TUFF
BUT EVENTUALLY, EVEN PREPARATION AND CONDITIONING...
...WILL BE OVERWHELMED BY **PAIN**.

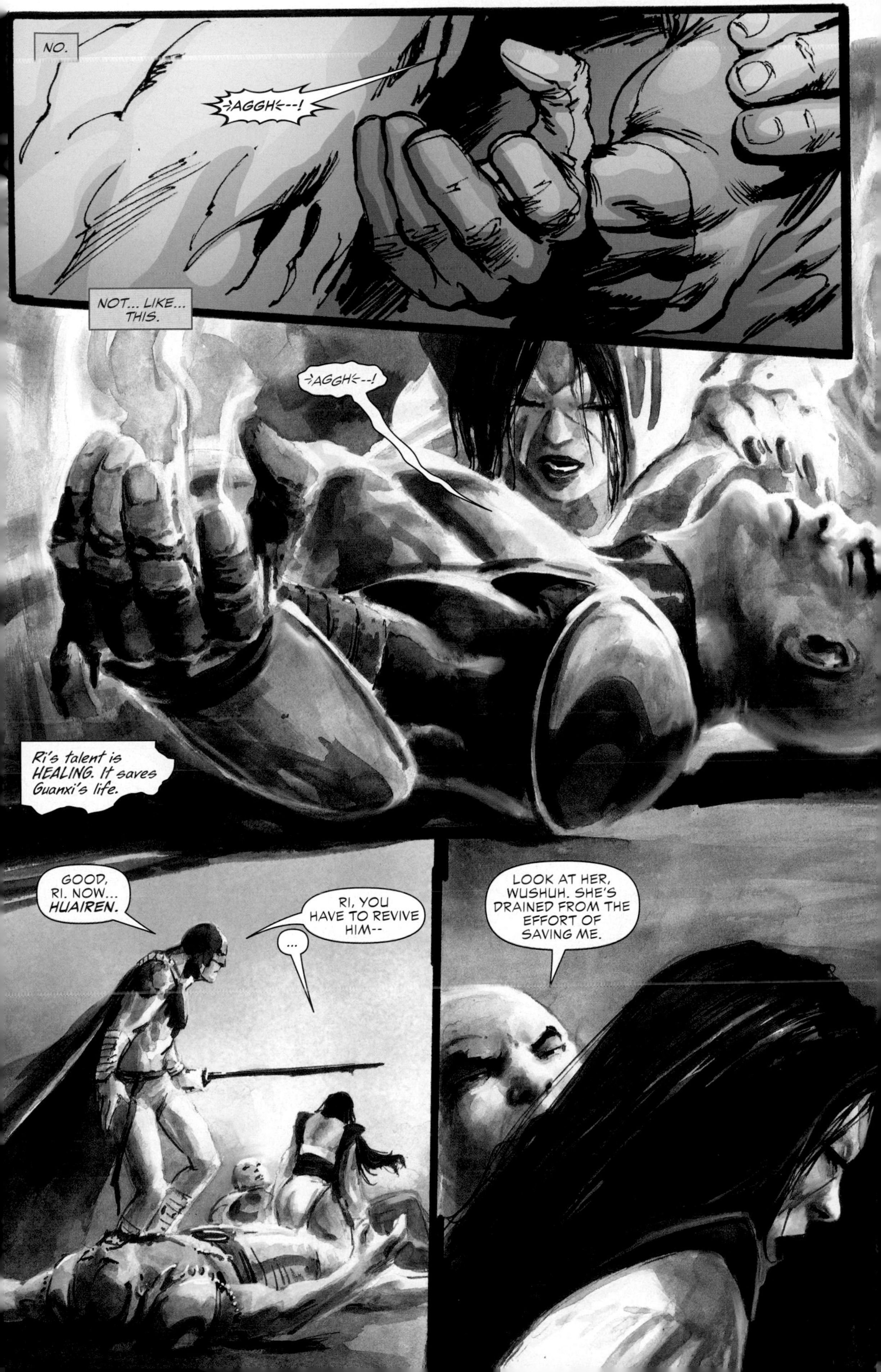
NO.
AGGH--!
NOT... LIKE... THIS.
AGGH--!
Ri's talent is HEALING. It saves Guanxi's life.
GOOD, RI. NOW... HUAIREN.
RI, YOU HAVE TO REVIVE HIM--
...
LOOK AT HER, WUSHUH. SHE'S DRAINED FROM THE EFFORT OF SAVING ME.

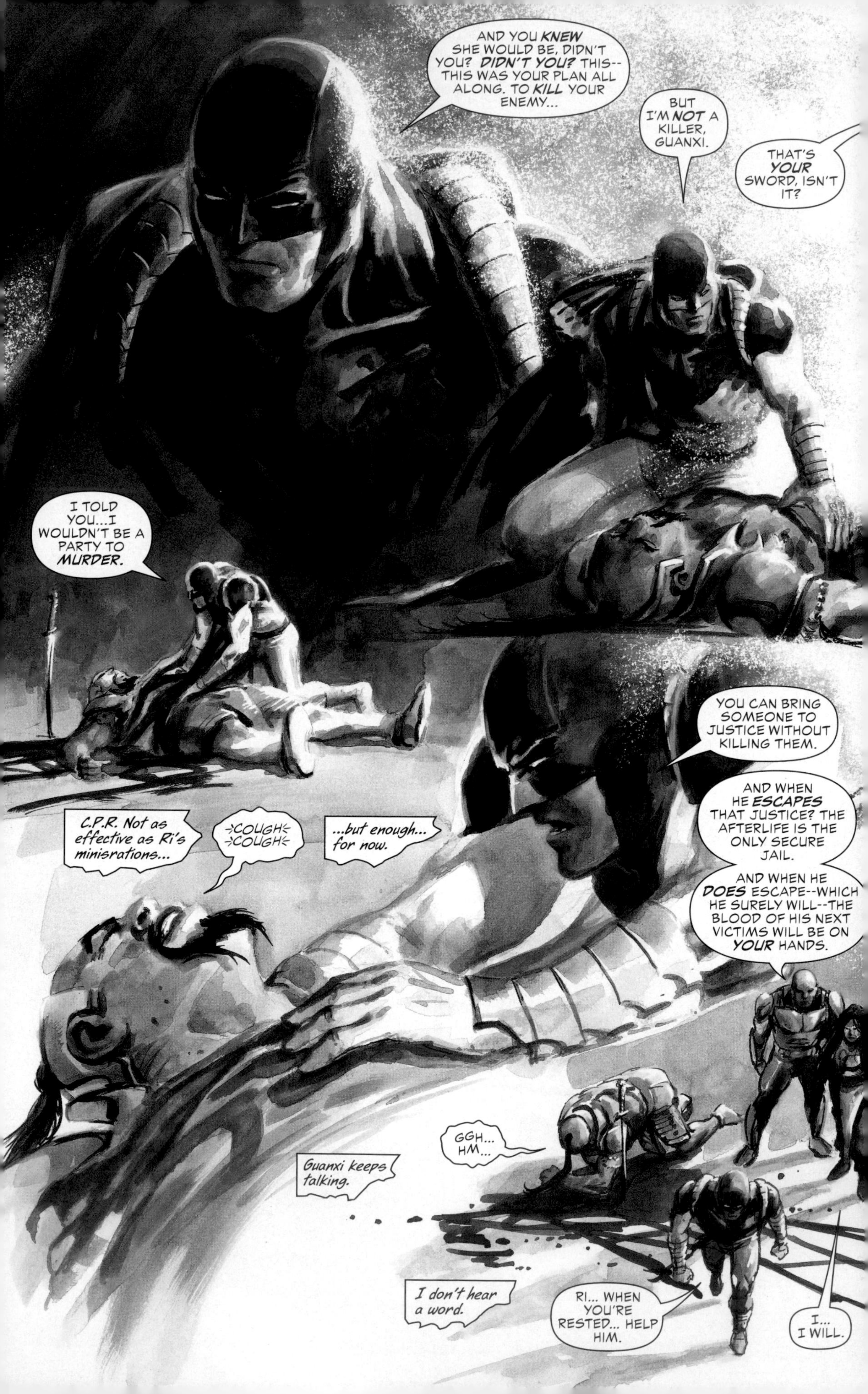
AND YOU KNEW SHE WOULD BE, DIDN'T YOU? DIDN'T YOU? THIS--THIS WAS YOUR PLAN ALL ALONG. TO KILL YOUR ENEMY...
BUT I'M NOT A KILLER, GUANXI.
THAT'S YOUR SWORD, ISN'T IT?
I TOLD YOU...I WOULDN'T BE A PARTY TO MURDER.
YOU CAN BRING SOMEONE TO JUSTICE WITHOUT KILLING THEM.
AND WHEN HE ESCAPES THAT JUSTICE? THE AFTERLIFE IS THE ONLY SECURE JAIL.
AND WHEN HE DOES ESCAPE--WHICH HE SURELY WILL--THE BLOOD OF HIS NEXT VICTIMS WILL BE ON YOUR HANDS.
C.P.R. Not as effective as Ri's minisrations...
COUGH COUGH
...but enough... for now.
GGH... HM...
Guanxi keeps talking.
I don't hear a word.
RI... WHEN YOU'RE RESTED... HELP HIM.
I... I WILL.

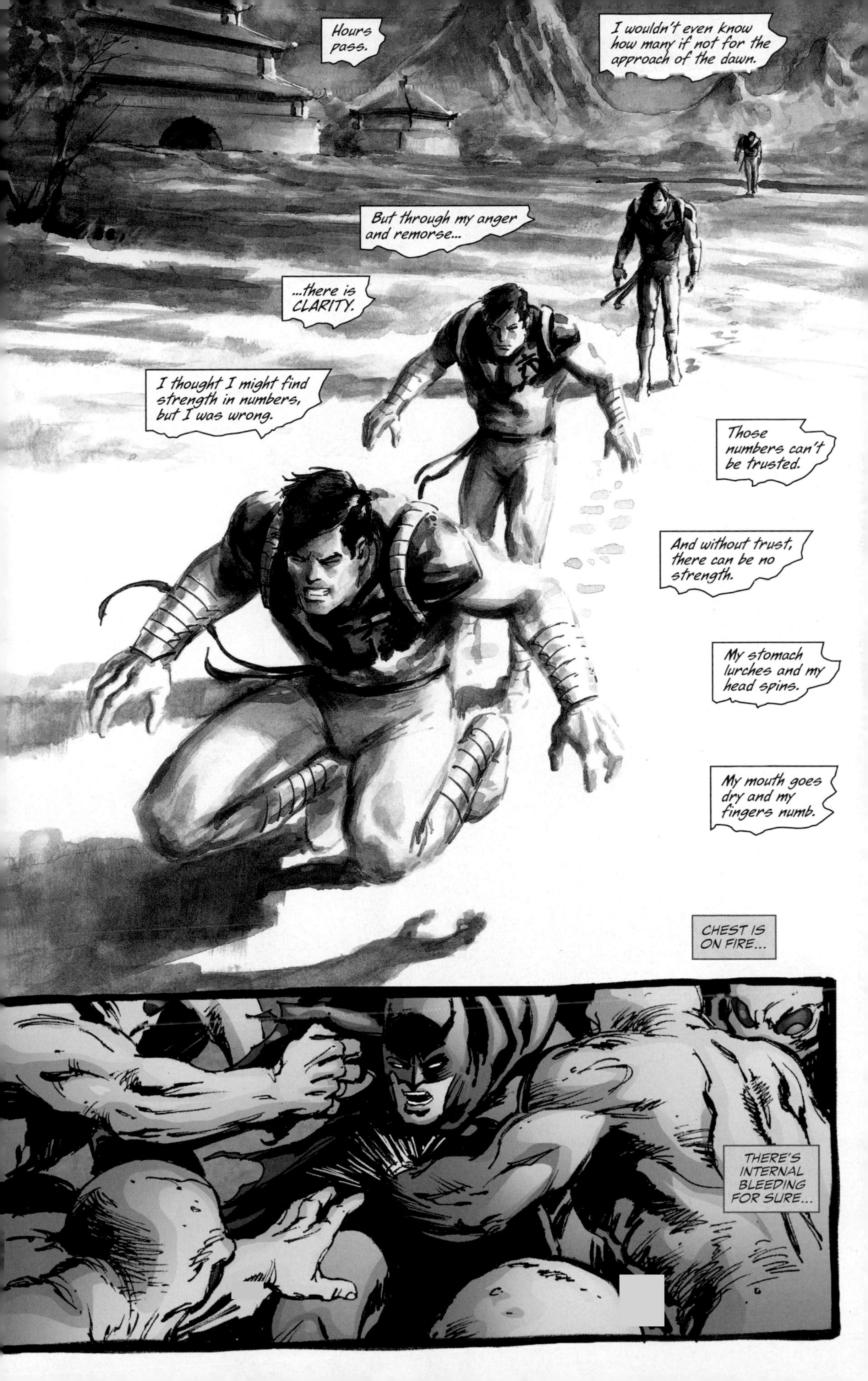
Hours pass.
I wouldn't even know how many if not for the approach of the dawn.
But through my anger and remorse...
...there is CLARITY.
I thought I might find strength in numbers, but I was wrong.
Those numbers can't be trusted.
And without trust, there can be no strength.
My stomach lurches and my head spins.
My mouth goes dry and my fingers numb.
CHEST IS ON FIRE...
THERE'S INTERNAL BLEEDING FOR SURE...

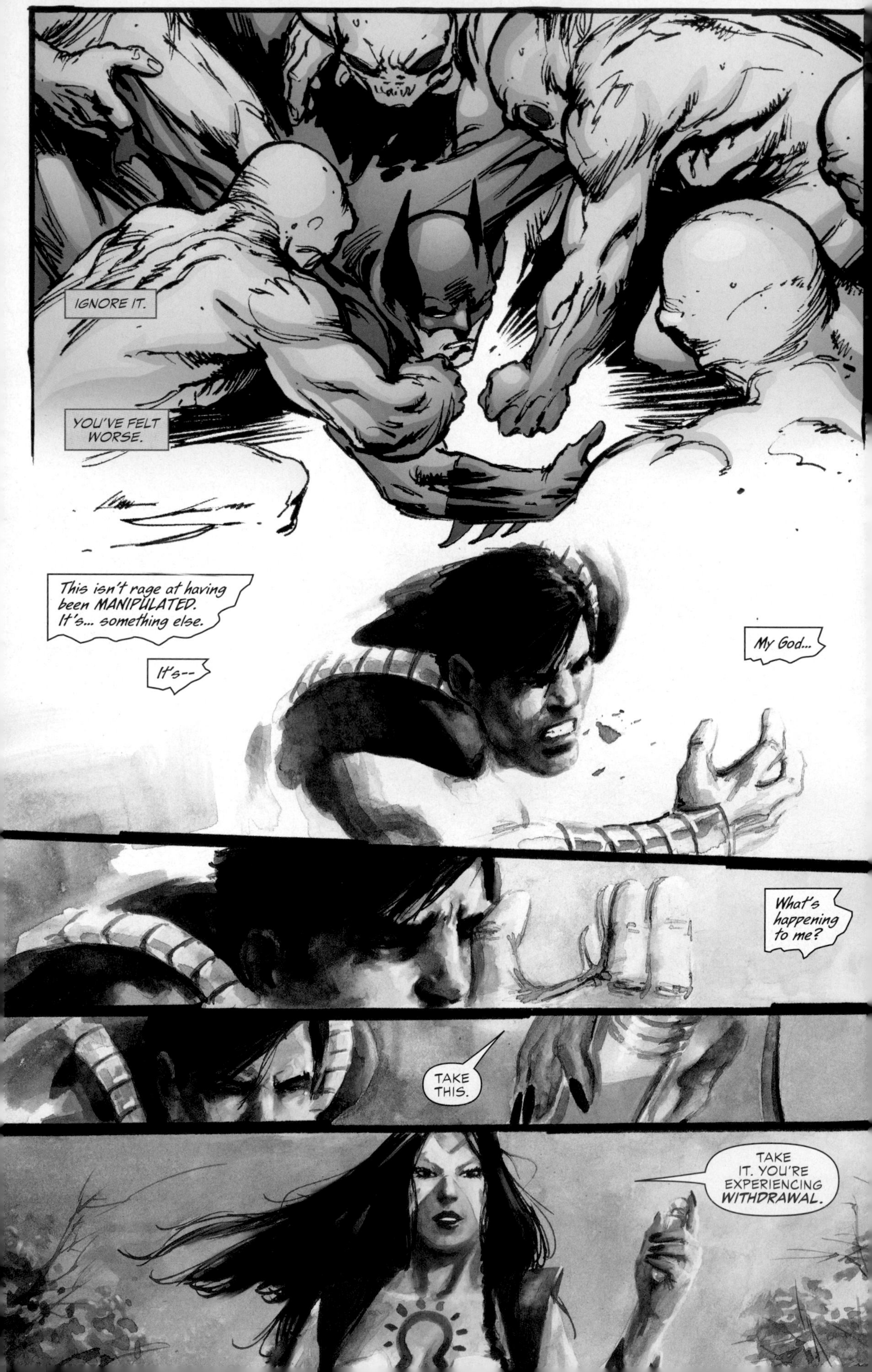
IGNORE IT.
YOU'VE FELT WORSE.
This isn't rage at having been MANIPULATED. It's... something else.
It's--
My God...
What's happening to me?
TAKE THIS.
TAKE IT. YOU'RE EXPERIENCING WITHDRAWAL.

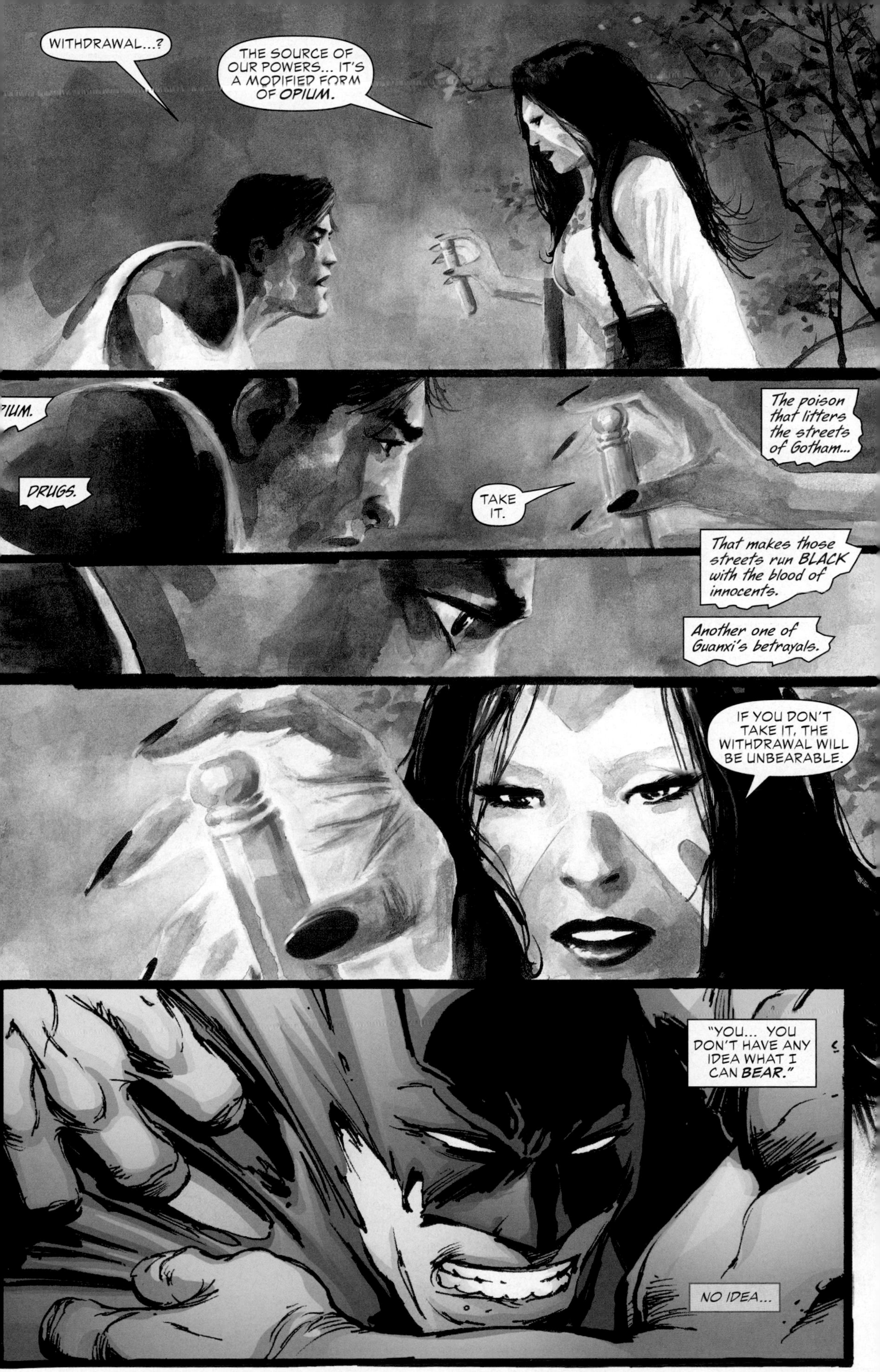
WITHDRAWAL...?
THE SOURCE OF OUR POWERS... IT'S A MODIFIED FORM OF OPIUM.
PIUM.
DRUGS.
TAKE IT.
The poison that litters the streets of Gotham...
That makes those streets run BLACK with the blood of innocents.
Another one of Guanxi's betrayals.
IF YOU DON'T TAKE IT, THE WITHDRAWAL WILL BE UNBEARABLE.
"YOU... YOU DON'T HAVE ANY IDEA WHAT I CAN BEAR."
NO IDEA...

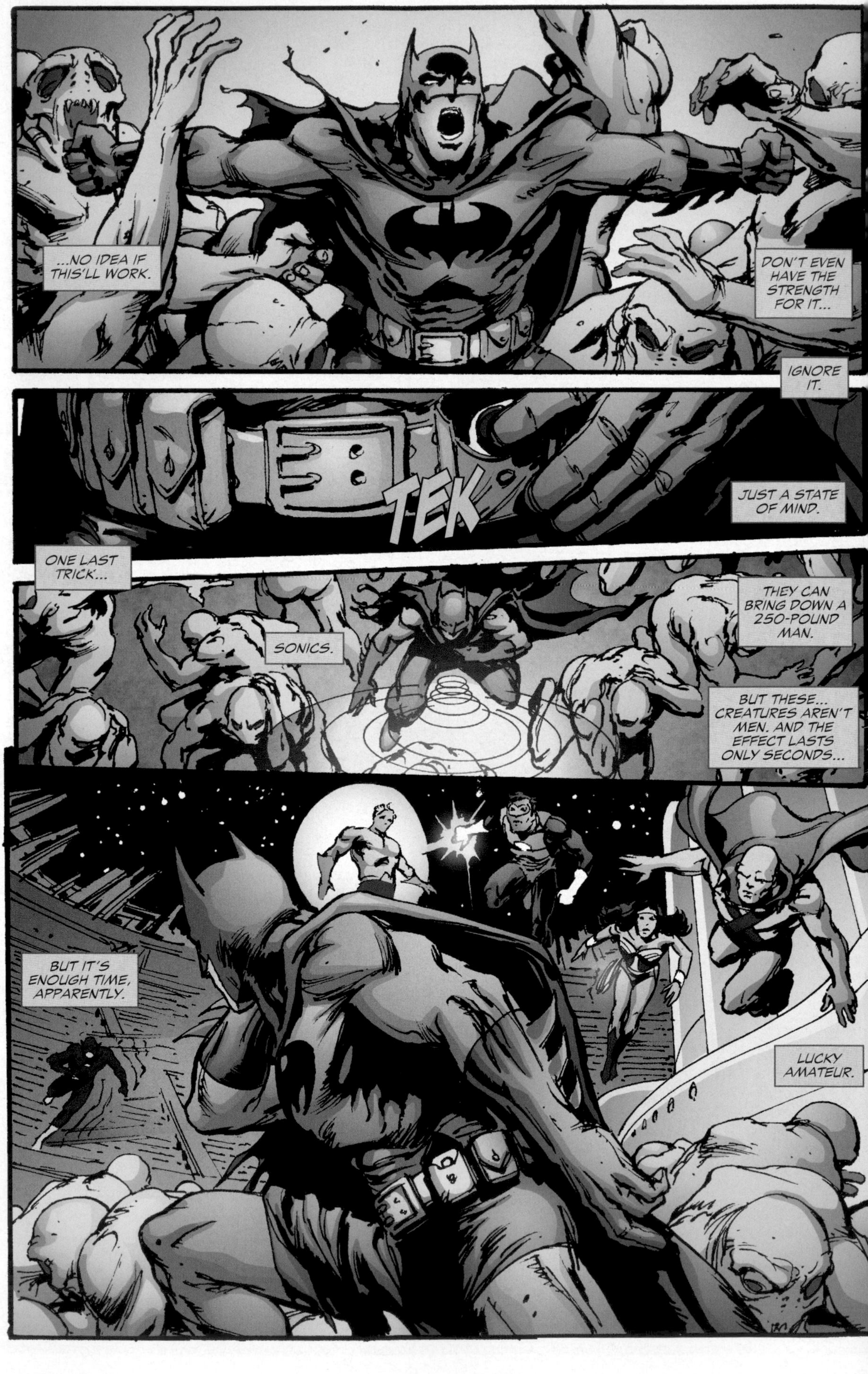
...NO IDEA IF THIS'LL WORK.
DON'T EVEN HAVE THE STRENGTH FOR IT...
IGNORE IT.
TEK
JUST A STATE OF MIND.
ONE LAST TRICK...
SONICS.
THEY CAN BRING DOWN A 250-POUND MAN.
BUT THESE... CREATURES AREN'T MEN. AND THE EFFECT LASTS ONLY SECONDS...
BUT IT'S ENOUGH TIME, APPARENTLY.
LUCKY AMATEUR.

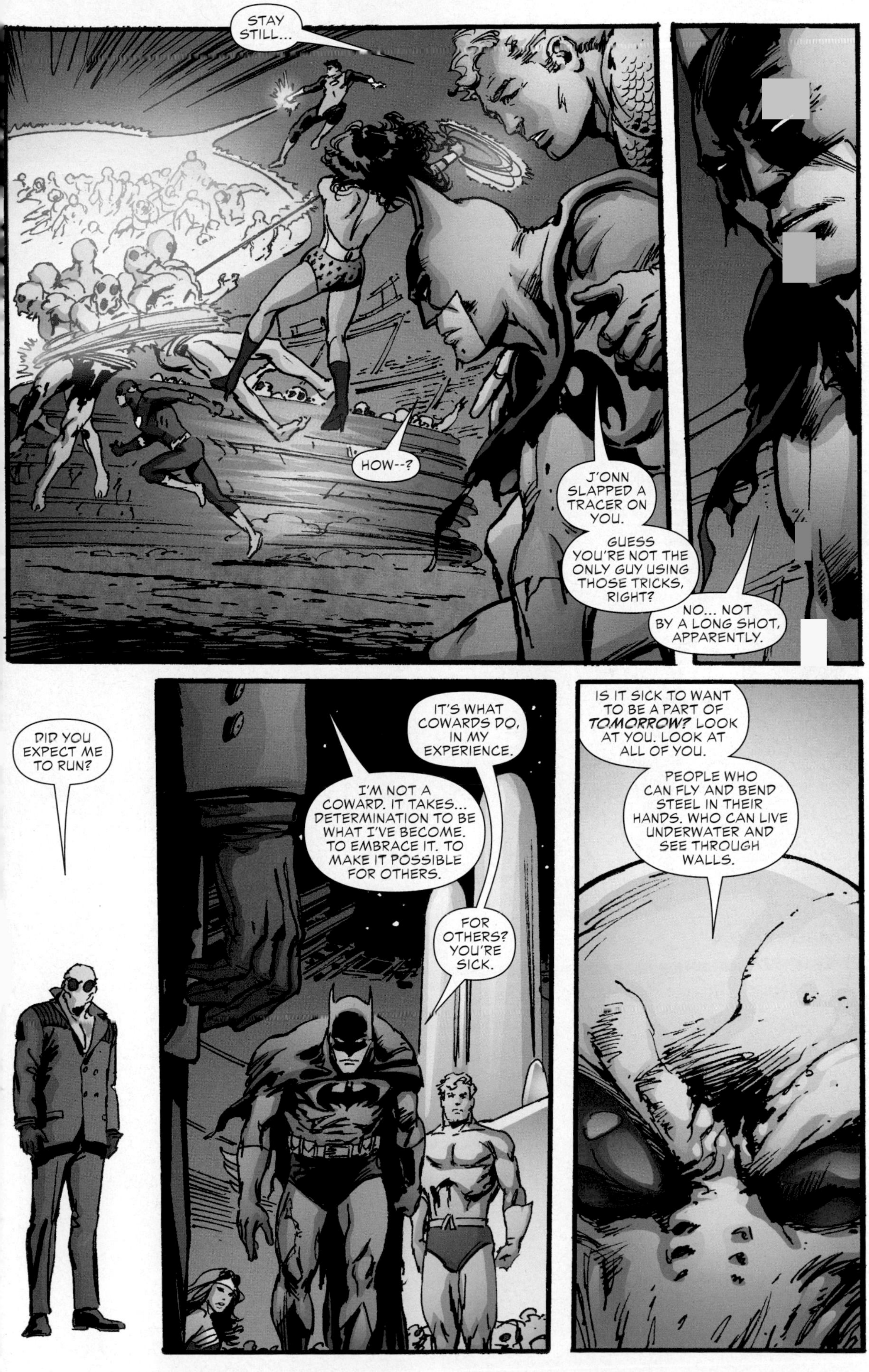
STAY STILL...
HOW--?
J'ONN SLAPPED A TRACER ON YOU.
GUESS YOU'RE NOT THE ONLY GUY USING THOSE TRICKS, RIGHT?
NO... NOT BY A LONG SHOT, APPARENTLY.
DID YOU EXPECT ME TO RUN?
IT'S WHAT COWARDS DO, IN MY EXPERIENCE.
I'M NOT A COWARD. IT TAKES... DETERMINATION TO BE WHAT I'VE BECOME. TO EMBRACE IT. TO MAKE IT POSSIBLE FOR OTHERS.
FOR OTHERS? YOU'RE SICK.
IS IT SICK TO WANT TO BE A PART OF *TOMORROW?* LOOK AT YOU. LOOK AT ALL OF YOU.
PEOPLE WHO CAN FLY AND BEND STEEL IN THEIR HANDS. WHO CAN LIVE UNDERWATER AND SEE THROUGH WALLS.

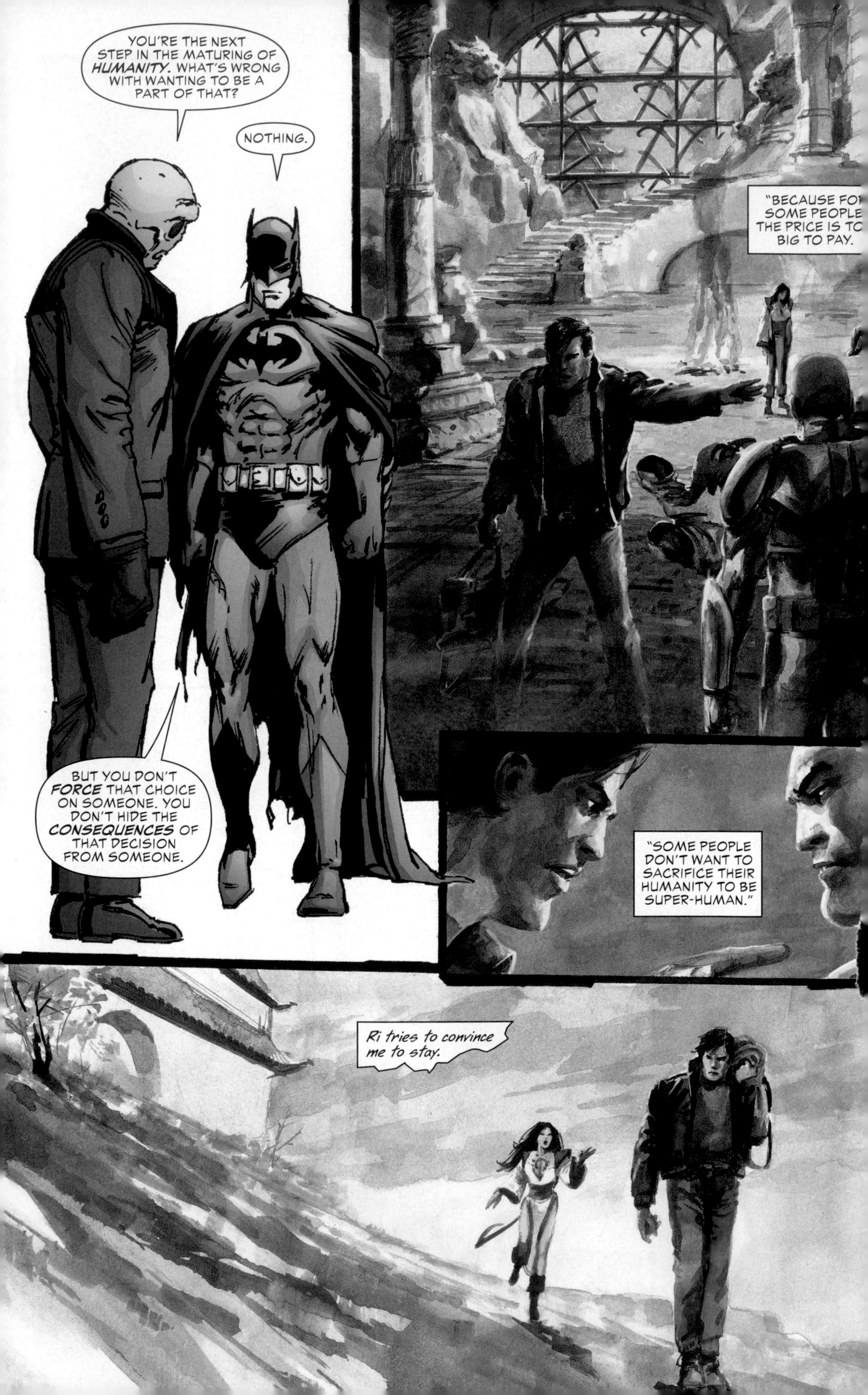
YOU'RE THE NEXT STEP IN THE MATURING OF HUMANITY. WHAT'S WRONG WITH WANTING TO BE A PART OF THAT?
NOTHING.
"BECAUSE FO SOME PEOPLE THE PRICE IS TO BIG TO PAY.
BUT YOU DON'T FORCE THAT CHOICE ON SOMEONE. YOU DON'T HIDE THE CONSEQUENCES OF THAT DECISION FROM SOMEONE.
"SOME PEOPLE DON'T WANT TO SACRIFICE THEIR HUMANITY TO BE SUPER-HUMAN."
Ri tries to convince me to stay.

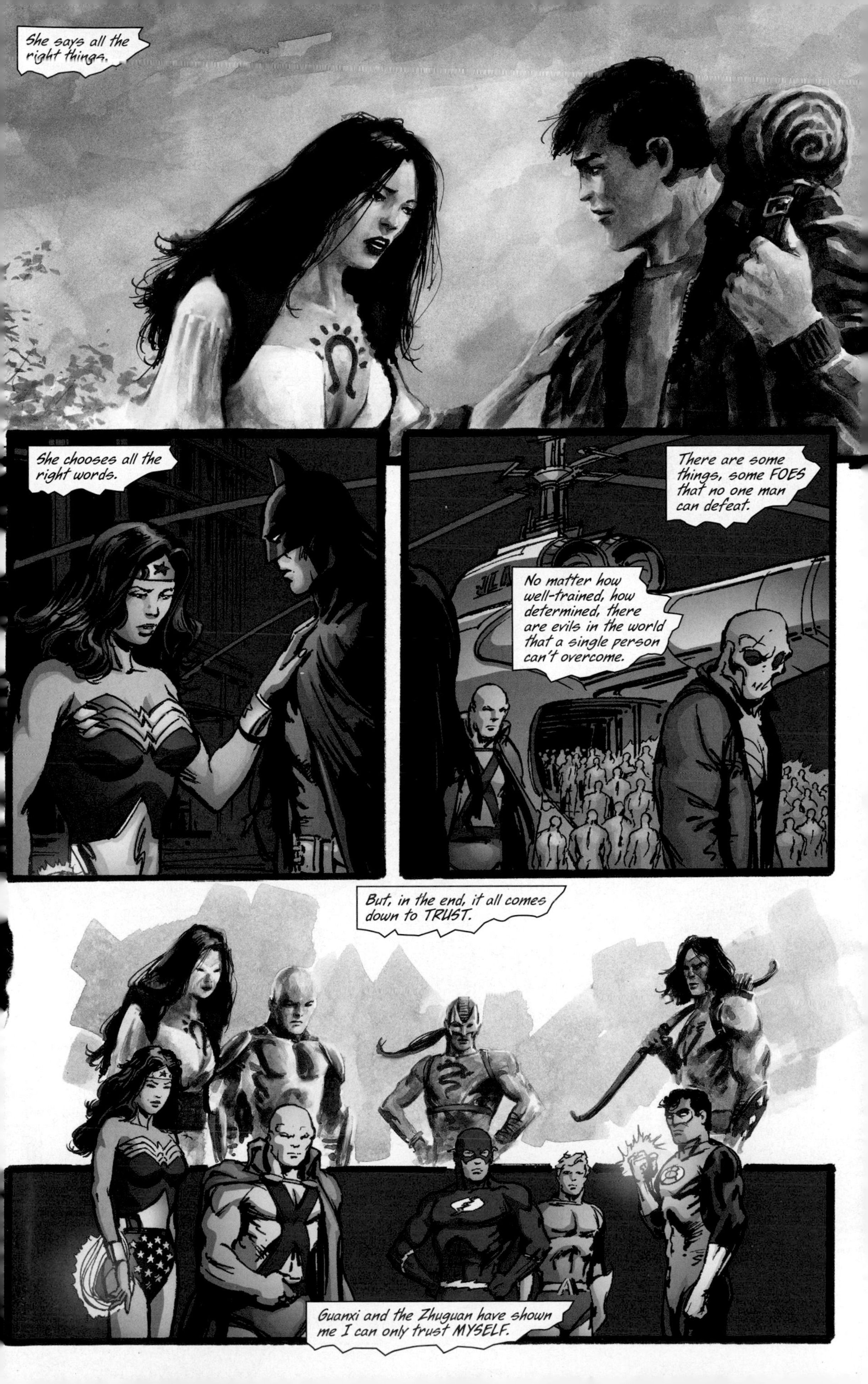
She says all the right things.
She chooses all the right words.
There are some things, some FOES that no one man can defeat.
No matter how well-trained, how determined, there are evils in the world that a single person can't overcome.
But, in the end, it all comes down to TRUST.
Guanxi and the Zhuguan have shown me I can only trust MYSELF.

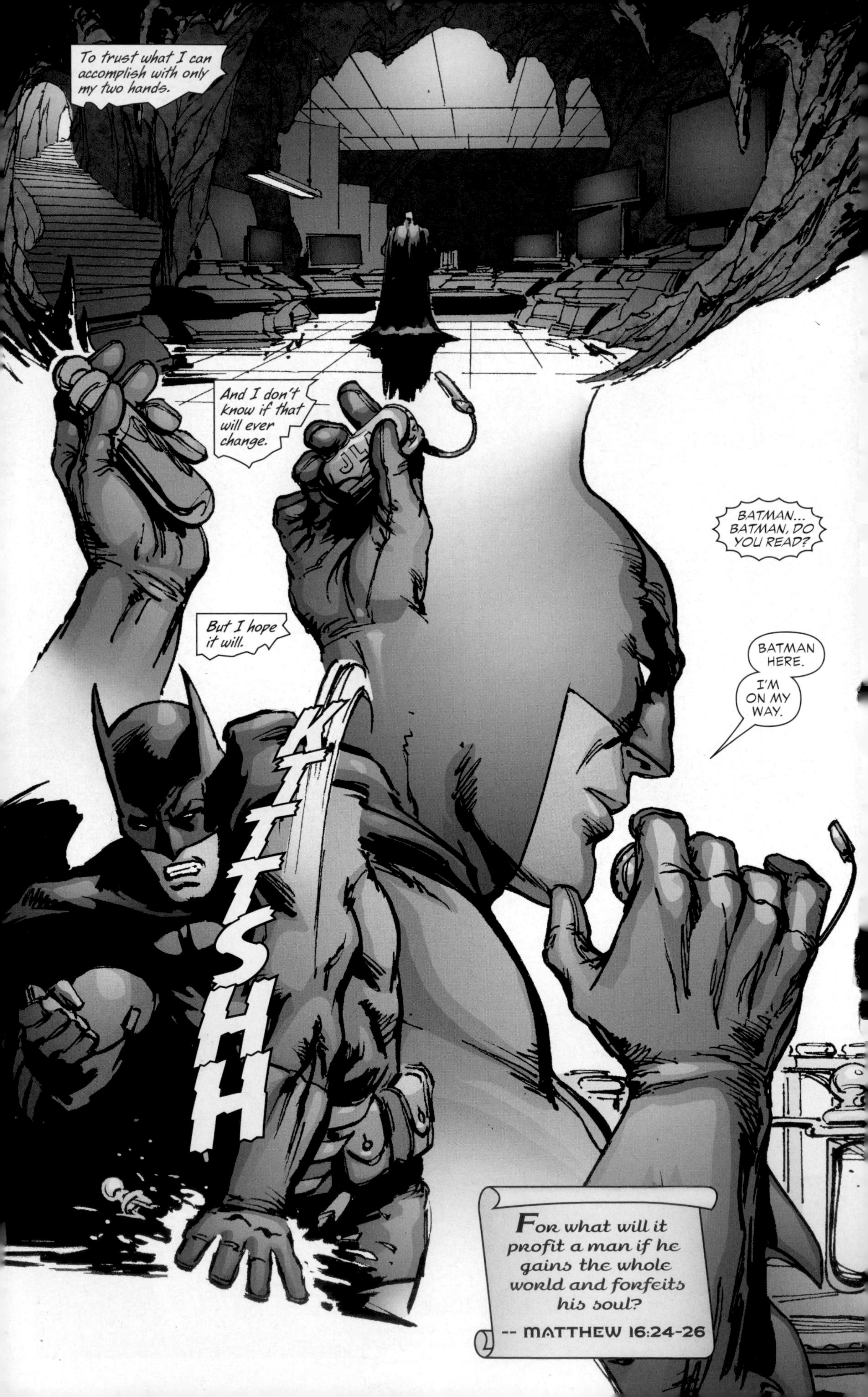
To trust what I can accomplish with only my two hands.
And I don't know if that will ever change.
But I hope it will.
BATMAN... BATMAN, DO YOU READ?
BATMAN HERE.
I'M ON MY WAY.
KTTTSHHH
For what will it profit a man if he gains the whole world and forfeits his soul?
-- MATTHEW 16:24-26